Samuel Butler and the Earl of Rochester

a reference guide

*A
Reference
Guide
to
Literature*

Arthur Weitzman
Editor

Samuel Butler and the Earl of Rochester

a reference guide

GEORGE WASSERMAN

G.K.HALL &CO.
70 LINCOLN STREET, BOSTON, MASS.

All Rights Reserved
Copyright © 1986 by George Wasserman

Library of Congress Cataloging in Publication Data

Wasserman, George Russell, 1927-
  Samuel Butler and the Earl of Rochester.

  (A Reference guide to literature)
  Includes indexes.
  1. English literature—Early modern, 1500-1700—
History and criticism—Bibliography. 2. Butler,
Samuel, 1612-1680—Bibliography. 3. Rochester, John
Wilmot, Earl of, 1647-1680—Bibliography. I. Title.
II. Series.
Z2012.W37 1986   [PR437]   016.821'4'09   85-24885
ISBN 0-8161-8625-1

This publication is printed on permanent/durable acid-free paper
MANUFACTURED IN THE UNITED STATES OF AMERICA

Contents

The Author vi

Preface vii

Introduction ix

Early Published Writings by the Authors xvii

Abbreviations xix

Writings about Samuel Butler, 1692-1984   1

Writings about the Earl of Rochester, 1680-1985 67

Index to Butler 161

Index to Rochester 169

The Author

Educated at the University of Pittsburgh and the University of Michigan, George Wasserman is professor of English at Russell Sage College. He is the author of <u>John Dryden</u> (1964), <u>Samuel "Hudibras" Butler</u> (1976), <u>Roland Barthes</u> (1981), and numerous articles on Restoration literature.

Preface

This reference guide provides an annotated chronological survey of the studies of two Restoration writers, Samuel Butler and John Wilmot, Earl of Rochester. It attempts to supply abstracts of books, articles and notes, parts of books and articles, and dissertations that focus distinctly on one or the other writer or on one or more of their works to enable students both to locate information and to determine its usefulness. The more than customary fulness of the annotations (particularly of twentieth-century materials) should also allow the reader to detect the main patterns of interest in the study of Butler and Rochester and of the Restoration generally.

The annotations are based upon fresh readings of the materials. Those of dissertations, however, are based upon published abstracts. (Norma Bentley's oft-cited Syracuse dissertation on Butler [1944.2] is an exception.) I have not included references to dictionaries or encyclopedias, to biographical handbooks and bibliographical registers, or to materials in student anthologies. Reviews and literary histories are not systematically recorded unless, in the first instance, they offer information on the primary author or, in the second, make a noteworthy statement of the consensus or signal a departure from it. I cite editions of the authors only where they are accompanied by substantial introductions or (in the case of the widely used Cambridge edition of Butler) where omission would seem eccentric. Again in the case of Butler, the lives and memoirs prefacing some nineteenth-century editions of the poet do not vary sufficiently to warrant distinction; I have, however, included those that constitute important links in the biographical tradition, under the year of the edition in which they first appeared, though I have usually read these in reprintings that are not separately listed. All other items I have not personally read are preceded by an asterisk. I cannot claim completeness even within these stated limits beyond 1983; both surveys, however, include more recent items that have come to my attention.

The critical literature of Butler and, until very recently, of Rochester has not received quite this degree of attention. The New Cambridge Bibliography is unannotated and makes no attempt at com-

Preface

pleteness in its coverage of secondary materials. David Farley-Hills's valuable <u>Rochester: The Critical Heritage</u> (1972.5) reprints materials of a peripheral and occasional sort that I do not include; but as its focus is upon the early reputation of the poet--the heritage of the modern critical tradition--it ends with the beginnings of the twentieth century. James Thorson's attempt at a complete bibliography of Butler (1973.4), while including eighteenth- and nineteenth-century items and a survey of noteworthy editions, offers only cursory annotation and is already ten years old; and David Vieth's bibliography of "Rochester Studies: 1925-1967" (1968.4)--extended to 1975 in another publication (1976.11)--also scants annotation, although its thoroughness has made it an indispensable tool to students of Rochester. (Since these words were written and after my manuscript had been sent to the publisher, Professor Vieth's own reference guide to Rochester studies has appeared.) As my annotations are nonevaluative, I take this opportunity to acknowledge my indebtedness to professors Thorson and Vieth for providing the bibliographical foundations of the present volume, and to Professor Farley-Hills, whose anthology of criticism supplied the texts of a number of rare items.

Though Butler and Rochester both died in 1680, tradition has assigned them rather widely separated places in literary history. Strictly speaking, they were not contemporaries, Rochester having not yet lived half as long as Butler when he predeceased the elder by two months; they illustrate a sort of generational fault (peculiar, we fancy, to Rochester's generation) that allows fathers (figuratively speaking) to survive sons. But the distinctness with which older literary history treated these two satirists was not simply a function of chronology. Criticism isolated Butler as the most inimitable as well as the most imitated poet in the language; on the other hand, it seemed to deny Rochester's individuality by identifying the flagrancies of his character and writing with those of a group of court wits, between whom a sort of shared poetic patrimony existed. Modern criticism has not only challenged these views--integrated Butler into the Restoration literary scene and differentiated Rochester's talent from that of his social peers--but has begun to draw Butler and Rochester together in relations of mutual significance. In coupling them here, this volume hopes to further this movement.

Introduction

Modern literary opinion is largely self-generating, a response not merely to primary works, but to prior responses to those works, and it is this reactive or revisionist function of criticism--as much as any inherent quality of the writer or work--that accounts for the extraordinary activity in twentieth-century Rochester studies and, until recently, for the lack of such activity in Butler studies. This is not to deny the fact that Hudibras achieved something like institutional status in the nineteenth century. A tradition of Hudibras commentary extended from Zachary Grey's eighteenth-century edition of the poem down to the very beginning of this century; but it was a commentary that so completely filled the gaps of the poem, so clarified a meaning in it, that it was repeated in edition after edition as a virtual part of the text. As the Butler material in the early issues of Notes and Queries suggests, Hudibras had become a poem about which there was too little to disagree; commentators turned to hair-splitting arguments on the etymology of Butler's word "breese," or to such wholly extratextual concerns as whether or not illustrations in eighteenth-century editions of the poem were by Hogarth. Before there could be the sort of critical activity that itself calls for commentary, Hudibras had to be returned to a "less finished" state the reading of which might again be problematic. It is possible that A. R. Waller's unannotated edition of the poem, published in 1905--the only modern text for a generation of readers--helped to perform this service; at least by 1967, when John Wilders produced the now standard Oxford edition of Hudibras, annotation had become sufficiently detached from the text to prompt one reviewer (Earl Miner [1969.4]) to recommend supplementing Wilders with Grey.

Rochester, on the other hand, seems always to have provoked differences of opinion. Tradition's atheistic sensualist became for Vivian de Sola Pinto (1935.6) an intellectual adventurer in quest of the "divine element" in the world; for David Vieth, writing in 1963, Rochester was a "complete Augustan"; for Paul Davies, in 1972, a Restoration liberal. The obscenity that prompted Graham Greene to shelve a study of the poet (1974.6) for forty years was redefined the year following its eventual publication as a "rhetoric of realism" (see Wilcoxon [1971.7; 1975.8]); and the lyrics that Samuel

Introduction

Johnson (1779.1) relegated to the category of "smooth and easy" have come to rival Donne's in complexity and subtlety. Rochester himself may have established the precedent for such revisions with his fondness for role-playing and his death-bed recantation of all that had gone before. Butler, by contrast, seems never to have changed his mind about a thing.

But the popular view of Butler as an inflexible mind, self-alienated from every institution, amusing itself in obsessive repetition, is surely incomplete--the product of a remarkably voluminous record of the world internalized in writing, further unbalanced by a dearth of information on the poet's day-to-day activities. Butler's biographers have had little success in correcting this imbalance. Thanks to the recent investigations of Ricardo Quintana (1933.2), Norma Bentley (1944.1-2; 1945.1), and Michael Wilding (1966.4-5; 1971.12), it is now possible to accept or reject certain claims made in E. S. de Beer's cautious, but largely inferential account of Butler's later life (1928.3); but just as de Beer added little to the accounts of his predecessors (the value of his investigation consists chiefly in its skeptical questioning of the Butler of tradition), so more recent biographers have added little to his account. As a consequence, Butler's manuscript notebooks (available only in excerpts until A. R. Waller's edition in 1908 and now, in vastly improved form, in an edition by Hugh de Quehen [1979.2]) have become the chief source of opinion on the poet.

Questions about origins have also preoccupied students of Butler's poems. Jan Veldkamp (1923.2) and Albert West (1931.1) devoted chapters to the problem of literary influences on Hudibras; and although argument on the identity of the historical model of Sir Hudibras abated after Ricardo Quintana published the Butler-Oxenden correspondence (1933.2), that on the models of Sidrophel and the characters in "The Elephant in the Moon" continues--see Curtiss (1929.1), Spence (1961.1), Nicolson (1965.3), Brunn (1969.1), and Laprevotte (1972.5). Related to these concerns is the attempt to read Hudibras as a consistent allegory, to find some Commonwealth tenor for its fictive vehicles, Hudibras, Ralph, the bear-baiters (Craig [1923.1]), and for larger narrative figures like the physical and verbal disputes in the poem (Miller [1955.4; 1958.3]). Since identifying an author's literary influences and the historical referents of his characters is also a way of locating him in the worlds of books and men, the source-hunting enterprise in Butler studies seems also to be an attempt to compensate for the absence of biographical information about the poet.

The practical counterpart of this strong historical bent in Butler studies is a scarcity of poetic analysis. Hudibras and Butler's miscellaneous satires have resisted the explicatory techniques of both the new criticism, which work best on short, highly compressed lyrics, and rhetorical criticism, which is a way of dealing with the explicitness and referentiality of satire by focusing

Introduction

upon its speaker or persona. Formalist considerations appear, however, in discussions of the style and genre of Butler's work--first on nationalist grounds (in Dryden's use of Boileau's neoclassical objections to burlesque [1692.1]--which Dennis [1693.1] turned to the advantage of the English poem), and then as yet another variety of source study (in Albert West's 1931 investigation of French influence on English burlesque and in Richmond Bond's definition of the genre as a species of literary imitation [1932.1]). But although Bond began by treating Hudibras as imitation, he quickly recognized that the poem does not conform to his definition, that the term "Hudibrastic" fits the imitations of Butler's poem, but fails to include what is most distinctive in the work from which it takes its name.

Bond's failure to reduce the complexities of Hudibras to a system set the poem, however, in a new critical light, focusing attention on the relation between subject matter and its treatment, and presenting the poem as an original (though flawed) creation rather than an imitation existing primarily in its relations with the world. Edward Ames Richards's study of Hudibras as the model for other burlesques (1937.1) was the first of several studies that took up this new perspective. In contrast to the partisan works of Butler's imitators, Hudibras seems to Richards oddly detached from circumstance, unrealistic, committed less to political causes than to its own principles of artistic invention. Ian Jack and Ellen Leyburn's interpretations of Hudibras also begin with concerns about the form of the poem, though they arrive at conclusions quite different from Richards's. For both, the inconsistencies of Butler's formal design seriously modify its function as burlesque. Jack (1952.1) attempts to simplify the poem's method: it is not indirection, the contrast of subject and style, but straightforward diminution--the method of "low satire"; Leyburn (1953.2), on the other hand, further complicates it: the satire is both direct and indirect, and, in the latter respect, allegorical as well.

Leyburn's designation of Hudibras as a satiric allegory is not, it should be noted, a reversion to an older referential reading of the poem, but an attempt to read it poetically; the meanings of Leyburn's allegory (and the targets of Jack's satire, he points out) are not particular individuals (like those adduced by Craig and Miller), but general human faults and habits of mind. This tendency to cultivate generality in interpretations of Restoration literature-- a way of transcending the "unpoetic" materials of political satire and occasional poetry--has been criticized for producing partial, dogmatic readings. In the study of Butler, however, the emphasis upon general meanings was a long delayed reaction to the nineteenth-century emphasis upon particularity; it has, moreover, a worthy precedent in Samuel Johnson's praise of the poem (1779.1) for its knowledge of human nature and its defense of metaphysical order (though Johnson himself did not consider discord and usurpation matters of general significance). Over all, the "poeticizing" of Hudibras has been stimulating. It brought Butler's satire--in prose as well as

Introduction

verse—closer to the center of current critical interests (between 1965 and 1975, for instance, it was the subject of sixteen doctoral dissertations) and it supplied the thesis of a dialectic for subsequent discussions of the poet.

One consequence of the view of Butler as a student of general human nature was a renewed interest in his prose characters, examined not individually, in relation to models in contemporary society or in literary traditions (as in Benjamin Boyce's discussion of Butler's polemic characters [1955.1]), but as a group comprising a systematic anatomy of mankind. Charles Totten's dissertation (1972.6) and later article (1975.2) are exemplary: Butler's characters are seen here as constituting a satiric hierarchy determined by patterns of complicity and by interrelations between the represented types. K. M. P. Burton (1958.2) made even greater claims for the characters, maintaining that they more clearly expressed the general satirical point of Hudibras—that man is "an undignified creature"—than the poem managed to do itself; and Arnold Asrelsky, in a dissertation entitled "The Forgotten Augustan" (1971.1), brought this line of argument to its logical conclusion by stating that Hudibras fails as an Augustan satire in the Menippean mode precisely because it lacks the variety of the prose characters and, further, that the failure of readers to grasp this purpose gave rise to the earlier allegorical readings of the poem.

By 1970, an Augustan or "poetic" reading of Hudibras as a broadly philosophical satire of human nature was well established. Recent studies of Swift, whose kinship to Butler had long been recognized (see, for example, Dowden's essay of 1901, the notes by Webster [1932.2] and Kulischeck [1951.1; 1954.1], and Quintana's influential "Samuel Butler: A Restoration Figure in a Modern Light" [1951.2]), now became the interpretive models for discussions of Butler. W. O. S. Sutherland's "Hudibras and the Nature of Man" (1965.5), for instance, not only viewed the poem as a philosophically coherent satire—its three parts dealing respectively with the nature of man, relations between men, and relations between men and women—but arrived at this view by means of an analysis of the "voices" of the poem, a technique made familiar in new-critical analyses of Swift's personae. My own three part study of Butler (1970.6; 1973.6; 1976.4) follows, I now recognize, the pattern of Sutherland's analysis, though it was shaped by generic rather than rhetorical considerations; its concern with feminism and theriophily grew out of the problematic status of a satirical norm that makes a general indictment of human beings, the so-called "satire against mankind."

This "Augustan" Butler—seriously intellectual, deeply pessimistic, academically serviceable (since adaptable to certain established formal and thematic patterns)—has little place in the latest studies of the poet, however. In part, this is due to the waning influence of the new criticism that helped to produce it; at the same time, it must be attributed to a new awareness of Restoration literature as

Introduction

a body of writing that may be read on its own terms--however topical or doctrinaire--rather than those of an unformulated and emerging Augustanism. To read Hudibras on its own terms is still to read it as a poem, however--not, that is, as an allegory that is complete only after it has been placed in a context external to itself. If the "pre-Augustan" reading of Butler's work remained faithful to its satirical texture at the expense of its poetic value, and if the "Augustan" reading tried to transcend the unpoetic texture in the interest of its poetic value, the latest "Restoration" readings attempt to poeticize that texture. Susan Staves (1979.5), for instance, flatly denies the value of Hudibras as a general or philosophical satire; the poem is undemocratic, an unfashionable attack upon Parliament and praise of monarchy. Nevertheless, the terms of Butler's satire for her are literary (or cultural, rather than political), having to do with the relations between words and actions, with oaths, or the "fictions of authority." Michael Seidel's second essay on Hudibras (1979.4) is a sort of "limit case" of the allegorical reading of the poem. The narrative of Hudibras imitates the history of the Revolutionary years; but because the historical scene is schismatic, and because satire violates narrative generation, the poetic record of historical details is meaningless as history.

Similarly, essays like Nicolas Nelson's investigation of the Puritan debate on astrology in Hudibras (1976.2) and the recent studies by William Horne and Ken Robinson (1983.1, 3) of Butler's satires on science sharply point up the difference between this new critical interest in history in the poem and an older sort of historical detective work in the world--"micro-criticism," to use Horne's word. In another study (1983.2), Horne tracks the Restoration world in the very fabric of Butler's writing, his language, which, Alvin Snider points out (1984.3), exploits an already existing gap between words and things in order to produce "an aesthetic of anti-style." What, in varying degrees, these new studies deal with is the history the Restoration did not record about itself, but simply took for granted--the doxa or received opinion that generated satire and exists there as paradox. The Butler revealed in these studies--the "Restoration" Butler--is more "Modern" than "Ancient," more comic than serious--Swiftian to the extent that Swift retains a Restoration sensibility, or, as David Vieth has suggested, to the extent that Butler (and Rochester) fathered a literary lineage that culminates in Swift and that blurs the traditional "official" distinctions of literary history.

Vieth's predication of an "unofficial," but natural literary affiliation between Butler and Rochester and certain Augustan writers resolves a difference of opinion in Rochester studies that parallels the opposition just described in the studies of Butler. In the case of Rochester, however, the reconstruction of the poet along Augustan lines takes the form of a more sharply defined debate since it occurred within (and challenged) a more fully established body of critical opinion and, perhaps too, because it has been identified with the two leading authorities on Rochester, Vivian de Sola Pinto and David M. Vieth, though it should be added that, after Pinto's initial reaction to Vieth's views (1964.8), this debate has been carried on less by the protagonists than by their English and American, their old and new-critical advocates. Indeed, in an essay published in 1961, Pinto had himself regarded Rochester and Dryden as "the first real Augustan poets."

Vieth's "Augustan" Rochester made its appearance in an essay appropriately subtitled "A Crux for Critics and Scholars," an analysis of the personae of "An Epistolary Essay from M. G. to O. B." and "A Very Heroical Epistle in Answer to Ephelia," and the first of a series of studies dealing with problems of attribution in Restoration poetry (1963.2). A model of new-critical lucidity and an admirable example of the complimentarity of interpretation and traditional scholarship (ironically, the essay aimed at being conciliatory), Vieth made the case for the priority in the two poems of two distinctively Augustan satirical devices: the self-satirizing speaker and the inversion of satirical norms. Though these conclusions would provide the starting point of a new direction in Rochester studies--a general concern with the formal features of the poems and, in particular, the investigation of the problematics of the poet's irony--it was Howard Erskine-Hill, in an essay called "Rochester: Augustan or Explorer?" (1966.1) published in a festschrift for Vivian de Sola Pinto, who articulated the polarity within which many of the subsequent studies would be written. If we are to interpret Rochester's irony as an inversion, for satirical purposes, of traditional values, we must be prepared to believe, Erskine-Hill argued, that he accepted those values to begin with, a notion that was sharply at odds with the widely accepted views of Rochester as a skeptic or restless intellectual adventurer.

The principal source of the "accepted" view of Rochester (the source too of Erskine-Hill's word "Explorer") was Vivian de Sola Pinto's 1935 study of the poet, revised in 1962. Both books consolidated information produced in the first phase of modern Rochester studies, efforts to sift biographical fact from rumor and popular legend, to plot the unstable relationships that constituted the literary community of the time, and to establish the canon of Rochester's poems--efforts, that is, to determine at least the poet's social presence in the Restoration world. Pinto sought to establish Rochester's intellectual presence there; his Rochester is a student in search of the right teacher--Hobbes, Blount, Burnet--too serious a thinker to be satisfied with any but perhaps the last of them. The most typical poetic production of this Rochester is his most explicitly philosophical poem, that poem too which rewards the investigation of his sources or the demonstration of his originality: the "Satyr against Reason and Mankind" became sine qua non Rochester --no mere dilletante imitation, but a serious statement rooted in philosophic traditions, as S. F. Crocker (1937.1) and Thomas Fujimura (1958.2) argued, a work of "eclectic originality," in John Moore's words (1943.1).

Introduction

The reclassification of the "Satyr against Reason and Mankind" as an imitation, in 1969, signals the rival presence of Vieth's Augustan Rochester. Though Harold Brooks had included Rochester's poem in his important study of the genre of imitation (1949.1) and C. F. Main had examined it as an example of formal satire (1960.2), Paul Davies's reassertion of Boileau's influence on Rochester (1969.2) sounds a regressive note that is surprising in literary study until we notice that in the same year he published an article entitled "Rochester: Augustan and Explorer." Although Davies's title appears to recommend a combination of the two views of Rochester, the article leaves little doubt of his polemical intention to support Vieth against Erskine-Hill (if not against Pinto). Dustin Griffin's book on Rochester (1973.4) represents another position on this question: rejection of both terms--"Augustan" and "explorer"--and along with them the notion that the libertine poems are spoken by either a persona or the poet himself. Griffin sees Rochester as a product of the Restoration. Davies, in 1972, appears to have made a similar adjustment, reformulating his 1969 interpretation of the poet's complex attitude toward traditional values as an expression of "Restoration liberalism," a position that points up the difference between Vieth's Rochester-as-Augustan and the "Augustan" Rochester that Erskine-Hill attributed to him. For Vieth, the term "Augustan" was a "new-critical" designation for a set of purely textual characteristics; for Erskine-Hill, it was a general ethical label that covered not only those characteristics, but their implications for the poet and his culture. Davies's Rochester is ambiguous, however: the "Restoration" label has a purely historical value since Rochester's liberalism is seen to connect him with the Augustan satirists. But although the term "liberalism" is denied its specific ideological sense in a later exchange with Arthur Weitzman (see 1973.12; 1974.2, 11), it obviously expresses the ethical implications that Vieth's term "Augustan" ignored. Vieth's later predication (1976.11) of an "unofficial" literary lineage that transcends the traditional distinctions between "Restoration" and "Augustan" just as clearly includes those values.

Vieth's analysis of Rochester's "Epistolary Essay" provided a model for a number of critical studies published in the next decade, analyses of individual or related works that demonstrated the impersonality of the poet and the ironic detachment of his poems. Even Rochester's borrowings from other poets came to be viewed as "satirical inversions" or parodies in two studies by Jeremy Treglown (1976.9; 1980.8). "Artemisia to Chloe," Rochester's most self-referential poem, begins to rival the "Satyr against Reason" as the focus of critical interest, and the latter itself becomes the site of ironic performance in Charles Knight's deconstruction of reason in the "Satyr" (1970.3) and Ronald Johnson's delineation of a "reflexively ironic narrator" in the poem, one who alternately alienates himself from the reader and evokes his sympathy (1975.2). But criticism that stresses the involvement of the reader in the work marks a sharp break with the new-critical principles that informed these studies, and that fact is shown in the variety of critical positions employed in the most recent studies of Rochester.

A concern with readers is perhaps understandable in the criticism of poetry that has been characterized as pornographic, but the role of the reader in these newer studies is that of a producer, not a consumer of the poem; their interest is in meaning, not effect, but a meaning that does not exist in the poem until it is read. David Vieth, again, forecast this new perspective as early as 1972 in an essay that articulated an "anti-Aristotelian poetic" behind the work of Rochester, Butler, and Swift (the essay provides the historical basis for this "unofficial" lineage), a poetic that sanctions discontinuities of various sorts and that consciously mocks the Aristotelian (new-critical) principle of poetic autonomy. Vieth's stance in 1972 was thus almost diametrically opposed to his position in 1963 --almost, but not quite. If he was no longer able to take the persona of Rochester's poems at face value, neither was he able to accept the speaker of the poems as a substitute for Rochester. Rather, this essentially unstable identity was the very condition of "Rochesterian irony." Interestingly, in his argument against Vieth's view of Rochester as an Augustan, Erskine-Hill had arrived at a similar understanding of the poet's relation to his poems--one that even drew the reader into a relationship with the unstable speaker of the poem. Modern Rochester studies appear to lend credence to the view that literary interpretations are authorized less by given texts than by the community of professional readers who agree on the ways of reading (or producing) those texts.

Early Published Writings by the Authors

1660   "To His Sacred Majesty, on His Restoration in the Year 1660." Oxford. (Possibly by Rochester).

1662   Butler's <u>Hudibras: The First Part</u>. London.

1663   Butler's <u>Hudibras: The Second Part</u>. London.

1671   Butler's <u>To the Memory of the Most Renowned Du-Vall</u>.

1672   Butler's <u>Two Letters, One from John Audland . . . the Other, William Prynne's Answer</u>.

1677   Butler's <u>Hudibras: The Third Part</u>. London.

1679   Rochester's <u>A Satyr against Reason and Mankind</u>. (Broadside).

1679   Rochester's <u>Artemisia to Chloe: A Letter from a Lady in the Town, to a Lady in the Country</u>. London. (Broadside).

1679   Rochester's <u>A Very Heroical Epistle in Answer to Ephelia</u>. London. (Broadside).

1679   Rochester's <u>Upon Nothing</u>. London. (Broadside).

1679   Rochester's <u>My Lord All-Pride</u>. (Broadside).

1680   <u>Poems on Several Occasions by the Right Honourable, the E. of R----</u>. "Antwerp."

Abbreviations

AL	American Literature
BC	Book Collector
BLR	Bodleian Library Record
CL	Comparative Literature
CLAJ	College Language Association Journal
DA	Dissertation Abstracts
DAI	Dissertation Abstracts International
DNB	Dictionary of National Biography
DUJ	Durham University Journal
EA	Etudes Anglaises
ECLife	Eighteenth Century Life
ECS	Eighteenth Century Studies
EdL	Etudes de lettres
EIC	Essays in Criticism
ELH	English Literary History
ELN	English Language Notes
ELWIU	Essays in Literature
EnlE	Enlightenment Essays
ES	English Studies
ESC	English Studies in Canada
HLQ	Huntington Library Quarterly
JEGP	Journal of English and Germanic Philology
JHI	Journal of the History of Ideas
JWCI	Journal of the Warburg and Courtald Institutes
KR	Kenyon Review
Lang&S	Language and Style
LC	Library Chronicle
MLN	Modern Language Notes
MLQ	Modern Language Quarterly
MLR	Modern Language Review
MP	Modern Philology
N&Q	Notes and Queries
PAPS	Proceedings of the American Philosophical Society
PBSA	Papers of the Bibliographical Society of America
PLL	Papers on Language and Literature
PMLA	Publications of the Modern Language Association

Abbreviations

PQ	Philogical Quarterly
PULC	Princeton University Library Chronicle
RES	Review of English Studies
RS	Research Studies
SAR	South Atlantic Review
SCN	Seventeenth Century News
SEL	Studies in English Literature, 1500–1900
SP	Studies in Philology
TLS	Times Literary Supplement (London)
TSL	Tennessee Studies in Literature
TSLL	Texas Studies in Language and Literature

Writings about Samuel Butler, 1692-1984

1692

1 DRYDEN, JOHN. "Discourse concerning the Original and Progress of Satire." In <u>The Satires of Decimus Junius Juvenalis: Translated into English Verse</u>. London: Printed for Jacob Tonson [dated 1693].
   Decrees hudibrastic meter and rhyme, in any but Butler's hand, beneath the dignity of "Manly Satire." Even Butler would have given us "a better, and more solid" delight in another verse form. Numerous reprints. Cf. 1693.1.

1693

1 DENNIS, JOHN. Preface to <u>Miscellanies in Verse and Prose</u>. London: Printed for James Knapton.
   Vindicates burlesque in general--and Butler's in particular --against the strictures of Boileau and Dryden (1692.1). The French critic's general opposition to burlesque (which is just in respect to Scarron) does not extend to Butler, whose burlesque exhibits a "gentleman's manner"--good sense and linguistic purity. (Rochester's practice supports the claim: though an admirer of Boileau, he followed Butler's fashion in several of his satires.) Dryden's criticism of hudibrastic versification is contradicted by the very satisfaction of experiencing Butler's; his rhyme is "becoming of a Jest," conducive to quickness, and takes advantage of the peculiar resources of the language. The standard text is Edward Niles Hooker's edition of <u>The Critical Works of John Dennis</u>, vol. 1 (Baltimore: Johns Hopkins Press, 1939).

1704

*1 [ASTRY, SIR JAMES?]. Life of Butler. In <u>Hudibras</u>. London: G. Sawbridge <u>et al</u>.

The first life of Butler to be published in an edition of his works. If the short "Author's Life" in the first American edition of Hudibras (Troy: Wright, Goodenow, & Stockwell, 1806) is Astry's (and the attribution to Astry rests solely on a note attributed to William Oldys), he drew upon Wood (1820.1), even to the extent of suggesting his personal acquaintance with Aubrey.

1715

*1 [L'ESTRANGE, SIR ROGER?]. "An Alphabetical Key to Hudibras." Posthumous Works in Prose and Verse. Vol. 1. London: Printed for S. Briscoe.
Identifies the "originals" of the principal characters in the three parts of Hudibras. A second key to Parts II and III also ascribed to L'Estrange, was published in The Second Volume of the Posthumous Works (1715).

1733

1 AROUET, FRANÇOIS-MARIE [Voltaire]. "On Pope and Some Other Famous Poets" (Letter XXII). In Philosophical Letters. Translated by John Lockman. London.
Introduces Hudibras to French readers as a poem combining features of the Satyre Ménippée and Don Quixote, though it is as far beneath the latter in narrative skill and taste as it is above the former in wit. Paradise Lost provides another point of comparison. Though Hudibras is untranslatable and truly understandable only to readers familiar with the theological issues of the time, the first 400 lines of the poem are recast in eighty lines of French tetrameter rhyme. The French edition (frequently reprinted) appeared in 1734.

1744

1 GREY, ZACHARY, ed. Preface to Hudibras. 2 vols. London: W. Innys, A. Ward et al.
This edition establishes the Tory view of Hudibras, identifying names and events to which Butler alludes. The preface presents information on the organization of Presbyterianism and Independency as a background to the detailed annotation of the text, and discusses the burlesque style of the poem, drawing upon Dennis's arguments (1693.1) to answer Dryden's criticisms of the form (1692.1). Frequently reprinted.

1759

1 THYER, R[OBERT], ed. Preface to The Genuine Remains in Verse and Prose. 2 vols. London: J. & R. Tonson.
 Certifies the genuineness of the papers from which the "Remains" are printed, and justifies the publication here of Butler's unfinished work. For a recent consideration of the Butler canon, see 1982.1.

1779

1 JOHNSON, SAMUEL. "Butler." In The Works of the English Poets, With Prefaces, Biographical and Critical, by Samuel Johnson. 68 vols. in 58. London: Printed by H. Hughes for C. Bathurst et al., 1779-81. [Lives of the Poets.]
 Reproduces and evaluates available information on Butler's life--chiefly that in Wood (1820.1) and the anonymous biography attributed to Astry (1704.1)--continuing the tradition of the poet's association with Sir Samuel Luke, his neglect by the king and subsequent poverty, but casting doubt on the poet's academic credentials and suggesting that Hudibras remains unfinished. Butler's poem is criticized for its want of variety: its hero is irredeemably contemptible, its action a succession of incidents overshadowed by conversations which lack "dramatick spriteliness" --the very inexhaustibility of its wit is wearying. The poem is praised for its learning and, especially, its practical knowledge of human nature. Hudibras is the product of both meditation and the promptings of occasion, but to the extent that it records the particular manners of its time, its humor is lost to later readers. Lost too is the seriousness of its attack upon the "insubordination" of Commonwealth society. The shortcomings of Hudibras are finally blamed on the burlesque form, which ultimately "detects itself" and reminds the reader of art, not nature. The standard edition of the Lives of the Poets has been edited by George Birkbeck Hill, 3 vols. (Oxford: Clarendon Press, 1905).

1793

1 NASH, TREADWAY RUSSEL, ed. "On Samuel Butler, Esq., Author of Hudibras." In Hudibras. London: T. Rickaby.
 Presents available information on Butler's life and writings, discusses the mock-heroic antecedents of Hudibras, and offers general observations on the plot and style of the poem. Nash's notes are indebted to Grey (1744.1). Frequently reprinted.

1819

1 HAZLITT, WILLIAM. Lectures on the English Comic Writers: Delivered at the Surry Institute. London: Taylor and Hessey. Reprinted in The Complete Works of William Hazlitt, ed. P. P. Howe (London: J. M. Dent & Sons, 1931).
   Though the "greatest single production of wit" in the seventeenth century, Hudibras nevertheless lacks pathos and humor; it has no story, and its characters have nothing to redeem them. The widow's sarcastic account of love is false. Butler "carried his private grudge too far into his general speculations."

1820

1 WOOD, ANTHONY à. Athenae Oxonienses. Edited by Philip Bliss. Vol. 3. London: F. C. & J. Rivington et al., 1813-20, pp. 874-76. Facsimile reprint. New York: Burt Franklin, 1967.
   Supplies available information on Butler's life. Since (on the authority of Butler's brother) he was a student at Cambridge, not Oxford, his life is included, paradoxically, under the name of the Puritan William Prynne, as the author of Two Letters, wrongly attributed to Prynne, according to Wood.

1821

1 "Imitations of Hudibras." Retrospective Review 3, article 7: 317-35.
   Surveys avowed imitations of the style and plan of Hudibras from the counterfeit second part of the poem--described as "contemptible and worthless"--to William Meston's The Knight of the Kirk--a "tolerably successful imitation" of Butler's style--noticing among others D'Urfey's Butler's Ghost, Hudibras at Court (unextractable), William Moffett's Irish Hudibras, Samuel Colvil's Scotch Hudibras, and Roger L'Estrange's Pendragon.

1846

*1 RAMSAY, ALEXANDER. Samuel Butler and His "Hudibras" and Other Works. London: Charles Knight & Co.
   Cited in 1973.4

1850

1 A., J. T. "Hogarth's Illustrations of Hudibras." N&Q 2 (26 October):355-56.

Identifies the designer of the illustrations in Grey's edition of Hudibras (1744.1) as Isaac Wood, who did nothing more than "remove some glaring indecencies" in the original plates engraved by Hogarth in 1726. The engravings are judged "very spiritless and indifferent productions."

2   DESCONOCIDO. "Note on a Passage in Hudibras." N&Q 2 (29 June):68-69.
    Supplies a possible source for Sir Hudibras's single spur: a jest-book entitled Gratiae Ludentes, by H. L. Oxen., published in 1638.

1852

1   CUNNINGHAM, PETER. "The Author of Hudibras at Ludlow Castle." N&Q 5 (3 January):5-6.
    Reprints a passage from Lord Carbery's account book revealing Butler's tenure as steward of the castle (January 1661-January 1662) and the nature of his duties.

1853

1   MITFORD, JOHN. "Life of Samuel Butler." In The Poetical Works of Samuel Butler. Vol. 1. Boston: Little Brown & Co., pp. vii-xxxvi.
    Reproduces familiar information on Butler's life and summarizes critical opinions of Hudibras, a poem that exhibits the same merits and defects as Young's Night Thoughts: "copious invention . . . and brilliant thoughts," but little coherence in the subject and progress in the story.

1854

1   GILFILLAN, GEORGE, ed. Introduction to Poetical Works. Vol. 1. Edinburgh: James Nichol.
    Reviews the familiar notions of Butler's life and works, summarizes the three parts of Hudibras, and compares it to the burlesque of Swift and Byron.

1857

1   A HERMIT AT HAMPSTEAD. "Butler's Hudibras." N&Q, 2d ser., 4 (5 September):191.
    Answers Deva's query (1857.5). The engraver of the illustrations in a 1720 edition of Hudibras was doubtless Hogarth; it is likely that he also engraved those in the 1732 edition. See also 1857.7, 11.

2 B., A. "Butler's Hudibras." N&Q, 2d ser., 4 (19 September): 230-31.
   Describes another 1732, 12mo. edition of Hudibras. See 1857.8, 10.

3 C., A. B. "Butler's Hudibras." N&Q, 2d ser., 4 (19 September): 230.
   Estimates the 1726, 12mo. edition (see 1857.7) "the most valued" of the small editions of Hudibras.

4 DE MORGAN, A. "Butler's Hudibras." N&Q, 2d ser., 4 (19 September):229-30.
   Accounts for errors in pagination in the 1726 edition of Hudibras.

5 DEVA. "Butler's Hudibras, 1732." N&Q, 2d ser., 4 (15 August): 131.
   Queries the identity of the engraver of illustrations in a 1732 edition of Hudibras. See 1857.1, 7, 10-11 for replies.

6 _____. "Butler's Hudibras." N&Q, 2d ser., 4 (19 September): 230.
   Further description of the pagination and engravings of the 1732, 12mo. edition of Hudibras.

7 F., P. H. "Butler's Hudibras." N&Q, 2d ser., 4 (5 September): 191.
   Replies to Deva's query (1857.5), explaining differences in the placing of illustrations in the 1726 and 1732 editions of Hudibras. See also 1857.1, 11 and 1965.4.

8 HENRI. "Butler's Hudibras." N&Q, 2d ser., 4 (19 September): 230.
   Further comment on the 1732, 12mo. edition of Hudibras. See also 1857.2, 10.

9 J., C. J. "Butler's Hudibras." N&Q, 2d ser., 4 (19 September): 229.
   Conjectures that the illustrations in a 1710 edition of Hudibras were not originally by Hogarth, but that he was employed to "improve" them. Cf. 1965.4.

10 MAYHEW, T. "Butler's Hudibras." N&Q, 2d ser., 4 (19 September):231.
    Another description of a 1732, 12mo. edition of Hudibras. See also 1857.2, 8.

11 N., G. "Butler's Hudibras, 1732." N&Q, 2d ser., 4 (29 August): 160.
    Answers Deva's query (1857.5). The plates in this edition, engraved by Hogarth, were reproduced in a 1732 Dublin edition. See also 1857.1, 7 and 1965.4.

1858

1 Ache! "Butler and Waller: Howard's 'British Princes.'" N&Q, 2d ser., 6 (28 August):164.

Queries Gilfillan's careless attribution (1854.1) to both Butler and Waller of the palinode on Howard's poem, and comments on his poor annotation of the lines on the "insect breeze" in Hudibras.

2 YEOWELL, J. "Hudibrastic Couplet." N&Q, 2d ser., 6 (29 August):161-62.

Summarizes suggested sources of the well-known lines "he that fights and runs away, / May live to fight another day" in Hudibras, III.iii.243.

1860

1 TANSWELL, J. "Notes on Hudibras." N&Q, 2d ser., 9 (25 February):138-39.

Reprints a "key" to the characters in Hudibras from an 1800 edition of the poem. Butler is said to be the source of the identifications which are "nearly identical" to those of Roger L'Estrange (1715.1).

1863

1 "Oldys's Notes on Hudibras." N&Q, 3d ser., 3 (7 February): 101-2.

Reprints annotations of Hudibras by William Oldys, found in a 1726 edition of the poem. "The Author's Life" included in the volume is attributed to Sir J. Anstrey [sic], the "alterations" of the text to Thomas Durfey.

2 TAINE, HIPPOLYTE ADOLPHE. Histoire de la littérature anglaise. Paris: Hachette, 1863-67.

Indicts Hudibras as an example of Restoration insipience, wanting action, simplicity, wit, and art. The poem recalls Cervantes less than it does Avellaneda, an imitator of Cervantes. The English translation by H. van Laun first appeared in 1871.

1866

1 B., W. C. "Butler's Hudibras." N&Q, 3d ser., 10 (1 September): 180.

Replies to Rix (1866.2) with a description of an earlier 8vo. edition of Hudibras. The title page of Part I is missing; Parts II and III are dated 1693 and 1694 respectively.

2 RIX, JOSEPH. "Butler's Hudibras." N&Q, 3d ser., 10 (21 July): 57.
    Notes a 1709 8vo. edition of the three parts of Hudibras not mentioned by Lowndes. See 1866.1.

1867

1 G., J. A. "The Name Hudibras." N&Q, 3d ser., 12 (21 December): 507-8.
    Adds Spenser's Faerie Queene to the list of early references to the name "Hudibras." See 1867.2, 3.

2 IRVING, GEORGE VERE. "Butler's Hudibras." N&Q, 3d ser., 12 (9 November):368.
    Surveys early references to the name "Hudibras" in Taylor, the Water Poet, Jonson, and Gifford. See also 1867.1,3.

3 LAELIUS. "The Name Hudibras." N&Q, 3d ser., 12 (21 December): 507.
    Notes Milton's reference to "Rudhuddibras or Hudibras," the grandfather of King Lear, and translates the meaning of this Welsh name as "Run of the powerful spear." See also 1867.1.

1868

1 BATES, WILLIAM. "MS. Annotations to Butler's Hudibras." N&Q, 4th ser., 1 (22 February):167-68.
    Reprints marginalia to the poem from a 1710 18mo. edition; the information supplied differs or augments that given by Grey or L'Estrange's "Key."

1869

1 ANTHONY-JOHNSTON, R. "Butleriana." N&Q, 4th ser., 4 (11 December):516.
    Queries the origin of Butler's reference to "sly surveyors who stole a shire" in "The Elephant in the Moon." William Petty's survey of Ireland is quoted. See 1879.1.

1870

1 BLAIR, D. "Butler and Remy Belleau: A Poetical Parallel." N&Q, 4th ser., 5 (9 April):358.
    Notes a parallel between Butler's description of the mob in Hudibras (I.ii.535ff.) and Belleau's comedy La reconnue.

1873

1 RIMBAULT, EDWARD F. "Hudibras." N&Q, 4th ser., 11 (19 April): 332.
   Confirms Solly's note (1873.3) that Hogarth's illustrations of Hudibras appeared first in the 1726 edition of the poem.

2 SOLLY, EDWARD. "Hudibras." N&Q, 4th ser., 11 (1 February): 103.
   Comments that the letters "E.C." on the whipping-post in Hogarth's illustration of the 1726 edition of Hudibras refer to the lord of the manor, possibly Earl Carbery, or to Earls Croom, where Butler was clerk to Justice Jefferey. See also 1873.1, 3-4.

3 _____. "Hudibras." N&Q, 4th ser., 11 (29 March):263.
   Points out that Hogarth was only an apprentice of eighteen in 1716, and so could not have designed the plates for the 1716 edition of Hudibras. See 1965.4.

4 STEPHENS, F. G. "Hudibras." N&Q, 4th ser., 11 (19 April):332.
   Maintains that the illustrations in the 1716 edition of Hudibras are copies of plates by an anonymous artist, not Hogarth, and were first published in the edition of 1710. Hogarth's illustrations of 1726 are traced through the 1739 edition of the poem. Cf. 1965.4.

1874

1 C., W. A. "Hudibras." N&Q, 5th ser., 2 (11 July):35.
   Identifies Sidrophel as William Lilly.

2 WILLIAMS, SPARKS HENDERSON. "Hudibras." N&Q, 5th ser., 2 (8 August):114-15.
   Cites Grey's notes on Hudibras to prove that Butler's reference to "matter . . . undress't (I.i.559-62) does not allude to Cleveland's description of a diurnal or to Regnier's Satire X, but simply ridicules "Hermetick Gibberish."

1875

1 MALCOLM, E. H. "Musical Revenge: Hudibras." N&Q, 5th ser., 4 (2 October):277-78.
   Maintains that after the Restoration, Hudibras "could not have been generally read." Its popularity in the nineteenth century was due to Cooke's illustrated edition of 1803. Cf. 1875.3.

1875

2   SOLLY, EDWARD. "Musical Revenge." N&Q, 5th ser., 3 (24 April): 325-26.

   Refers to a unique illustration in an 1800 edition of Hudibras (a woodcut by C. Nesbit) to interpret Crowdero's "vengeance" (I.iii.995-99) as fiddle playing.

3   STEPHENS, F. G. "Musical Revenge: Hudibras." N&Q, 5th ser., 4 (9 October):295-96.

   Disputes Malcolm's claim (1875.1) that Hudibras waned in popularity after the Restoration by referring to the frequency with which it was reprinted in illustrated editions. See also 1876.2.

1876

*1 BOXBERGER, RUDOLF. Butler's "Hudibras," ein echtes Zeit-und-Sittengemalde. Leipzig: Teubner.
   Cited in 1973.4.

2   MALCOLM, E. H. "Musical Revenge: Hudibras." N&Q, 5th ser., 5 (8 January):32.

   Answers Stephen's rebuttal (1875.3) by maintaining that the frequency of illustrated editions of Hudibras proves not the poem's popularity, but the need to make it popular.

1877

1   SOLLY, EDWARD. "Hudibras." N&Q, 5th ser., 7 (27 January): 71-72.

   Studies the illustrations in seven editions of Hudibras published from 1710 to 1726 (one of them dated 1709). Those in only the last of these editions are by Hogarth, though they are apparently redrawings of plates in the earliest edition. See also 1965.4.

1879

1   SOLLY, EDWARD. "Butler on Irish Surveyors." N&Q, 5th ser., 12 (26 July):75-76.

   Supplies information on Dr. Petty as annotation to Butler's reference to the "sly surveyors" of Ireland in "The Elephant in the Moon." See 1869.1.

1881

1   BEDE, CUTHBERT. "Samuel Butler's House." N&Q, 6th ser., 4 (10 December):469-70.

Presents information on "Butler's Cot"--the house in Strensham in which he was born--from a report of the Worcestershire Naturalists' Club (1855), John Noake's Rambler in Worcestershire (1848), and James Thorne's Rambles by Rivers: the Avon (1845).

2 LANGSTON, F. W. "Samuel Butler's House." N&Q, 6th ser., 4 (12 November):387.
   Discovers that Butler's house in Strensham was demolished by the squire, a Mr. Taylor.

1882

1 INGLEBY, C. M. "Butler's Hudibras, Part III., 1678." N&Q, 6th ser., 6 (30 September):276.
   Claims existence for a third version of Part III printed in 1678.

2 _____. "Butler's Hudibras, Part III., 1678." N&Q, 6th ser., 6 (4 November):370-71.
   Maintains that his variant copy of Part III is distinct from and intermediate between the two that Solly (1882.3, 4) differentiates.

3 SOLLY, EDWARD. "Butler's Hudibras, Part III., 1678." N&Q, 6th ser., 6 (19 August):150-51.
   Points out differences between two 1678 printings of the third part of Hudibras, arguing that the printings should be regarded as separate editions rather than two states of a single edition, as Lowndes described them.

4 _____. "Butler's Hudibras, Part III., 1678." N&Q, 6th ser., 6 (14 October):311-12.
   Reiterates his argument (1882.3) for two distinct issues of Part III printed in 1678, and suggests that other texts of this date (see 1882.1) may be variant states of one of them.

5 _____. "Butler's Hudibras, Part III., 1678." N&Q, 6th ser., 6 (2 December):454.
   Concludes that Ingleby's problematic 1678 printing of Part III (see 1882.2) is a copy of what he takes to be the first edition (see 1882.3), "but not in its first state."

1884

1 WARD, C. A. "Samuel Butler." N&Q, 6th ser., 10 (18 October): 301-2.
   Reviews the confusing details of Butler's biography: his birth date, his father's position, the poet's university, his

talent in painting, the model for Sir Hudibras, Butler's income from the crown, etc.

1893

*1 JOHNSON, REGINALD B., ed. <u>Poetical Works</u>. 2 vols. London: G. Bell and Sons.
Cited in 1973.4.

1895

1 GARNETT, R[ICHARD]. "Poets Contemporary with Dryden." In <u>The Age of Dryden</u>. London: G. Bell and Sons, pp. 53-56, 248-51.
Reviews the biography of Butler and surveys his writings in verse and (in the later passage) prose. Pope, who condensed a couplet from Butler's manuscript observation on the best and worst governments, may have known the manuscript material through Atterbury. Butler's satire, along with Marvell's, forms a transition between Donne's satire and Dryden's.

1898

1 AUBREY, JOHN. "Samuel Butler." In <u>"Brief Lives," chiefly of Contemporaries, set down by John Aubrey, between the Years 1669 & 1696</u>. Edited by Andrew Clark. 2 vols. Oxford: Clarendon Press, 1:135-38.
Personal notes on Butler's life and death compiled by a contemporary (one of the poet's pall-bearers): the starting point of most early biographies of the poet. Reprinted in <u>Aubrey's Brief Lives</u>, ed. Oliver Lawson Dick (London: Secker and Warburg, 1950).

1899

1 ELTON, OLIVER. <u>The Augustan Age</u>. New York: Charles Scribner's Sons, pp. 222-26.
Finds Butler's work an "annulment of the aesthetic feeling," the consequence of his dissatisfaction with both the old and new "inspirations." His travesty therefore lacks humanity, his wit humor.

1900

*1 HARDER, BRUNO. <u>Die Reime von Butlers "Hudibras."</u> Königsberg: Hartungsche buchdr.
Cited in 1973.4.

1901

1 DOWDEN, EDWARD. "Samuel Butler." In <u>Puritan and Anglican: Studies in Literature</u>. New York: Henry Holt & Co., pp. 279-310.
   Reviews Butler's works as an expression of Swiftian gloom. Though reason was the only basis of security in his views, it was destructive, chiefly useful in detecting unreason in politics and religion, bestiality in courtly life, madness and self-interest in science, and nonsense in literature. The ridicule of his satire is therefore intellectual ("wit," as he defined it), as demonstrated by "The Elephant in the Moon" and the ode "Upon a Hypocritical Nonconformist." Although <u>Hudibras</u> is a drollery, it has a serious intention--the recommendation of good sense; the second canto of Part III is Menippean (having "much in common" with the "Two Speeches made in the Rump Parliament" and in the "Speech made at the Rota"). The witty thoughts of Selden are also suggested as a source of <u>Hudibras</u>.

1902

1 CHEW, BEVERLY. "Some Notes on the Three Parts of <u>Hudibras</u>." <u>Bibliographer</u> 1 (April):123-38.
   Describes in detail three authorized and three unauthorized editions of Part I of <u>Hudibras</u>, two genuine and two spurious editions of Part II, and two genuine editions of Part III, supplying facsimiles of their title pages. Reprinted: 1926.1.

1903

1 COURTHOPE, W. J. <u>A History of English Poetry</u>. Vol. 3. London: Macmillan, pp. 355-77.
   Defends <u>Hudibras</u> against the criticisms of Johnson (1779.1) and Dryden (1692.1). Butler's satiric "design"--ridicule of a political party--was radically different from Cervantes's. His conception of the hero, therefore, owes nothing to the Spanish knight; it is drawn from a living original (Sir Samuel Luke): the more unlike a champion of romance, then, the more pointed the satire of Presbyterianism. The epic quarrels between the knight and squire also function satirically by differentiating between Presbyterian and Independent. Butler was less successful at designing epic actions that would function satirically; he would better have left the poem a fragment after the second canto. Finally, the style of the poem, combining burlesque manner and doggerel versification (and drawing upon Butler's "metaphysical fancy"), is also well adapted to its satiric purpose. Butler's satire is not limited by its occasion, however; like Cowley, he gives us "the last accents" of the Middle Ages, but his poem still speaks to us. See also 1901.1.

1904

1 WENDELL, BARRETT. The Temper of the Seventeenth Century in English Literature. New York: Charles Scribner's Sons, pp. 335-37.
   Argues that Hudibras was animated by the temper of a "fashionable class." The expression of this temper may have been insincere and cynical, but not dishonest; it implied that "it is better to recognize that whatever is is right than to pretend any longer that the only right things are things which can never exist in such a world."

1905

1 WALLER, A. R., ed. Hudibras. Cambridge: Cambridge University Press.
   Lacks commentary and introduction, though for many years the standard edition of Butler's poem. Supplanted by 1967.3.

1907

1 MAYHEW, A. L. "'Breese' in Hudibras." N&Q, 10th ser., 7 (29 June):515.
   Maintains that there is no such word as brimsa in Old English (1907.2) and that "'Breeze' reprents O.E. briosa."

2 PALMER, A. SMYTH. "'Breese' in Hudibras." N&Q, 10th ser., 7 (8 June):446.
   Interprets the word "Breese" (III.ii.1) as meaning "gadfly" (O.E. brimsa), not "breeze" as traditionally annotated.

3 _____. "'Breese' in Hudibras." N&Q, 10th ser., 8 (27 July): 77-78.
   Points out that the dialect occurrence of brimse or brimsey for gadfly suggests that it is an Old English word.

4 YARDLY, E. "'Breese' in Hudibras." N&Q, 10th ser., 7 (29 June):515.
   Contradicts Palmer's inference (1907.2) that the word "breese" was obsolete in the time of Zachary Grey (who misinterpreted it): it is included (with the meaning "gadfly") in Johnson's dictionary.

1908

1 SAINTSBURY, GEORGE. "The Octosyllable and the Anapest--Butler, Swift, and Prior." In A History of English Prosody from the

Twelfth Century to the Present Day. Vol. 2, From Shakespeare to Crabbe. New York: Macmillan Co., pp. 413-17. Reprint. New York: Russell & Russell, 1961.

Praises Butler's use of octosyllabics (and pentameters), but objects to the metrical label "hudibrastics." With Butler's example, the meter was "appanaged . . . against the tyranny of the heroic" and became the vehicle of prosodic independence.

2   WALLER, A. R., ed. Characters and Passages from Note-Books. Cambridge: Cambridge University Press.

For many years the only available source of Butler's prose characters and manuscript notebook materials. Incomplete and lacking commentary and introductory materials, this edition has been supplanted by 1970.2 and 1979.2.

1910

1   PREVITE ORTON, CHARLES WILLIAMS. Political Satire in English Poetry. Cambridge: At the University Press, pp. 84-91. Reprint. New York: Russell & Russell, 1968.

Characterizes Butler as a disciple of Cleveland and a practitioner of an old-fashioned mode of satire--hence the failure of his imitators and his kinship to Cervantes. The breadth of its scope has made Hudibras "a classic of the older English literature."

2   PRIDEAUX, W. F. "Hudibras: Earliest Pirated Edition." N&Q. 11th ser., 11 (10 September):211.

Questions the DNB's use of the word "pirated" to describe three "unauthorized" editions of Hudibras, each bearing the imprimature of Birkenhead, 11 November 1663, and seconds Chew's suggestion (1902.1) that the advertisement of a "false" copy in the Intelligencer may have been a sales gimmick. The spurious impression of Part II was a work by an unknown imitator of Butler, and hence not a piracy either.

3   ROBBINS, ALFRED F. "Hudibras: Earliest Pirated Edition." N&Q, 11th ser., 11 (20 August):142-43.

Explains the DNB's statement that the pirated edition of Hudibras, Part I, appeared before the authorized edition: the advertisement of the piracy appeared in The Kingdome's Intelligencer which, in the British Museum collection, is "bound in the first volume for 1662."

1911

1   BALDWIN, EDWARD CHAUNCY. "A Suggestion for a New Edition of Butler's Hudibras." PMLA 26:528-48.

Recommends using Butler's prose characters to clarify his satiric method and allusions in a new edition of Hudibras. The characters "prove" that the poem primarily satirizes the pretensions to godliness in Puritan and sectarian society and the hypocrisy of learning, politics, and medicine. The poem employs the satirical method (representations of a particular vice) of the characters, which is the method of the Roman satirists. As Butler dismembered the poem to write the characters, study of the latter reveals the method of the poem's construction--adaptation of the character sketch in prose to the purposes of political satire, thus combining the general and particular modes of the genre. To illustrate the usefulness of the characters for annotating the poem, passages of the former are set beside excerpts of the poetic portrait of Ralph.

1912

1 SMITH, WILLIAM FRANCIS. "Samuel Butler." In The Cambridge History of English Literature. Edited by A[dolphus] W[illiam] Ward and A[lfred] R[ayney] Waller. Vol. 8, The Age of Dryden. New York: G. P. Putnam's Sons, pp. 65-90.

Surveys available information on Butler's career and literary productions, and summarizes the three parts of Hudibras. The roots of the poem are traced to medieval satire of women and the mendicant orders. Butler's mock-heroic intention probably envisioned a fourth part, bringing the total number of cantos to the conventional dozen.

1920

1 CLOUGH, BEN C. "Notes on the Metaphysical Poets." MLN 35 (February):115-17.

Identifies two allusions in Hudibras, one (I.i.649-50) to Donne's "Progress of the Soul" (lines 511-12), the other (I.i. 165-66) to the epigram "Disputandi pruritus ecclesiarum scabies," attributed to Sir Henry Wotton.

1921

1 HANCOCK, C. V. "The Schools of Samuel Butler." N&Q 140 (5 February):107.

Offers indirect verification of the tradition that Butler attended the King's School at Worcester. Though Butler's name is not found in the register of the school (because he was not elected to a King's scholarship), that one of his classmates (according to John Aubrey) is: Mr. Richard Hill. (This note appears to be the obscure article published by "C. V. H." in the

Vigornian for November 1921 to which DeBeer 1928.3 refers.) See also 1952.3.

1923

1 CRAIG, HARDIN. "Hudibras, Part I, and the Politics of 1647." In The Manly Anniversary Studies in Language and Literature. Chicago: University of Chicago Press, pp. 145-55. Reprint. Freeport, N.Y.: Books for Libraries Press, 1968.
   Attempts to determine when Part I of Hudibras was written and what political significance it might have had at that time. Evidence that the first canto was composed before the execution of Charles I is suggested by the triviality of the implied cause of the war (misguided ignorance) and by echoes of the propositions presented to the king at the Treaty of Oxford. Allusions in the second canto are generally later than those in the first, although the king is still referred to as if alive; indications of the impending quarrel between Presbyterians and Independents and of Parliament's attempt to get rid of the army suggest a composition date of 1647-48. The third canto also contains references to this period. The faint outlines of a political allegory are defined: the flight of the bear may represent the king's flight from Hampton Court; the interference with the bear-baiting suggests the overthrow of the Presbyterians by the leaders of the army. The rabble and its leaders suggest the new model army and its leaders (Talgol:Fairfax, Magnano:Skippon, Cerdon:Ireton, Colon:Cromwell, Crowdero:Lilburne, Orsin:Prince Rupert). A portion of the second part of the poem was probably also written before the execution of the king (see also 1929.1); the remainder, together with the first and third cantos of Part III, was written during the Interregnum. Cf. Veldkamp (1923.2), who finds three distinct time references in the second canto of Part I; see also 1933.2 for evidence suggesting a later composition date for Part I.

2 VELDKAMP, JAN. Samuel Butler: The Author of "Hudibras." Hilversum: "De Atlas," 239 pp.
   Collects available information on Butler's life and works, discusses the political role of the various sects within English Puritanism in the seventeenth century, and assesses the influence of Cervantes and Rabelais on Hudibras and Butler's miscellaneous writings. Don Quixote was the model for Hudibras in both the general design (the adventures of a mock knight errant and his squire as a vehicle for satire) and--following Sancho's observation that Quixote was "fitter to be a Preacher, then for a Knight Errant"--in the conception of the hero as both Presbyterian and knight. In tone and spirit--e.g., in the coarse ridicule of women, occult learning, the law, Scholasticism--Butler is more akin to Rabelais (whom he read in the original) that to Cervantes. (Butler did not, however, take his famous analogy

of a boiled lobster and the sunrise from Rabelais; Pierre Motteux, whose English translation of the latter Butler did not live to see, took that from him.) However, Butler lacks the humanity of Cervantes and the redeeming laughter of Rabelais. His wit is intellectual, "metaphysical" in Johnson's sense; nothing escapes it and it affirms nothing. Butler is the complete skeptic, without faith in or sympathy for mankind, without love of religion-- Puritan or Anglican. His treatment of the former is here regarded as unfair--unloading on the Puritans all the follies of the age, which might as well be attached to their enemies. (Cf. 1933.1 on Restoration satire of Puritan ignorance.) The reader is admonished to beware the Puritan mythology created by Clarendon, Burnet, and (it is implied) Butler. This book was originally a Ph.D. dissertation completed in 1923 at the University of Amsterdam.

1924

1 LAMAR, RENÉ. "Du nouveau sur l'auteur d'Hudibras." Revue anglo-americaine 1:213-27.

Presents documentary evidence (some of it new because related to family connections in Defford) concerning the mystery of Butler's origin, the social status of his parents, and the question of his education, providing also grounds for probable conclusions on his early years. The poet's father, heir to a farm in Strensham and to property in Barbourne, was one of the most important men in the parish; capable and well-educated (designated "Gentleman" in a document of the period), he may have served the lord of the manor, Sir Thomas Russell, as secretary or steward, and succeeded his father as church-warden in Strensham. (Cf. the traditional view of Butler's humble origin in 1923.2.) The parish register for 14 February 1612 records the baptism of the poet (the second son of eight offspring), though not, as previously supposed, in his father's hand. Young Samuel was brought up in loyalist, if not royalist surroundings, and was instructed in the commonsense piety and discipline of an Anglican household. At age nine, when he entered the King's School in Worcester, his parents moved to Defford, where in November 1626 his father died. At the end of the following year, at age fifteen, he terminated his studies and became secretary to Leonard Jefferey, justice of the peace at Earle's Croome Court. His inheritance included a portion of his father's holding in Barbourne and, as the most erudite member of the family, his library. For information on Butler's later career, see 1928.3.

1925

1 WALKER, HUGH. English Satire and Satirists. London: J. M. Dent & Sons, pp. 127-44.

Restates the view that Butler was a one-poem poet, maintaining that he could not have written another way as well as he did in Hudibras. Proof appears in a comparison of the "short" and "long" verse versions of "The Elephant in the Moon"; the latter is described as "'short verse' and gas." Butler did one thing (political-religious satire) supremely well, and he did it one way, the medieval way. His ease in working without an artistic design (enabling him to include in a poem almost anything in his mind) and his whimsical and grotesque rhymes makes him "the last as well as the greatest of the medieval satirists"; he shows hardly a trace of the classical tradition. The failure of Butler's many imitators does not contradict this view. They failed not because Hudibras was too original to be repeated, but because "there could be but one Hudibras before medieval satire flickered out."

1926

*1 CHEW, BEVERLY. "Some Notes on the Three Parts of Hudibras." In Essays and Verses about Books. New York: Privately printed, pp. 64-95.
    Reprints 1902.1.

1928

1 "Hudibrastics." TLS, 16 August, p. 59.
    Comments (in a review of Lamar's edition of Butler's Satires and Miscellaneous Poetry and Prose [1928.5]) on the virtue (its hatred of pedantry, quackery, and snobbery, its exhilerating raciness and linguistic inventiveness in prose and verse, and its hearty, commonsense comedy) and faults (its pursuit of common sense beyond the limit of common sense, its inability to leave well enough alone, and its occasional silliness) of Butler's satirical writing. As a literary critic, Butler's common sense aligns him with the school of Rymer, though (given his hatred of pedantry) as one who sided with the Moderns; as a critic of the learning of his time, he wished to destroy not fact, but pretense, the abuse of learning. For a second opinion on Lamar's edition, provoked by this review, see 1928.4; see also 1969.2.

2 BLUNDEN, EDMUND. "Some Remarks on Hudibras." London Mercury 18:172-77.
    Samples the "permanent wit and poetry" (as opposed to the ephemeral topicality) of Hudibras. Selections illustrate four characteristics of the poem: the cinematic rapidity of comparisons; imagery that speaks the simple intelligence of the countryman (the ability to create "original proverbs"); the occasional music of delight and beauty; and the mastery of the odd and whimsical.

3 DE BEER, E. S. "The Later Life of Samuel Butler." RES 4 (April):159-66.

Brings together documented facts of Butler's later career and the publication of the three parts of Hudibras, and attempts to date the minor writings produced between 1667 and 1680. The earliest of the latter are the prologue and epilogue to Habington's Queen of Aragon, presumably written for a performance of the play on the Duke of York's birthday (14 October) in 1668. An uncomplimentary reference to Butler's interest in the theater is cited in an anonymous Session of the Poets (ca. 1665), and the manuscript of an unfinished tragedy entitled "Nero" testifies to this interest, as do two poems on Edward Howard's British Princes (early 1669), and the "Satirical Epistle to a Bad Poet" (also on Howard). The "Repartees between Cat and Puss," satirizing heroic tragedy, is associated with Dryden's Conquest of Granada, produced in December 1670, and, according to Wood, Butler had a hand in composing The Rehearsal. (He was acting as Buckingham's secretary in June 1673, during the latter's tenure as chancellor of Cambridge University, and may have accompanied him on an ambassadorial visit to France in the summer of 1670. The visit is unconfirmed here, but see 1945.1.) The satire "Upon Critics Who Judge of Modern Plays" was provoked by Rymer's Tragedies of the Last Age (1680). After the publication of the third part of Hudibras, Charles granted Butler 100 pounds and an annual pension of an equal amount, mitigating the tradition (to which Butler himself seems to have contributed) that the king was neglectful (see also 1944.1).

4 GREG, W. W. "Hudibrastics." TLS, 23 August, p. 605.

Criticizes Lamar's edition of Butler's fragments in verse and prose (1928.5) on the grounds that it does not follow the order of subject groupings in the manuscript and makes no reference to the folios on which they occur. Moreover, the edition is incomplete, takes no account of Butler's alterations in the course of composition, and offers readings that are "not correct." See also 1928.1, 1969.2, and 1979.2.

5 LAMAR, R[ENÉ]. Satires and Miscellaneous Poetry and Prose. Cambridge: Cambridge University Press.

The most complete edition of Butler's miscellaneous poetry and prose writings (excluding the characters and notebook materials). Reviewed: 1928.4. The attribution to Butler of many of the works in this volume is judged in 1982.1.

1929

1 CURTISS, JOSEPH TOY. "Butler's Sidrophel." PMLA 44:1066-78.

Accounts for inconsistencies in the character Sidrophel—part fraudulent astrologer, part silly Royal Society experimenter—by postulating two dates, sixteen years apart, for its composition. Allusions to the witch-finder Mathew Hopkins, near the beginning of the third canto of Part II of Hudibras, and to John Cleveland's attacks upon William Lilly in Mercurius Pragmaticus indicate that Butler originally proposed--perhaps as early as 1647 (see 1923.1) and perhaps at Cleveland's prompting--a satiric portrait of Lilly, the Puritan astrologer. This portion of the canto was apparently shelved until the success of the First Part of the poem (1662-63) was assured, by which time the Royal Society had replaced astrology as the object of Butler's satiric attention, and Sidrophel became a virtuoso. Allusions to the spurious Second Part of Hudibras, to Robert Hooke's microscopic observations of insects (which Butler could have known only in manuscript), and to Sir Kenelm Digby's The Powder of Sympathy indicate a date of 1663 for this part of the canto (see also 1965.3). The argument explains in a similar way the inconsistencies in the character Wachum, Sidrophel's servant--originally a portrait of Lilly's associate, John Booker, and later a composite portrait of Booker (who, like Wachum, wrote verse) and the unknown author of the spurious Second Part of Hudibras. In "The Heroicall Epistle of Hudibras to Sidrophel," added to the Second Part of the poem in 1674, Sidrophel is clearly a portrait of the Royal Society member, Sir Paul Neile.

2 QUINTANA, RICARDO. "John Hall of Durham and Samuel Butler: A Note." MLN 44 (March):176-79.
    Points out similarities of phrasing, style, and movement in Hall's "A Satire" (published in the 1646 edition of his Poems) and Butler's Hudibras, and suggests Hall's general contribution, "as an essayist," to the development of a central concern of Butler's thought: the defense of a theory of intellectual values. Butler may have learned more from Hall about the matter, manner, and spirit of satire than has been recognized. See also 1933.3.

1931

1 WEST, ALBERT H. L'influence française dans la poésie burlesque en Angleterre entre 1660 et 1700. Paris, pp. 105-55. Reprint. New York: Burt Franklin, 1971.
    Reviews the evidence of Butler's knowledge of French (he translated Boileau's second satire as a "Satirical Epistle to a Bad Poet") and his disapproval of the Francomania in English society (in the ode "To the Memory of . . . Du-Val," for instance). His dislike of things French did not, however, prevent him from popularizing the French burlesque in England. His immediate models in burlesque, though, were Cervantes and Rabelais, not Scarron; similarities between Hudibras and the Satire Ménippée are also discounted. Butler is regarded as a "rare and exceptional" genius, capable of writing a serious poem. See also 1932.1.

1932

1 BOND, RICHMOND P. English Burlesque Poetry: 1700-1750. Harvard Studies in English. Cambridge, Mass.: Harvard University Press, pp. 3-17, 145-54.

Situates Hudibras and the term "Hudibrastic" within a classificatory scheme of burlesque, a genre in which (imitated) matter and (imitated) manner are associated in order to create an incongruity between subject and style. Two generic classes are differentiated on the basis of method: one in which style is lower in dignity than subject and diminishes the latter, and one in which subject is lower than style and magnifies the former-- low burlesque and high burlesque respectively. These two classes are in turn subdivided on the basis of the generality of the imitation: travesty and parody imitate particular works or styles; Hudibrastic and the mock poem are generic imitations. But Hudibras, which imitates serious chivalric romance in a comic verse medium, seems too complex to submit to such a classification. The poem is both satire and burlesque; its hero is both caricatured and placed in a heroic framework. Moreover, the concept of the Hudibrastic was based not upon Butler's manner, but upon the productions of its imitators, for whom it became purely a medium of ridicule. But the original manner is more than that; however much it is able to diminish what it touches, its wit and power make it admirable in itself. The short couplet, using unexpected rhymes and odd comparisons, existed in England before Butler; the latter's debt to Scarron is broadly stylistic, extending to the habit of digression and the whimsical citation of authority (cf. 1931.1). Butler's imitators first appeared with the counterfeit second part of Hudibras (1663) and continued through the middle of the next century; American imitations appeared at the time of the Revolution.

2 WEBSTER, C[LARENCE] M. "Hudibras and Swift." MLN 47 (April): 245-46.

Cites Swift's allusion to "English Mall" in "Baucis and Philemon" as a borrowing from Hudibras I.ii.367, and as "one very obvious proof that Swift had carefully read Hudibras." See also 1951.1, 1954.1, and 1958.1.

1933

1 GIBSON, DAN, JR. "Samuel Butler." In Seventeenth Century Studies. Edited by Robert Shafer. Princeton: Princeton University Press for the University of Cincinnati, pp. 277-335. Reprint. Freeport: Books for Libraries Press, 1968.

Extracts Butler's views on society, the state, the church, science, and literature from his notebooks and posthumously published writings. Butler regarded wealth as both the measure and guarantee of moral behavior. This practical concession to power is closer to Stoic individualism than to Hobbes's egotism. Self-love nevertheless underlies relations between the sexes and the institution of marriage. In political theory, Butler was a conservative. Contemptuous of the ignorance of the masses, his outlook was aristocratic and absolutist--though not by necessity, as was Hobbes's; a parliament is, however, a necessary safeguard against arbitrary power. Butler would limit the power of the monarch, but would also have that monarch grant as little real liberty to the people as possible. His views on the place of law in government are similarly complex: those mockingly ascribed to the Royalist-Puritan lawyer William Prynne in Mola Asinaria might be Butler's own. Of the Anglican Church, Butler is often as critical as he is of Puritanism: he was Anglican by convention. Hypocrisy, he believed, was a fault of all churches, but chiefly of the Roman Church. His criticism of religious superstition (including Puritan inspiration), of magic, astrology, and alchemy, and his total disbelief in "the visible supernatural" is a measure of his rationalism. But there is also an empirical strain in Butler's thought. Knowledge was "a right observation of Nature"; it was immediate and practical: Hudibras's words to Sidrophel speak Butler's mind (cf. 1976.2). Rationalism determined his views on literature. Above all, he reacted against the tyranny of the Ancients, except where they happened to agree with his own commitment to Nature. Butler adopted Hobbes's subordination of fancy to judgment and the Royal Society's recommendation of the plain style. His later literary opinions "definitely announce the advent of a new age."

2 QUINTANA, RICARDO. "The Butler-Oxenden Correspondence." MLN 48 (January):1-11.

Attempts to find evidence of the date of composition of the First Part of Hudibras and of the identity of Sir Hudibras in three pieces of hitherto unpublished correspondence between Richard Oxenden and his cousin George, president of the East India Company, living at the time in Surat. Richard's letter (dated 30 March 1663) includes another by Butler, accompanying a copy of the First Part of Hudibras sent him by another relative. It identifies the poet as one with whom Sir George had spent some time on an earlier visit to England (probably between June 1659 and May 1660, though possibly as early as 1653-56), "not long" before which, according to Butler's letter, the First Part of Hudibras "was written." (For an earlier dating of Part I, see 1923.1.) It is possible, however, that Butler's "written" may refer to a redaction of earlier written materials. Butler's statement that the model for Hudibras was a "West Countrey" knight and a committeeman suggests an identification with Sir Henry Rosewel of Devonshire rather than Sir Samuel Luke of Bedfordshire. The preferred identification here is attributed to a contemporary bencher of Gray's Inn, a figure with whom Butler is associated in Richard's letter and in Aubrey's brief life of the poet. The correspondence is reprinted in 1967.3.

3 _____. "Butler." MLN 48 (November):486.
    Corrects a misstatement in the preceding article (1933.2). The reference to "Gray's Inn Walkes" in Richard Oxenden's letter does not associate Butler with Gray's Inn. Rather, the reference makes Butler's association with certain men (the Oxendens, Cleveland, John Hall, the bencher who provided an identification of Hudibras) "seem quite certain."

1935

1 BENSLY, EDWARD. "The Name Hudibras." N&Q 168 (2 March):160.
    Objects to Duffett's positiveness (1935.2) about Butler's having taken the name of his hero from Jonson's Sir Rud Hughdebras in The New Inn, and recommends Zachary Grey's inclination to regard Spenser as Butler's source.

2 DUFFETT, G. W. "The Name Hudibras." N&Q 168 (9 February):96.
    Cites a reference in Jonson's The New Inn (I.ii) to an unknown "Sir Hughdebras," perhaps a Cornish knight of popular ballad, and concludes that this was "doubtless" Butler's source for the name of his hero. Cf. 1935.1.

1936

1 HINDLE, C. J. "A Broadside by Samuel Butler." TLS, 21 March, p. 244.
    Notes the existence of Butler's "A true and perfect Copy of the Lord Roos His Answer to the Marquesse of Dorchester's Letter written the 25. of February 1659," the second of three exchanges published as broadsides and then collected in a quarto pamphlet (1660). Butler's authorship of the second letter is confirmed by Elias Ashmole, and is so attributed by John Aubrey.

1937

1 RICHARDS, EDWARD AMES. Hudibras in the Burlesque Tradition. Columbia University Studies in English and Comparative Literature, no. 127. New York: Columbia University Press, 186 pp.
    Considers the relation of hudibrastic burlesque to political and social phenomena between 1680 and 1830. Hudibras, the source of this tradition, is less a partisan satire than the expression of a peculiarly independent temperament--isolated from all parties and churches, cut off from every means of social identification. Butler's mind is the authority of the satire. His imitators, however, regarded his poem as a satire of dissent and as the model of partisan verse. Written after the defeat of the forces of dissent, Hudibras takes a retrospective stance; but Thomas D'Urfey's Butler's Ghost and Collin's Walk (typical of

these imitations) are nothing if not partisan and current. In a
number of hudibrastic productions of the 1680s, Catholicism or
Jacobitism is linked with the sects in a common effort to overthrow the government. In England, the tradition draws to a close
in the first decade of the eighteenth century with Edward Ward's
Vulgus Britannicus. It continues, however, in Scotland in the
productions of Samuel Colville, Archibald Pitcairne, William
Meston, and William Cleland, the last having the distinction of
being Presbyterian and turning hudibrastics against the Angli-
cans and Tories, and in Ireland hudibrastics became a weapon
against Methodism. Since hudibrastic burlesque appears wherever
the ruling class feels threatened by democratic or populist tendencies, in America it voiced loyalist sentiments, a notable exception being John Trumbull's M'Fingal, a satire of High Church
monarchism (see 1956.1). Butler's influence all but ends with
Matthew Prior's transformation of octosyllabics into an instrument of polite philosophical satire in Alma. The distance between Butler's burlesque and that of his realist imitators is
epitomized in Hogarth's illustrations of Hudibras, representations of real people instead of the fantastic inventions of his
text (cf. 1971.8).

1939

*1 BÜELER, SIGISBERT. "J. H. Waser, 1713-1777, Diacon in Winter-
thur, als Ubersetzer des 'Hudibras' von Samuel Butler." Ph.D.
dissertation, University of Freiburg.
Cited in 1973.4.

1940

1 BROOKS, HAROLD F. "Gift to Samuel Butler." TLS, 6 July,
p. 327.
Adds to the list of Butler's grants and pensions in 1674-77
(see 1928.3) the payment of 20 pounds "as free guift and royal
bounty" from the Secret Service funds. The item appears in
Henry Guy's account, passed 10 May 1680. Guy's previous account
was passed 10 April, for notice of which, see 1944.1.

1943

1 RICHARDS, GERTRUDE R. B. "Butler's Hudibras." More Books:
The Bulletin of the Boston Public Library 18 (November):407-10.
Presents available information on the publication and re-
ception of the three parts of Hudibras. Three editions of Part
I are listed--one of them spurious (cf. 1967.3)--all of them
dated 1663 but published by the end of 1662. The original of
Sir Hudibras is believed to be Sir Samuel Luke (cf. 1933.2).

1944

1 BENTLEY, NORMA E. "A Grant to Hudibras Butler." MLN 59 (April):281.

Casts further doubt on the tradition of Butler's abject poverty (see 1928.3) by bringing to light evidence of Charles's "free guift" to the poet of 20 pounds, ordered 10 May 1680. See also 1940.1.

2 ———. "Hudibras Butler." Ph.D. dissertation, Syracuse University, 236 pp.

Draws upon Butler's manuscript materials (both the British Museum manuscripts and the Rosenbach commonplace book) to fill out the poet's biography and to interpret his thoughts on religion, government, and science. The greater part of the commonplace book is judged to be in Butler's hand, parts of it written as early as the 1650's, most of it between 1667 and 1669. A reference to Samuel Parker's Case of the Church of England may have been made by the poet in the last year of his life--assuming that the printed date (1681) of the Case was anticipated, as those of the three parts of Hudibras were (see also 1947.1). Central to the interpretations of Butler's thought and of Hudibras is his longing to identify himself with the leisured class and his hatred and fear of war. Butler's rationalism led him in the direction of deism, though he accepted revelation and, as his notebook quotations of seventeenth-century theologians suggest, found the Church of England "more satisfying" toward the end of his life. His satire of the virtuosi was not a blanket condemnation of science, but "constructive advice" to scientists (see also 1983.1). The satire of Hudibras is "probably more general" than the poem's focus on Puritanism suggests. Sir Hudibras was Butler's (and England's) scapegoat; abuse of the Puritans asuaged the nation's sense of war guilt. But the knight was also an aristocrat, and in berating him, Butler also berated the court.

1945

1 BENTLEY, NORMA E. "Hudibras Butler Abroad." MLN 60 (April): 254-59.

Supplies evidence from Butler's unpublished commonplace book proving that he traveled to France in 1670. The evidence consists of a partially compiled English-French dictionary and firsthand observations of France and the French people including references to the building by Louis XIV of the Arc de Triomphe du Trone (under construction in 1669) and an observatory (completed in 1672). The evidence also supports the contention that Butler was part of the company (including Thomas Sprat and Joe Haines) that preceded or followed Buckingham on a diplomatic mission to the Court of Louis in the summer of 1670. Butler's notes make passing references to "the King's houses" and to the summer vacation of the French parliament.

1946

1 ALLEN, DON CAMERON. "Donne, Butler, and ?" MLN 61 (January): 65.
 Points out a similarity between Butler's notebook opinion of John Donne (his "writings are like Voluntary or Prelude . . .") and an observation on the pulpit style of Donne and Andrews published in The Surfeit to A.B.C. (1656), attributed to either Philip King, Philip Kynder (a friend of John Selden's), or Philip Kirk. The clarity of the latter remark suggests its priority. Butler's criticism is the response of a reader, not a listener, and probably refers to Donne's poems rather than to his sermons. See 1946.2 for a response to the last remark.

2 BENTLEY, NORMA E. "In Defense of Butler." MLN 61 (May):359-60.
 Argues that Butler's recorded opinion of Donne (see 1946.1) refers to the latter's poems, not his sermons. Butler used the word "scope" in this note and also in his character of "A Small Poet." Moreover, although Butler's notebooks contain many references to seventeenth-century divines (but none to Donne in this respect), his interest in them was in their theology, not their style. It is unlikely, then, that in his one reference to Donne he would be thinking of his pulpit style. Butler's opinion (of Donne's poetry) may be completely original (as may also be that of the author of The Surfeit to A.B.C.); Butler's opinion is also just.

1947

1 ANDERSON, PAUL BUNYAN. "Anonymous Critic of Milton: Richard Leigh? or Samuel Butler?" SP 44 (July):504-18.
 Arguing that Butler was an ally of Andrew Marvell's opponent, Samuel Parker, Anderson believes that Butler, not Leigh (as Anthony à Wood believed), was the author of The Transproser Rehears'd (1673) and, because of their similarity to this work, of The Character of the Rump (1660) and The Censure of the Rota upon Mr. Milton's Book (1660), here claimed to contain "the most cogent" criticism of Milton produced in the period. Marvell himself, it is argued, attributed The Transproser to Butler by ironic denial. External evidence supporting Butler's authorship includes his familiarity with pre-Restoration theological controversy, his affiliation with Buckingham in the composition of the original Rehearsal (cf. 1982.1), and a relationship with Parker sufficiently close and sympathetic to account for Butler's manuscript summary, shortly before his death, of two as yet unpublished works of Parker's. Internal evidence includes the re-

petition in The Transproser and The Censure of certain figures and ideas found in Butler's published and manuscript writings: e.g., the expression of his dislike of Dryden and his admiration of Donne (see 1946.1); similar analogues are adduced for the criticism of Milton's argumentative style, his versification and "Babylonish dialect." Butler was qualified to be Milton's "most vigorous critic" because--as Richards (1937.1) demonstrated--he was Milton's opposite. Cf. 1972.7.

1948

1 BAUER, JOSEPHINE. "Some Verse Fragments and Prose Characters by Samuel Butler Not Included in the Complete Works." MP 45 (February):160-68.

Describes the contents of five articles from the London Magazine of 1825-26 containing twenty prose characters and 582 lines of verse taken apparently from folios that are now lost from the Butler manuscript collection currently in the British Museum (cf. 1979.2). Eight of the characters ("A Self-Conceited Man," "A Bawd," "An Ambitious Man," "A Vapourer," "A Morose Man," "A Railer," "A Drunkard," and "A Master of Arts"), not included in Waller's edition of Butler's characters, and a number of passages of couplet verse that do not appear in Lamar's edition of the miscellaneous verse are reprinted here. The second article in the series consists of a long (252 lines) but incomplete verse narrative entitled "The Doctor and His Wife's Pin Money," not present as such in Lamar's volume, but (with the exception of a "very few figures and only a dozen and a half couplets") found there under the heading "Physique" and scattered throughout the miscellaneous materials--such was Butler's method of composition (cf. 1969.2). The character of "A Self-Conceited Man" may be an earlier version or revision of "The Self Conceited or Singular" in Waller's edition, but "it is a distinct character."

2 BENTLEY, NORMA E. "Another Butler Manuscript." MP 45 (November):132-35.

Announces the discovery of an unpublished manuscript commonplace book in the A. S. W. Rosenbach collection. The book was apparently part of Butler's bequest to William Longueville, and it contains entries by the latter and perhaps others, one of which dispels the notion that Butler had begun a tragedy called "Nero" (see, e.g., 1928.3), here identified as "a series of quotations from a play of that name first published in 1624." The greater part of the manuscript is in Butler's hand, however, most of it written between 1667 and 1669, though the range of references extends from the "present usurpacon" (1650s) to Samuel Parker's Case of the Church of England (1681), published the year after Butler's death (see also 1947.1). The volume contains two of Butler's characters, "A Lawyer," which "differs somewhat" from the printed version, and a "Schoolmaster," which is printed here for the first time.

1951

1 KULISCHECK, CLARENCE L. "Hudibrastic Echoes in Swift." N&Q 196 (4 August):339.
   Cites Swift's use of the rhyme "philosopher"/"gloss over" in "An Epistle to a Lady" as evidence of Butler's influence on Swift. See also 1932.2, 1954.1, and 1958.1.

2 QUINTANA, RICARDO. "Samuel Butler: A Restoration Figure in a Modern Light." ELH 18 (March):7-31.
   Traces in Butler's notebooks a "reasonably . . . self-consistent philosophic system" underlying his moral and religious views. Butler begins from the traditional distinction between truth and opinion. Truth results from the proper function of reason; confirmed by demonstration, the product is knowledge--opinion is the product of unassisted fancy. Unlike Hobbes, Butler does not naturalize human defects; rather, the defects make man unnatural. Learning is corrupted either by failing to observe the limits of understanding or by bogging down in trivialities. True wisdom disillusions (Butler anticipates Swift's definition of happiness as the ability to be well deceived, and his awareness of the inconsistency between surfaces and depths). Butler nevertheless preferred Moderns to Ancients; his cosmology reflects the new astronomy; his intellectual values resemble those of the Baconians. His religious views have more in common with Anglican rationalism (see 1946.2) than with deism even though he considered a rational understanding of God sufficient for human purposes. In politics, Butler was conservative by instinct. His theory of literature also affirms his concept of a rationally ordered world; since the product of reason, truth, cannot be depicted by analogy, literature must deal with types of ignorance, folly, and knavery. The images of heroic poetry are unnatural. There is, however, a controlled use of falsehood, wit, a means of distorting truth to advantage. Butler's use of such wit is noted in the parody and impersonations of Mola Asinaria, the Two Letters, and the mock-Pindarick ode to Du-val. Witty distortion is found even in the prose character of "A Modern Politician," where an ethical statement is made by the subject's self-description--a foreshadowing of the technique and spirit of the next age.

3 SMITH, HAROLD WENDELL. "'Reason' and the Restoration Ethos." Scrutiny 18 (Autumn):118-36.
   Defining the Restoration ethos as a change, in society and religion, from a static order protecting and protected by the Old Monarchy to a state of dynamic flux advanced by (and in turn maintaining) progressive Puritan theology and bourgeois commer-

cial enterprise, Smith argues that criticism of abstract reason and espousal of the sensory and the natural in the writings of Sprat, Dryden, Rochester, and Butler represent their reactions to this historical phenomenon. Paradoxically, it was abstract intellectualism (Aristotelianism) that led to both the "mystical riddles" (antirationalism) of Butler's Fifth Monarchy man and, in the form of the mental science of capitalist economics, to the very material effects of the bourgeoisie upon the old order. Butler's mock-romance Hudibras (the very form of which attacks the traditional use of language divorced from things) provides the clearest view of these paradoxical relations between abstractness and chaos, words and deeds.

1952

1 JACK, IAN. "Low Satire: Hudibras." In Augustan Satire: Intention and Idiom in English Poetry: 1660-1750. Oxford: Clarendon Press, pp. 15-42.

Classifies Hudibras as low satire rather than burlesque. The latter term--as the designation for a work marked by incongruity of subject and style (see 1932.1)--would be appropriate only if the world of the entire poem symbolized the civil wars; but this is true only of the initial impetus of the poem--Butler's application of Spenser's Sans-loy/Huddibras contrast to the opposition of the Royalists and the Parliamentary party. But the general satire of Hudibras exceeds its burlesque of political parties. Again, like Spenser's heroes, Butler's hero functions allegorically--but as the embodiment of the all-encompassing sin of hypocrisy rather than the cardinal virtues. Hudibras and his adventures are undignified; the style--harsh enjambments, odd rhymes, low diction--is also undignified: there is no inconsistency between subject and style. The method is straightforward diminution--the opposite of the mock-heroic. But the poem is also parodic, as another aspect of the diction illustrates; the satire is literary as well as moral. Butler was a typical Augustan conservative; he was respectful of ancient models (cf. 1951.2) and suspicious of "modern" innovation--hence the parody of romantic epic, medieval metrical romance, and seventeenth-century prose romance. He was "a thoroughly traditional humanist," concerned with the propriety of the vernacular--hence the parody of rhetorical affectation, professional and religious cant, and logical sophistry. The realistic bent (cf. 1937.1) of Butler's imagery--parodying the "Metaphor-mongers" of dissenting pulpits, and imitating the witty extravagances of metaphysical poets--distinguishes Hudibras "most sharply" from burlesque; its adaptation of wit to the purposes of low satire earns it an important place in the evolution of the Augustan idiom.

2 LAMAR RENÉ. "Samuel Butler à l'école du Roi." EA 1 (February):17-24.

Offers information on the King's School in the seventeenth century as a context for Butler's remarks on education in the characters, notebooks, and miscellaneous satire. Butler was extremely critical of his own education. He regarded Henry Bright, the principal of the King's School, and his assistant Henry Randolph (both were probably Butler's teachers), as vain, ignorant tyrants. Latin was a "detested memory" for Butler, Greek a useless labor, Hebrew, at best, an occasion for vanity. Thomas Hall, a student of King's in Butler's time who later marshaled the full weight of his learning to prove the "Loathsomeness of Long Haire," is cited as an example of the actual effect of such an education on a mediocre mind; Sir Hudibras was its literary caricature. Nevertheless, the King's School left its mark on Butler; his lifelong habit of keeping a commonplace book was a product of the scholastic habit of recording and classifying rhetorical examples. So was the erudition with which he stuffed his satires. Butler never ceased to reread and admire the ancients, Ovid, Virgil, Cicero, Horace, and the Roman historians. Not from Rabelais (whom he does not mention in the commonplace book), but from Erasmus (whom he would have read in the sixth year curriculum), he took his style of burlesque and perhaps received his satiric calling.

3 NATAN, ALEX. "Samuel Butler's School." TLS, 11 January, p. 25.
    Establishes again (see 1921.1) the right of King's Cathedral School over Worcester Royal Grammar to claim Butler as a scholar. The authority cited here is Alec Mackonald, the historian of King's, and the fact that the school owns an old engraving of Butler as an "O. V.," i.e., "an old boy of the Regia Schola Vivorniensis." See also 1952.2.

1953

1 CONNELLY, KENNETH AMOR, JR. "A Preface to Hudibras." Ph.D. dissertation, Yale University, 295 pp.
    Discusses obstacles to the modern reader's appreciation of Hudibras: first, understanding Butler's thought (he was a conservative moralist whose values were close to those of orthodox Christianity); second, understanding the genre of the poem (mock-romance, a "special type" of mock-heroic that revealed the impossibility of heroism in the Commonwealth period); and third, understanding the parodic methods of the poem and their relation to literary and social circumstances (e.g., Butler's comic adaptation of the devices of metaphysical poetry). See also DAI 30 (1969):5403-4A.

2 LEYBURN, ELLEN DOUGLASS. "Hudibras Considered as Satiric Allegory." HLQ 16 (February):141-60.
    Reads Hudibras as a satiric allegory not of particular persons (cf. 1929.1) or events (cf. 1923.1), but of the general

human faults and habits of mind that most repelled Butler and that he saw illustrated in the quarrels of the Puritan sects. Butler's critical comments on the moral effectiveness of allegory and metaphor recorded in his notebooks justify such a reading; the validity of these comments is in turn confirmed by the recognition that the indirect (allegorical) satire of the poem is more convincing than the direct (nonallegorical) satire of the prose characters. The mode of indirection (the mock-heroic) in Hudibras is peculiarly complex because the two levels of allegory (representation and meaning) are not widely separated in the poem as they are in the beast fable: the fantastic distortions of the burlesque vehicle are very close to the real intellectual distortions of the Puritan tenor. Butler emphasizes this distinction by first surveying the mental confusion of his hero (tenor), and then presenting his bodily awkwardness (vehicle) as a sign of the former. Viewed this way, Veldkamp's charge (1923.2) that Butler is unfair in mocking the Puritans as lechers, cowards, and believers in astrology and chivalry is off the mark: Butler is satirizing hypocrisy, irrationality, and avarice; the extravagances ridiculed are simply the means of expressing those faults. The weakness of the poem consists of its failure to digest all that is satirized into the allegorical framework. Thus, because Hudibras's harangue to the rabble mentions actual events of 1638 to 1643, the controversy over breaking up the bear-baiting is linked to the historical events-- becomes, that is, a vehicle for an actual quarrel among the saints. Similarly, the debate between Hudibras and Ralpho over "'Synods or Bears' repeatedly jerks us back and forth in the two modes of conception," indirect allegory and direct satire. Reprinted in slightly altered form in 1956.2.

1954

1 KULISHECK, CLARENCE L. "Swift's Octosyllables and the Hudibrastic Tradition." JEGP 53 (July):361-68.
   Locates similarities between Swift's hudibrastics (i.e., octosyllabic couplets) and Butler's in matters of technique-- especially in the repeated use of the hypercatalectic line (with double and triple rhyme)--and in the expression of "direct and simple contempt." Swift added variety and movement to Butler's uniform couplets.

2 LAMAR, RENÉ. "Samuel Butler et la justice de son temps." EA 7, no. 3:271-79.
   Draws upon Butler's characters of legal types and his notebook observations of legal practices to describe the English institution of law in the poet's time. Butler's legal knowledge was acquired firsthand in his service with Leonard Jefferey, and although he applied himself diligently at the outset, his natural honesty soon recoiled at the conventional practice of

justice; the faults in the system shocked his reason. Butler therefore brought to the English tradition of legal satire a surprising harshness. Nevertheless, the judicial world haunted him; its language is everywhere in his work. When, however, it became necessary to side with either the mysteries of the law or common reason, with the judges or the king, he chose the latter in both cases.

1955

1 BOYCE, BENJAMIN. "Postscript: From Polemic Character to Verse Satire." In The Polemic Character: 1640-1661. Lincoln: University of Nebraska Press, pp. 115-23.
   Points out resemblances between anti-Puritan witticisms in Hudibras and in polemical characters published after 1640. Cleveland's Character of a London Diurnall (1645), for example, may have supplied the image of formless "First Matter" (which Ralpho had "seen undrest"), or that of the "upstart sect'ry" that erupts like a wen. Also to Cleveland (who spoke of the parliamentary diurnals as "Quixotes . . . fighting with the windmills of their own heads") may be due the association of Presbyterianism and knight-errantry. Hudibras's well-stocked breeches are similar to those of the character of an "Upstart Pragmatical" (1661), and his dogmatism and disputatiousness are typical features of other characters of Puritans. Butler breaks with the stereotype, however, in not making his Presbyterian a psalm-singer or an advocate of predestination and in making him "learnedly foolish," an innovation that broadens his satire to cover more than a specific class of fools. This is regarded as a fault rather than a virtue--but a fault Butler shared with the polemical character writers: they all said too much.

2 BRINKLEY, ROBERTA FLORENCE, ed. "Samuel Butler." In Coleridge on the Seventeenth Century. Durham: Duke University Press, pp. 614-17.
   Brings together five comments by Coleridge on Butler's satire (which is serious and provokes sardonic laughter), his wit (which arises from the surprising identity of dissimilar thoughts), his poetic manner (which is characterized by too great a fullness in the parts to permit a unity of impression in the whole), and his value as a moral teacher (which, as also in Swift, consists of the satirical representation of spiritual pretense).

3 KER, W. P. "Samuel Butler." In On Modern Literature: Lectures and Addresses. Edited by Terence Spencer and James Sutherland. Oxford: Clarendon Press, pp. 1-12. Reprint. Folcroft, Pa.: Folcroft Press, 1969.
   Locates Butler, along with Rabelais, Jonson, and Browning, in the tradition of the "lonely scholar," characterized by in-

satiable and unsystematic reading, and by "a sort of drunken exhileration of learning" that never sinks to pedantry. A humorist--in the sense of one "who would follow his own bent, and choose his own mode of behavior"--Butler expressed himself by old-fashioned literary modes. Yet, as his notebooks indicate, his mind and thought are representative of a modern cooling down of Renaissance enthusiasm due to an awareness of human limitations. The paradox of Butler's work, then, is that he expresses by antiquated methods the thought of the century that succeeded him.

4 MILLER, WARD SEARING. "The Allegory in Hudibras." Ph.D. dissertation, State University of Iowa, 318 pp.
Argues that until 1645 Butler's views of current affairs were influenced by John Selden, "an impartial constitutionalist," and that Hudibras, which was conceived and "no doubt largely written" before that date, had to be adapted for Royalist purposes when public opinion and Butler's own views shifted toward the king. Viewed in this way, the "alleged allegory" of Hudibras is described as follows: Hudibras is the Presbyterian Long Parliament; Ralpho, the Parliamentary armies; Crowdero (the fiddler), Cavalierism; Orsin, the Scots (who shifted from the popular side to the king's); Bruin, the idea of kingship; Talgol, Magnano, and Cerdon are also Royalist in sympathy; Colon suggests Cromwell, but also the force of "rampant Independency" that "abetted the King's forces"; Trulla is a burlesque goddess personifying "loyalty or providence bringing Restoration." The skimmington of Part II allegorizes the tendency of rebellion to condone "tyrannical usurpation by church power." The obscurity of this allegory is due to the imperfect adaptation of a Parliamentary poem for Restoration readers. See DA 15 (1955): 1614-15. This interpretation of Hudibras is published in 1958.3.

1956

1 GRANGER, BRUCE INGHAM. "Hudibras in the American Revolution." AL 27 (January):499-508.
Reviews the hudibrastic tradition in America between 1765 and 1783. Seventy-seven hudibrastic satires treating political matters appeared during these years, ten of them by Philip Freneau. These poems exploit low-burlesque situations, travesty heroic allusions, and practice the prosodic and linguistic features of their model. In few of them, however, does a fully drawn hero emerge. Moreover, because American society was in some respects "more complex than the Restoration," the imitations take different points of view: forty-five of them attack the English; twenty-one, American patriots; ten, American loyalists; one attacks both the English and loyalists. John Trumbull's M'Fingal is the most literary of these poems; its model, according to the author, was Swift and Churchill, not Butler,

whose wit, he wrote, was "never well imitated by any man, nor ever will be." See also 1937.1 and 1971.6 for more on the American hudibrastic tradition.

2   LEYBURN, ELLEN DOUGLASS. Satiric Allegory: Mirror of Man. Yale Studies in English, edited by Benjamin Christie Nangle, vol. 130. New Haven: Yale University Press, pp. 37-52.
    Reprints in slightly altered form 1953.2. Hudibras is classified here as a Varronian satire "in Dryden's sense of the term."

1957

1   JACK, IAN. "Samuel Butler and 'Hudibras.'" In From Dryden to Johnson. Pelican Guide to English Literature, edited by Boris Ford, vol. 4. London: Penguin Books, pp. 114-24.
    An abbreviated version of 1952.1.

1958

1   "A Note on Samuel Butler (1612-80) and Jonathan Swift." N&Q 203 (July):294-96.
    Points out several "close resemblances" between passages in Gulliver's Travels and Butler's characters and miscellaneous works. Most of the former are found among the absurd projects of the scholars and scientists of the "Voyage to Laputa"; the latter are drawn from Butler's notebook observations on Aristotelian philosophy and the ignorance of government, and from his characters of "An Hypocrite," "A Hunter," and "A Pedant." For other possible borrowings from Butler by Swift, see 1932.2 and 1951.1.

2   BURTON, K. M. P. "Samuel Butler." In Restoration Literature. London: Hutchinson & Co., pp. 118-26.
    Discusses Butler's satire on mankind in general (in Hudibras, and in the prose characters) and on the virtuosi in particular in "The Elephant in the Moon." Butler became so fascinated with the techniques of low satire in Hudibras that he often lost sight of his satiric point--that man is "an undignified creature who deserved to be exposed." The satire is best expressed in the prose characters which are "unencumbered with the consciousness of his personal ingenuity."

3   MILLER, WARD S. "The Allegory in Part I of Hudibras." HLQ 21 (August):323-43.
    Reproduces the interpretation appearing first in 1955.4.

1960

*1 JACK, IAN. "'The True Raillery.'" Cairo Studies in English, pp. 9-23.
   Cited in 1973.4.

2 WEDGWOOD, C. V. Poetry and Politics under the Stuarts. Cambridge: At the University Press, pp. 130-36.
   Describes Hudibras as the "sneering voice" of a moment of "moral exhaustion" and therefore finds "something ugly" in it that is not present in the earlier, cruder Royalist satire of Denham and Cleveland. Though Butler's poem is a product of Civil War satire, its morality of emptiness and disillusion is that of a generation bored with the arguments and ideals of its fathers.

1961

1 SPENCE, ALEXANDER C., ed. Introduction to Samuel Butler: Three Poems. Augustan Reprint Society, no. 88. Los Angeles: University of California.
   Provides information on To the Memory of the Most Renowned Du-vall, "Satyr on Our Ridiculous Imitation of the French," and "The Elephant in the Moon," reprinted here. The French highwayman Duval's execution in 1670 and the printing of Butler's Pindaric mock-eulogy in 1671 provide limit-dates for the composition of the first of these, and as Butler's chief satiric object in this ode is the "Francomania" of the time, 1670 is also offered as the composition date of the "Satyr." The year 1676 or a bit earlier is the suggested date of "The Elephant in the Moon" (cf. 1965.3), which appears to voice Henry Stubbe's opinion of the deceptiveness of the telescope, the position he took in a controversy with Royal Society member Joseph Glanvill in 1670 and 1671. Butler was too much the man of reason to ridicule science or its instruments, however; his satire is focused upon incautious enthusiasm in learning. His use of the heroic couplet in a second, later version of "The Elephant in the Moon" may be ironic, as was certainly his intention in using the Pindaric ode to celebrate a highwayman.

2 WILLIAMSON, GEORGE. The Proper Wit of Poetry. Chicago: University of Chicago Press, pp. 92-95, 106-7, 112-24, and passim.
   Discusses Butler's characters of "A Quibbler" and "A Small Poet" as criticisms of excessive wit (chiefly in the verse of Benlowes) and of wit that expresses sense by contradiction and riddle (the exemplar of which is Waller). Butler's inventory of "reprehensible wit" is compared to those of Sprat, Dryden, and Addison.

1962

*1 KRYNSKI, STANISLAW. "Rymy Komiczne angielsko-greckie i angielsko-*l*acinskie w Hudibrasie Butlera." Kwartalnik neofilologiczny 9:399-406.
In Polish. Cited in 1973.4.

1963

1 NEVO, RUTH. The Dial of Virtue: A Study of Poems on Affairs of State in the Seventeenth Century. Princeton: Princeton University Press, pp. 189-204, 221-40.
   Assigns Butler an important transitional place in the development of seventeenth-century English raillery--the term is distinguished from railing and preserves the traditional distinction between Horatian and Juvenalian, or, in social terms, between court wit and dogmatic enthusiasm. An essential feature of raillery is the burlesque similitude, a figure that exploits disparities of size or importance between vehicle and tenor, and that came to Butler from Donne through Cleveland. In Butler, this figure of burlesque description is enacted by syntax as well as image and underlies the sportive effects of both the prose characters and Hudibras, where it is used to expose sophistry. This combination of the mimetic and the rationalistic produced a "mixed style" capable of modulating between mockery and high seriousness; one would expect it to fulfill its enterprise as the mock-heroic in Hudibras, which denigrates its vulgar adversaries by treating them in the heroic manner to which they aspire. Butler's portrait of the knight exploits the incongruity between aristocratic chivalric ritual and bourgeois utilitarian purpose; honor and love, the most immaterial of knightly ideals, are invoked in terms of litigation and property. Nevertheless, Butler's attitude toward the relationship between true chivalry and the behavior of Sir Hudibras and his mistress is ambivalent: he mocks the high object of aspiration as well as the low aspirants. Butler is not an idealist but a rationalist critic; his thought runs close to the materialism of Hobbes's analysis of society, close to the economic realities that motivated the Puritan bourgeoisie he ridicules and that therefore compromise the heroic frame of the poem. Cf. 1932.1 and 1970.3.

1965

1 DAVES, CHARLES WARNER. "An Annotated Edition of the Characters of Samuel Butler (1612-1680) with Textual, Critical and Historical Introduction." Ph.D. dissertation, University of Minnesota, 594 pp.

Reviews the provenance of Butler's characters since Thyer's printing of 121 specimens; the present edition contains 195 characters (see 1948.1-2). For the published edition of Butler's characters, see 1970.2. See also DA 26 (1965-66):1019.

2 ERSKINE-HILL, H. H. "Edmund Waller and Samuel Butler: Two Poetic Debts to Hall's 'Occasionall Meditations.'" N&Q 210 (April):133-34.

Maintains that Butler's "Dark-Lanthorn of the soul" image (of the Puritan's inner light) is indebted to the "darke Lanthorne" of Joseph Hall's "Occasionall Meditations," XXXII.

3 NICOLSON, MARJORIE HOPE. Pepys' "Diary" and the New Science. Charlottesville: University Press of Virginia, pp. 122-57.

Starting with Thomas Sprat's claim that ridicule of the virtuosi by the wits ("these terrible men") was a major threat to the Royal Society, Nicolson supplies the background of allusions in five of Butler's works. Charles II's delight in Hudibras created considerable uneasiness for Society members since the second part of the poem used the coffeehouse laughter about scientific experiment as a background for Butler's ridicule of Sir Paul Neile in "An Heroical Epistle of Hudibras to Sidrophel." Butler's references to a deliberately outmoded astronomy in the third canto of Part II were probably directed at the astrologer William Lilly and would not have disturbed the Society; however, the passages on microscopy in the same canto are "remarkably up to date"; they probably reflect a general interest in Robert Hooke's reports to the Society during 1663 (see 1929.1). Less personal and less satisfactory (hence unfinished) is the "Satyr upon the Royal Society." On the other hand, Butler liked "The Elephant in the Moon" so well that he followed the octosyllabic version with another in "long verse." John Wilkins's A Discourse Concerning a New World and Another Planet (1638) provides the "scientific" basis of the poem, which Butler then updated by characterizing its speakers as contemporary members of the Royal Society. Reference to Henry Stubbe's attack on the Royal Society in 1670-71 provides one limit date for "The Elephant in the Moon"; but if Robert Thyer supplied the reference to Stubbe in the octosyllabic version from the long verse version, the date of the former could be as early as 1666 or 1665 (cf. 1974.1). The latter is given as the date of "An Occasional Reflection on Dr. Charleton's Feeling a Dog's Pulse at Gresham," Butler's parody of Boyle's rhapsodic prose style and satire of Charleton's infraction of Society rules.

4 PAULSON, RONALD, ed. Hogarth's Graphic Works. 2 vols. New Haven: Yale University Press, 1:31-34, 115-27; 2: plates 77-105.

Describes the printed states and supplies the printing history of Hogarth's drawings and engravings for Hudibras--the twelve large illustrations issued separately in 1726 and then

published in the 1793 edition of Hudibras, and the seventeen
small illustrations published after the former in the 1726 edition of the poem, but executed, it is claimed, "a year or so"
earlier. The small illustrations were based on two sets of
anonymous illustrations included in the two 1710 editions of
Hudibras. Hogarth's designs are "a completely new creation,"
however. The latter were used again in the editions of 1732,
1739, and (re-engraved) 1744, Grey's edition (see 1850.1; 1857.1;
1873.1-4; 1877.1). In the small illustrations, Hogarth adapts
baroque conventions to an "un-baroque" subject; the mode of the
large illustrations is mock-heroic: the ideal world of the Grand
Style both belittles Hudibras's world and expresses the heroic
distortions of his imagination (see 1971.8). Vol. 2 reproduces
both sets of illustrations. Revised edition correcting errors,
1970.

5   SUTHERLAND, W. O. S., JR. "Hudibras and the Nature of Man."
    In The Art of the Satirist: Essays on the Satire of Augustan
    England. Austin: University of Texas Press, pp. 54-71.
        Argues that the meaning of Hudibras (and of great satire
    generally) transcends the historical circumstances of its origin:
    the three parts of the poem express Butler's conception of the
    nature of man, of the relations between men, and those between
    men and women; read in succession, they reveal "the nothingness
    of human ideals." Part I of the poem is "anti-heroic," present-
    ing two points of view, Hudibras's and the author's, and reveal-
    ing that the ideal of conduct is a pretense, irrelevant to human
    nature, Cavalier as well as Puritan. The discrepancy in the
    poem exists between Hudibras's self-conception and the poet's
    portrayal of him, not between the heroic ideal and what Hudibras
    is. Butler presents a parallel discrepancy: "Ralph as the poet
    describes him"--argumentative, superstitious--and "Ralph as the
    poet presents him"--a skillful, logical arguer. Ralph, then,
    represents the general abuse of reason as well as the faults of
    Independency. Part II presents the equally pretentious romantic
    ideal in place of the heroic, Sidrophel's fraudulent astrology
    in place of religion. The point of view is single: Hudibras
    is described as a cheat, and he knows it. Though he achieves
    two victories--one over the widow, the other over Sidrophel--the
    first demonstrates his personal intellectual dishonesty, the
    second his lack of integrity. Part II expresses the meanness
    and selfishness of human nature; Part III intensifies this view,
    institutionalizing it in the character of the lawyer. Hudibras
    offers no positive norms; heroism, love, and justice in the
    world are just what they appear to be in the poem.

1966

1   SWARTCHILD, WILLIAM G., III. "The Character of a Roundhead:
    Theme and Rhetoric in Anti-Puritan Verse Satire from 1639

through Hudibras." Ph.D. dissertation, Columbia University, 291 pp.

Reconstructs the intellectual milieu of anti-Puritan satire from Royalist polemical poets like Cleveland, Denham, and Cowley and examines Hudibras as its most brilliant product. See also DA 27 (1967):3019A.

2 THORSON, JAMES LLEWELLYN. "A Definitive Text on the First Part of Hudibras." Ph.D. dissertation, Cornell University, 240 pp.

Establishes the bibliographical history of all editions of the First Part of Hudibras, providing that Richard Marriott's large octavo edition was the first and that the four unauthorized editions were reprinted from it (for additional detail, see 1966.3). The text produced here uses the first edition as copy-text, introducing substantive variants from the 1674 edition of Parts I and II which Butler revised. Cf. 1967.3; see also DA 28 (1967):205A.

3 _____. "The Publication of Hudibras." PBSA 60 (4th Quarter): 418-38.

Provides bibliography and descriptions of all editions of Hudibras published during Butler's lifetime. Nine editions of Part I (dated 1663) are differentiated, five of them authorized (designated A, B, C, D, E), four unauthorized (F, G, H, I). Comparison of the two groups confirms the contemporary description of an unauthorized edition as "most false [and] imperfect," and a newly discovered letter that refers to a "rogue printer" effectively removes the possibility of its priority. The postulated relationships between these editions are as follows: A, B, F (printed, perhaps, from A, following the page limits of B), G, H, I, C (deriving from B), D, E. In 1663, the spurious Hudibras: the Second Part appeared, going though at least four editions (J, K, L, M). The legitimate second part (dated 1664) exists in two editions (N, O). In 1674, an edition of the first and second parts together appeared with the author's corrections and additions, including "An Heroical Epistle of Hudibras to Sidrophel" (P); this edition was reprinted in 1678 (Q). There are two editions of Part III dated 1678 (R, S), one dated 1679 (T), and another 1680 (U). Editions A and P are determined "the only significant editions." Of the editions of Hudibras that appeared after Butler's death, all are reprints, mostly of Q and of the 1678 editions of Part III. A 1704 edition of the three parts was apparently the basis of Zachary Grey's edition of 1744, the basis of most nineteenth-century editions, and of T. R. Nash's edition of 1793. Cf. 1967.3.

4 WILDING, MICHAEL. "Samuel Butler at Barbourne." N&Q 211 (January):15-19.

Supplies two new pieces of documentary evidence relating to Butler's early years: one, the record, in the parish register at Barbourne, of the baptism, on 14 July 1621, of Margaret, the poet's youngest sister (see 1924.1); the other, three notes in the account book of the bishop of Worcester's lands, which list Samuel (the poet's father) and Richard Butler (the poet's cousin) as "free tenants" in 1615. As Samuel senior died in 1626, the Samuel mentioned under the year 1628 must be the poet, who now held the house and twenty acres of land in Barbourne; by 1637, however, Butler surrendered this property, which was being farmed by three tenants. Two conclusions are drawn from this discussion: first, it is unlikely that Butler would have been able to afford a university education; second, since Butler was at Barbourne in 1628, it is unlikely that he was clerk to Leonard Jefferey in 1627 or 1628. (It seems "certain," nevertheless, that Butler was employed by Leonard's son Thomas.) See also 1966.5.

5 _____. "The Date of Samuel Butler's Baptism." RES 17:174-77.
Concludes, from the Strensham parish register, that 14 February 1613 is the date of Butler's baptism, and on this account accepts the authority of John Aubrey over that of Charles Longueville on the dates of Butler's birth and death. See also 1966.4.

1967

*1 DE QUEHEN, ANTHONY H. "The Literary and Philosophical Opinions of Samuel Butler 1612-1680 as Seen in His Methods of Composition." Ph.D. dissertation, London University.
Cited in 1973.4.

2 KEENAN, HUGH T. "Another Hudibras Allusion in Byron's Don Juan." N&Q 212:301-2.
Notes Byron's allusion, in canto viii of Don Juan (lines 1103-12), to the argument of canto i, Part I of Hudibras--specifically, Butler's rhyming of "Fiddle" with "breaks off in the middle."

3 WILDERS, JOHN, ed. Introduction, Textual Introduction, and Appendices to Hudibras. Oxford: Clarendon Press, pp. xiii-xliii, xliv-lxi, 450-54.
Supplies a life of Butler, an account of his moral-philosophical views, and an interpretive essay on Hudibras; a textual introduction describes all editions of the poem published during Butler's life; appendixes reprint the Butler-Oxenden correspondence (see 1933.2) and survey the still inconclusive attempts to identify the model for Sir Hudibras. Butler's satire is an expression of his skepticism, the product of an empirical mind. Empirical also in literary criticism, Butler scorned the idea of poetic inspiration; the poet should imitate nature. The result in Butler's practice is mock-heroic and satire. The satire of Part I of Hudibras is philosophical as well as theological.

Butler's mock-heroic is ambivalent in effect: at times mocking the characters in contrast to their epic trappings, at others mocking the literary conventions. Internal evidence (supported by Butler's letter to Oxenden) suggests a composition date of 1658-60 for Part I. Part II probably existed in an unfinished state by the end of 1662, but part of the third canto was written in 1663. The "Epistle to Sidrophel" was written between 1672 and 1674, the bulk of Part III between 1663 and 1677. The descent of five authorized editions of Part I is described as a vertical line (cf. 1966.3) running from the large octavo (A1) through three duodecimo issues (A2-A4) to the small octavo (A5). Four unauthorized editions (A6-A9) are supposed to have preceded all four of the smaller formats (A2-A5) which were issued to compete with the pirated editions. There were three editions of Part III (D1-D3). The copy-texts chosen for this edition are A1 and B1 for Parts I and II, emended with substantive variants from the first edition of Parts I and II combined (C1); for Part III, D1 is the copy-text. Also included is a survey of principal editions after 1680. The edition is reviewed in 1969.3-4.

1968

1 LA COURREYE, CATHERINE CLOTILDE. "The Political Character, 1660-1685." Ph.D. dissertation, University of California, Los Angeles, 336 pp.

Discusses Butler's transitional place in the tradition of political character writing in the Restoration. Butler followed traditional patterns of form in writing the Theophrastan and polemical character, but also exploited the possibilities of burlesque wit wherever possible. See also DA 29 (1969):3102-3A.

1969

1 BRUNN, SV. "Who's Who in Samuel Butler's 'The Elephant in the Moon'?" ES 50:381-89.

Presents new information on the identity of characters in Butler's satire of the Royal Society. Comparison of the short- and long-verse portraits of the discoverer of the elephant indicates that Butler originally assigned this distinction to John Evelyn, but then gave it to Sir Paul Neile. A deleted couplet in the first version referring to the repair of St. Paul's and the paving of London streets "certainly" alludes to Evelyn, as Nicolson (1965.3) claimed; details in both versions--an astronomical interest in the moon and knowledge of cider making--fit both Evelyn and Neile; but one detail added to the long-verse portrait--the proposal to fine members of the Royal Society for not paying their dues--fits only Neile. That Butler could attribute the incident first to one and then another person suggests that it was pure invention, and the fact that Evelyn's name had not gotten attached to the incident (as Neile's had) indicates that the second version was written immediately after the first. The speaker who precedes Evelyn-Neile is identified as John Wilkins; the "microscopic Wit" who follows him is identified as Robert Hooke, the physically insignificant author of Micrographia. The details surrounding the final speaker in the poem--impeded speech, observations of vermin--caricature Robert Boyle, though Butler's further exposure of this character's intellectual dishonesty is contradicted by Boyle's own commitment to scientific probity.

2   DE QUEHEN, A. H. "Hudibrastic Drafts." TLS, 9 January, p. 39.
    Cautions against inferring, from parallel verse and prose passages in manuscript, a theory of Butler's method of composition--specifically that of "cross-hatching," the building-up of longer passages out of verse fragments, as Bauer (1948.1) assumes. Actual evidence of this sort of textual generation is rare; the result, when it does occur, is conspicuously incoherent. It is more likely that Butler was able to compose extended passages without the help of fragments, and then incorporated them later. Notice is taken of Lamar's failure, in his edition of the Satires and Miscellaneous Poetry, to identify the sequence of verses called "The Doctor and His Wife's Pin Money." See also 1972.2 and 1979.2.

3   HILL, CHRISTOPHER. "The End of Ideology." EIC 19:78-84.
    Asserts Butler's suspicion of ideology, a form of self-indulgence that leads to self-indulgent quarrels. He moved from an animus against parties--Presbyterians, Parliamentarians, the sectaries--to an animous against institutions--the church, the court, literature itself, law, and science, though toward the last his attitude was ambivalent. Between Ancients and Moderns, he sided with the latter. A review of 1967.3.

4   MINER, EARL. PQ 48 (July):340-42.
    Reviews Wilders's edition of Hudibras (1967.3), noting in particular his "alteration" of the Tory slant that Zachary Grey's commentary gave to the poem in eighteenth-century editions, and pointing out that the Clark Library copy of "The Third and Last Part," while bearing the title-page date 1678, is inscribed "December. 30th. 1677," and so "seems to be a state prior to the eight copies collated by Wilders." DeBeer (1928.3), Bentley (1944.2), Thorson (1966.3), and Wilders himself mention late 1677 as the issuing date of the Third Part.

5   SUTHERLAND, JAMES. English Literature of the Late Seventeenth Century. New York: Oxford University Press, pp. 157-60, 229-30.
    Comments, generally in the first passage, on Hudibras and Butler's minor satires, and, in the second, on his characters, "one of the outstanding contributions to Restoration literature."

Butler's combination of learning and wit isolated him from both the scholars and the wits. His failure to publish the characters suggests that the taste for Theophrastan characters had passed. Butler's output impresses one with "a sense of waste: so much wisdom embodied in a form that was already becoming old-fashioned."

1970

1 BRODSLEY, LAUREL HARRIET CHILK. "The Structure of Butler's Hudibras." Ph.D. dissertation, University of California, Los Angeles, 372 pp.
   Describes the structure of Hudibras as an adaptation of three genres: (1) debate and dialogue, (2) formal character, and (3) burlesque narrative. Debate--which "Butler believed . . . the most pernicious form of human communication"--is used to ridicule characters; dialogue (the simple language of truth-speaking) serves as the model of proper discourse. Butler's characters employ the conventions of English character writing and draw upon an iconographical tradition (see also 1972.1), which Hogarth also employed for his illustrations of the poem. The narrative of the poem gains coherence and decorum through the use of allusions and echoes of incidents in jest-book fiction. Satirical elements in the narrative "exploit the mock-heroic jargon of contemporary journalism and Royalist diatribe." Taken together, these elements earn Hudibras a place in the category Dryden called the Varronian. See also DAI 31 (1971): 5352A.

2 DAVES, CHARLES W., ed. Introduction to Samuel Butler 1612-1680: Characters. Cleveland: Press of Case Western Reserve University, pp. 1-27.
   Places Butler's characters in the history of seventeenth-century English character writing and defines their distinctive features and their relation to Hudibras. Though Butler's characters are structurally Theophrastan, reflecting ideas and phrases of his predecessors, Thomas Overbury and John Earle, they are more particularly indebted to the polemic character, especially as that was written by his near contemporaries, Richard Flecknoe and John Cleveland. Butler extended the limits of the character, however, lengthening the form through discursive consideration of ideas into something like a theoretical essay. See also 1965.1.

3 DAVIES, PAUL C. "Hudibras and 'the proper Sphere of Wit.'" Trivium 5:104-15.
   Examines Butler's concept of wit as the means of giving "Intelligence to Truth." Hudibras makes us aware of the disorder in the world by joining in an amusing and surprising way the disparities that exist there and by dissolving the distinctions that protect men from the truth. The two means of accomplishing

this end are the burlesque similitude which, like the metaphysical conceit, violently yokes heterogeneities and logical demonstration. Thus, distinctions between men and beasts are metaphorically blurred in the poem; Hudibras's argument against bear-baiting proves that beasts are superior to men; his comparison of synods and bears shows that the two are more alike than unlike. Burlesque similitudes in Hudibras's speeches parody the mental processes of the knight and condemn him as one attempting to conceal the truth of his motives; the similitudes do not, however—even when they play with heroic imagery—compromise the heroic frame of the poem as Nevo (1963.1) maintained; remove the distinction between man and beast and the worlds of heroes and butchers indeed become one.

4   PAULSON, RONALD, ed. Hogarth's Graphic Works. 2d ed. 2 vols. New Haven: Yale University Press, 1:31-34, 115-27; 2: plates 77-105.
    Reprint of 1965.4.

5   RAWSON, C. J. "Frozen Words: A Note to Idler, no. 46." N&Q 225 (August):300.
    Notes allusions to Zembla (where words congeal in the frigid air) in Idler, no. 46, Tatler, no. 254, and one of Chesterfield's letters (29 January 1748). The latter occurrences refer to Hudibras, I.i.148.

6   WASSERMAN, GEORGE R. "Samuel Butler and the Problem of Unnatural Man." MLQ 31 (June):179-94.
    Elaborates Quintana's thesis (1951.2) that man, for Butler, was "essentially unnatural," but argues that unnaturalness here is not equivalent to irrationality. The paradox of man's unnaturalness is related to the paradoxical place of reason in Butler's interpretation of the Fall. Man, he believed, was not created rational; the Fall was an intellectual error. But the reason man thereby gained was also a form of punishment: condemned to distinguish between truth and falsehood, Adam's first rational act was to clothe his fallen condition, that is, confound truth and falsehood. Butler differentiated three types of human nature on these grounds: (1) knaves, those who deceive others, (2) the ignorant, those deceived by knaves or by themselves, and (3) fools and madmen, those who by nature or accident lack the means of finding their proper places in nature. Most men are predisposed to error, a survival in the fallen world of Adam's original ignorance; knavery is their just punishment, but they are also likely to err through self-deception. Empirical evidence is the only check against error, opinion, or speculation (reflection of the mind's desire). The mistake of the virtuosos in "The Elephant in the Moon," a "discovery" designed to improve the image of a learned society, reveals a weakness of reason, not the eye; the empirical footboys discover the unflattering truth. Butler's awareness of this tendency to accept self-

favoring opinion before truth was the basis of his literary theory and practice. Rejecting the rational standards of Rymer's Aristotelian rules for a poetics of feeling, he inverted the hierarchy of poetic kinds, ranking realistic satire and comedy above idealized heroics and tragedy. If men prefer lies to truth, and if wit is a form of lying, it is possible to deceive them for their own good.

1971

1 ASRELSKY, ARNOLD. "The Forgotten Augustan: A Critical Study of the Works of Samuel Butler (1612-1680)." Ph.D. dissertation, New York University, 306 pp.

Attempts to place Butler among the Augustan satirists by revealing the broadly philosophical character of his notebook writings, prose characters, and minor verse satire (Butler, for instance, was opposed to notions of progress and perfectability); and explains the chief fault of Hudibras as an imperfect grasp of the requirements of Menippean satire. Missing in the poem is the variety of satiric character (present in the prose characters) that embodies the philosophical and moral vagaries typical of the mode. Efforts to compensate for this artistic flaw have given impetus to allegorical readings of the poem which are shown to be "self-contradictory." See also DAI 32 (1972):3943A.

2 CATLETT, LA RUE SCOTT. "An Odde Promiscuous Tone: A Study of the Prosody of Hudibras." Ph.D. dissertation, University of Wisconsin, 227 pp.

Concludes that Butler both accepted and rejected the restrictions of conservative prosodic theories. The former position is indicated by the poem's excessive elision and its unnatural stress contours, the latter by its frequent irreducibility to the octosyllabic norm and its disregard of stress alternation. The excessive counterpointing of metrical and rhetorical patterns produces a "jolting" effect; if the metrical pattern is permitted to dominate, the effect is described as "jogging." See also DAI 32 (1971):3244A.

3 EDWARDS, THOMAS R. "The Hero Emasculated: Hudibras and Mock-Epic." In Imagination and Power: A Study of Poetry on Public Themes. New York: Oxford University Press, pp. 39-44.

Cites Hudibras as an illustration of what happened to the Renaissance concern with public enterprise--that is, heroism. Butler, the "condescending ironist," invites the reader to regard the voice of the poem on a level with the actions it describes (see 1965.5); but it is also the right voice for locating what is objectionable in those actions as well as those in more serious heroic poems--the absence of common sense. The implied alternative to the false heroism of Hudibras (and Cromwell) is not real heroism but "inaction." The satire of the hero is less political than sexual, the "gelding of heroic potency."

4 HORNE, WILLIAM C. "Butler's Use of the Rump in Hudibras." LC 37:126-35.
    Suggests that Butler could have found the prototype for Sir Hudibras in conventional caricature of the Roundhead common in Royalist verse satire published in the anthology Rump (1662). Three examples of the prototype--identified as Puritan knight, stout Colonel, and Committeeman or Alderman--are cited: "A City Ballad" (the hero of which woos for wealth), Alexander Broome's "On Col. Pride" (who opposes bearbaiting), and "Upon Alderman Atkins bewraying his Slops on the great Training day." The third poem presents mock-romance elements, double rhymes, and an incident (a variation on the "Rump joke") that Butler may have used in the battle between Hudibras and the bear-baiters. Butler's development of this stereotype--by allowing his hero knowingly to degrade himself--transforms it into a burlesque image of the wrongheadedness of the Puritan cause. For Butler's use of other conventions in the Royalist Rump satires, see 1971.5 and 1983.2.

5 _____. "Violence in Hudibras: Wit, 'Hard Words,' and the Rump." Ph.D. dissertation, University of Pennsylvania, 292 pp.
    Maintains that Hudibras is a poem of violence on several levels: (1) the poem is a distillation of the violent wit of Royalist satire that appeared in the anthology Rump (see 1971.4); (2) Butler practices a sort of metaphysical wit (the violent yoking of heterogenous ideas) as a burlesque device; (3) Butler's use of distorted perspective, repetition, and "creative analogy" does violence to the reader by teaching him "lessons about human nature"; and (4) Butler's analysis of hypocrisy, the divorce between speech and action, is the ultimate manifestation of violence. See also DAI 32 (1972):4566-67A.

6 MORTLAND, DONALD EUGENE. "A Critical Study of Hudibrastic Satire in America, 1708-1806." Ph.D. dissertation, University of Oklahoma, 296 pp.
    Argues that American hudibrastic satire rarely achieved the artistic status of its original or even of English imitations (the exceptions are Ebenezer Cook's Bacon's Rebellion, John Trumbull's M'Fingal, and, in its limited scope, Joseph Green's Entertainment for a Winter's Evening) because it was unable to transcend the topicality that produced it, and failed to employ indirection, which would have curbed its tendency toward didacticism. See also Granger (1956.1), who directed this dissertation, and DAI 32 (1972):3959A.

7 NELSON, NICOLAS HARDING. "A Study of Hudibras: Satiric Theme and Form." Ph.D. dissertation, University of Wisconsin, 275 pp.

Argues that Hudibras is not a historical allegory (cf. 1923.1, 1955.4, and 1958.3), but a "general satire based on literary tradition," specifically, anti-Puritan satire and romantic epic. Hypocritical avarice, foolish zeal, specious ratiocination, contentiousness--the qualities for which Sir Hudibras is reviled--were all traits of the traditional Puritan stereotype. Combined with the themes of love and valor and with the formal elements of works like Orlando Furioso, Jerusalem Delivered, and Gondibert, these conventions of anti-Puritan satire invert the ideal of the romantic hero. See also DAI 32 (1971):393A.

8 PAULSON, RONALD. Hogarth: His Life, Art, and Times. Vol. 1. New Haven: Yale University Press, pp. 146-55.

Discusses William Hogarth's twelve large engravings of scenes from Hudibras, executed in 1725 (Hogarth had earlier produced a series of seventeen smaller illustrations for an edition of the poem). The large prints, which were to be sold independently, constitute the artist's initial statement about history painting. In the frontispiece, for instance, a cherub sculpts a scene in which Hudibras and Ralpho are lashed by a satyr; but the cherub's model for the scene is Butler's poem, held before him by another satyr, not Nature (cf. 1937.1). Balancing the composition is the figure of Britannia gazing at her undistorted image in a mirror held by a faun, the implication being that Hanoverian England no longer resembles Butler's. Hogarth wished to endow the baroque history painting with moral significance, the effect being similar to that of the mock-heroic. The composition of the print "Hudibras and the Skimmington," depicting rustics and buffoons, is based on Annibale Carracci's Procession of Bacchus and Ariadne. See also 1965.4.

9 POWERS, DORIS C. English Formal Satire: Elizabethan to Augustan. De Proprietatibus Litterarum, edited by C. H. Van Schoonveld, no. 19. The Hague: Mouton, pp. 126-69 passim.

Discusses distinctive features of Butler's formal satire, a genre distinguished by its attempt to duplicate the effect of thought verbalized as it forms. Butler's satires on the "Imperfection and Abuse of Human Learning" and on the "Licentious Age of Charles the 2nd" are typically post-Caroline in their use of generalizing structures, a reflection of neoclassical esteem for general truths. They invariably open sententiously rather than dramatically, and achieve versimilitude through the moral earnestness of the satirist-persona (which in Butler is conveyed through expressions of disgust and indignation) and through the urgent note sounded in rhetorical questions (as in his satire "Upon Modern Critics"). The "Satyr upon the Imperfection and Abuse of Human Learning," however, exemplifies the controlled style of formal satire. The satirist-as-stylist paces his discourse through dilation and compression and the connotations of homely images in summarizing analogies. Butler also uses laughter as a means of control; in the "Abuses of Learning--Part 2," ridicule is achieved through exaggeration, in "Upon Modern Critics," through reductio ad absurdum, and in the "Satyr upon Plagiaries," through mock approval and false analogy.

10 QUINN, JOHN DAVID. "A Study of Samuel Butler's Characters." Ph.D. dissertation, University of Notre Dame, 244 pp.
    Argues that Butler, alone among English character writers, succeeded in reuniting the ethical and entertainment value of Theophrastus's characters divided during the Renaissance. See also DAI 32 (1971):450A.

11 SEIDEL, MICHAEL A. "Patterns of Anarchy and Oppression in Samuel Butler's Hudibras." ECS 5 (Winter):294-314.
    Adduces Butler's theory of satire--"Controlled madness" (natural anger combined with rhetorical anger) that prevents a one-sided attack and produces an expansive vision--and goes on to illustrate its application by interpreting Hudibras as an attack on two social extremes: rebellion (signaled in the opening lines) and oppression (an image of which, in "The Ladies Answer," closes the poem). This pattern of anarchy and coercion --reenforced by analogous historical events that lie behind the poem, by mental "perturbations" that characterize the human condition in general, and by picaresque adventures parodied in the poem--comes together in the character of Sir Hudibras, who is both revolutionary and church and state tyrant. The pattern is also structurally articulated in each of the three parts of the poem: by the actions of the rabble and the burlesqued tyrant; by the crowd in the skimmington and its persecuted female tyrant (a symbol of church tyranny and its attackers); and (in the second canto of Part III) by the city mob and its tyrannic demagogues.

12 WILDING, MICHAEL. "Butler and Gray's Inn." N&Q 216 (August): 293-95.
    Adduces the dates 1645-58 as the period, mentioned in Butler's letter to Oxenden (see 1933.2), during which the former was living in Holborn, lodging with the model of Hudibras, and by the end of which had begun to write the first part of his poem (see also 1967.3). The basis of this calculation is Aubrey's reference to Butler's club with Cleveland, who lived in Gray's Inn in the fall of 1657 and died there in April 1658. It follows that Butler was still living in the neighborhood after completing Part I. That he was a lawyer himself may be suggested by Marvell's reference to Butler (in The Rehearsal Transpros'd) as "a man of the other [i.e., legal rather than ecclestiastical] robe."

1972

1 BRODSLEY, LAUREL. "Butler's Character of Hudibras and Contemporary Graphic Satire." JWCI 35:401-4.
   Considers the formal presentation of the character Hudibras as analogous to the techniques of contemporary graphic satire in narrative pictures, iconographical engravings, and broadside woodcuts. In all these models, disconnected elements are enclosed within a larger frame, requiring the observer to create his or her own pattern or organization of the whole. The epigrams comprising the character of Hudibras--in effect, a series of emblems--may be similarly interpreted as comprising a thematic type: e.g., Puritan Hypocrisy, Gluttony, the "Man-Monster." Hudibras exists, then, not as a portrait of an individual, but as "a creative exploration of closed systems."

2 DE QUEHEN, ANTHONY HUGH. "Editing Butler's Manuscripts." In Editing Seventeenth Century Prose. Edited by D. I. B. Smith. Toronto: A. M. Hakkert for the Committee of the Conference on Editorial Problems, pp. 71-93.
   Describes the sources of what may be called Butler's "genuine remains" and discusses two editorial problems in producing an edition of the prose passages in the British Museum Butler manuscripts: restoring the 95 folios to their original order and dating the composition of the folios. Butler's own subject headings are helpful in reordering the folios; internal allusions (to the period from October 1665 to the end of 1677) and a change in Butler's handwriting (occurring after 1668) assist in dating them. Consideration is also given to the ordering and duplication of individual passages for readers of a modern edition; in this connection, it is observed that Butler's best writing is at variance with his most constructive thought, that the nearer he brought his passages to the reading public, the more he withdrew himself and his personal beliefs. See also de Quehen's introduction to the published edition of Butler's Prose Observations (1979.2).

3 HORNE, WILLIAM C. "Violence in Hudibras and Hogarth's Illustrations." New Rambler 13 (Autumn):49-56.
   Uses Hogarth's illustrations for the 1726 edition of Hudibras as a commentary on the prominence of violence in the central episodes of the satire. Hogarth's emphasis reflects Butler's humanistic concern with the potential for violence in human nature.

4 JUMP, JOHN D. Burlesque. The Critical Idiom, edited by John D. Jump, no. 22. London: Methuen & Co., pp. 12-17.
   Applies Bond's designation "hudibrastic" to Butler's poem (see 1932.1): noting the incongruity between "throw-away doggerel" and an important and general subject (Puritan religious

and political attitudes), Hudibras is "a classical instance of the low burlesque."

5 LAPREVOTTE, GUY. "'The Elephant in the Moon' de Samuel Butler: Le context et la satire." EA 25 (October–December):465-78.

Locates the context of Butler's satire in the controversy between Joseph Glanvill and Henry Stubbe (see 1961.1), to which both the short and long versions allude; and disagrees, then, with Nicolson (1965.3) on several points: both versions were written after 1670, the publication date of Stubbe's Plus Ultra Reduced to a Non Plus; the speaker who magnifies his writing with "microscopic wit" is Thomas Sprat (cf. 1969.1), whom Stubbe had also criticized. But the satire is aimed as much at the institutional aspect of the Royal Society as at its individual members; Sprat's claim that an assembly of minds is a surer source of truth than an isolated mind merely associates the Society, in Butler's lines, with the crowd. Butler's irony uses the words of scientific apologists--Sprat, Bacon--against science, and allows the objects of his satire to voice his own skeptical thought.

6 TOTTEN, CHARLES FREDERICK. "The Prose Characters of Samuel Butler (1612-1680): A Critical Study." Ph.D. dissertation, Wayne State University, 209 pp.

Analyzes the form and content of Butler's characters, finding them unique in their dominating satiric purpose, unrelenting in their exposure of hypocrisy, and persistent in their use of two image patterns--one postulating the complicity between fools and knaves, the other reflecting the Renaissance concern "that words stretched too far from their meanings become themselves instruments for violence and deceit." Viewed as a whole, Butler's 196 characters constitute an anatomy of a world of madness and folly, and reveal a satiric hierarchy in which the highest places go to the basest hypocrites. See also DAI 33 (1972): 2346A, and 1975.2.

7 WILDING, MICHAEL. "The Last of the Epics: The Rejection of the Heroic in Paradise Lost and Hudibras." In Restoration Literature: Critical Approaches. Edited by Harold Love. London: Methuen & Co., pp. 91-120.

Compares Hudibras and Paradise Lost as reactions against the heroic tradition provoked by the realities of civil war. Both attack directly the heroic code and its conventions and derive their effects by interweaving the honorific terms of heroism with the "reductive language" of brutal action: the ambiguous description of the fighter Talgol (a butcher by trade) is exemplary of Butler's manner. For both, military heroism confuses spirit and matter (Hudibras's "Apostolick Blows and Knocks"; Satan's use of force in the war in Heaven). Milton magnifies the evil of the heroic by identifying it (until after the Fall) with Satan; Butler belittles it. Both degrade their heroes by involving them in the movement from actions to words, from violence to deceit and hypocrisy, and by directing their efforts against women who are ultimately the victors. In rejecting the old heroic values, Milton endorsed Christian values and domestic simplicity; the only positive in Hudibras is the rich texture of everyday life which was antithetic to the idealism of Puritanism and the heroic tradition.

1973

1 BENTLEY, CHRISTOPHER. "Samuel Butler and Jean-Louis Guez de Balzac." N&Q 218 (October):390-91.
   Points out Butler's indebtedness, in a short poem (beginning "No Jesuit e'er took in Hand, / To plant a Church in barren Land"), to Guez de Balzac's accusation, in Le prince (1631), that Catholics in the New World "sell their Gospel."

2 DONOVAN, J. "The 'Key to Hudibras' and Cleveland's 'The Character of a London Diurnall.'" N&Q 218 (May):175-76.
   Further weakens the authority of the identification of Ralpho as Isaac Robinson in the "Key" ascribed to Roger L'Estrange, by pointing out that the description of Robinson in the "Key" was drawn from "a fanciful creation" of John Cleveland's.

*3 LOBZOWSKA, MARIA. "Samuel Butler, the Author of Hudibras and the Leveller Pamphleteers." Kwartalnik Neofilologiczny 20: 3-20.
   Cited in 1973 MLA International Bibliography.

4 THORSON, JAMES L. "Samuel Butler (1612-1680): A Bibliography." Bulletin of Bibliography 30, no. 1:34-39.
   Attempts to provide a complete bibliography of biographical, bibliographical, and critical studies of Butler, together with a list of noteworthy editions of his works. Most items are briefly annotated.

5 WAGNER, JOSEPH B. "Samuel Butler's Satire of the Hermetic Philosophers." Ph.D. dissertation, Kent State University, 247 pp.
   Analyzes the "full scope" of Butler's antihermeticism and his satiric alliance of hermeticism and the new science, a distinction that was often unclear in the minds of the Royal Society itself. The antihermetic satire in Hudibras is more subtle and complex than is usually acknowledged: his masterful use of hermetic imagery (e.g., the hermaphrodite) and the balanced portraits of the Rosicrucian mystic (Ralpho) and the astrologer-turned-"new"-scientist (Sidrophel) are cited. The study also deals with Butler's characters of "An Astrologer," "A Virtuoso," and "An Hermetic Philosopher," and with "The Elephant in the

Moon" and the "Satyr upon the Royal Society." See also DAI 35 (1974):421A and 1982.4.

6   WASSERMAN, GEORGE R. "'A Strange Chimaera of Beasts and Men': The Argument and Imagery of Hudibras, Part I." SEL 8 (Summer): 405-21.

Interprets Hudibras, Part I as a satire on mankind, an attack upon that which differentiates humans and beasts, (i.e., reason). According to a typology drawn from Butler's notebooks, humans congenitally deprived of reason--that is, "natural madmen" or fools--are placed on a par with animals; on the other hand, types of corrupted rational nature--the accidentally "mad" and the ignorant--are placed beneath animals. To be human, then, is to use reason unnaturally (see also 1970.6). This sense of the unhumanness of "human" beings is consistently expressed in animal and mechanical imagery throughout the prose characters and Hudibras: Butler thus turns Descartes's antitheriophilist argument in defense of reason into a criticism of the misuse of reason. Ignorance, the impairment of reason by the want of empirical data, is the specific form of irrationality satirized in Hudibras: the knight has replaced sense with the machinery of rationalism; his squire has replaced it with imagination. Hudibras's argument against bear-baiting blinds him to the fact that his rational attempt to avoid strife actually promotes it. He fails to see the truth of what his logic denies: that man is "a strange Chimaera of Beasts and Men . . . Such as in Nature never met."

7   WILDERS, JOHN, and DE QUEHEN, HUGH, eds. Introduction to Samuel Butler: Hudibras Parts I and II and Selected Other Writings. Oxford Paperback English texts, edited by John Buxton. Oxford: Clarendon Press, pp. vii-xvii.

Presents the facts of Butler's life and works and provides a general view of his thought as an introduction to the content and style of his verse and prose writings. For a fuller introduction, see 1967.3.

1974

1   BRUNN, SV. "The Date of Samuel Butler's 'The Elephant in the Moon.'" ES 55 (April):133-39.

Uses La Fontaine's repetition of the central incident of "The Elephant in the Moon" in his fable "Un animal dans la lune" to establish the terminus ante quem of the first (short-verse) version of Butler's satire: early August 1676. French enthusiasm for England, reflected in La Fontaine's fable, would not have survived Sir William Temple's frustration of Louis's plans at Nijmegen at that date. November 1675 remains the terminus post quem. Cf. Nicolson's argument (1965.3) for a composition earlier than 1670.

*2 DONOVAN, J. "Hudibras and Sir Samuel Rolle." Recherches Anglaises et Americaines 3:39-55.
Cited in 1974 MLA International Bibliography.

3 FARLEY-HILLS, DAVID. "Hudibras." In The Benevolence of Laughter: Comic Poetry of the Commonwealth and Restoration. Totowa: Rowman & Littlefield, pp. 46-71.
Maintains that the view of Butler as a wholly negative satirist, an unqualified pessimist and total skeptic (see, e.g., 1933.1 and 1967.3) is one-sided, and to correct this imbalance points out the conflicting presence of a humane and benevolent comedy in his writing. Butler was, theoretically, a rational optimist; his pessimism was practical, based on his awareness of the disruptive effects of the passions. Unlike Rochester or Swift, however, he lacked the detachment necessary to translate personal dislikes into convincing general statements, becoming himself part of the chaotic world he ridicules while his hero, the satiric butt, becomes an alter ego whose "invincible vitality" finally wins the reader's sympathy. The comedy of the introductory description of Hudibras, of the fight with the bear-baiters (the "best part" because Butler has forgotten that he was writing satire), is farce in which a little man battles against circumstances beyond his control, but always comes back for more. Action, supported by rhythm, takes precedence over comment in such passages; we are "asked not to criticize, but to enjoy." So deeply does the farce undercut the satire, that the latter may be felt as an intrusion: Hudibras, the symbol of hypocrisy at the beginning of the poem, becomes the voice of "his own downright honesty" in admitting to the widow that it is her property he is after.

4 KELLY, ANN KLINE. "A Rowlands-Butler-Swift Parallel." N&Q 219 (March):101-2.
Questions whether Hudibras (III.i.1277-78) or Samuel Rowlands's "Epigram" (in Good Newes and Bad Newes [1622]) was the direct source of Swift's couplet, "I often wish'd, that I had clear / For Life, six hundred Pounds a year . . ." (in the "Imitation of Horace," 2.6).

5 MINER, EARL. "Butler: Hating Our Physician." In The Restoration Mode from Milton to Dryden. Princeton: Princeton University Press, pp. 130-36, 158-97, 407-12, 465-79.
Contemplates the opposed qualities contained in the judgments that Hudibras is "a terrible, terrible great poem" and Butler "indisputably one of the great poets in the language." The main target of the poem is mankind, not Puritanism (so there is little reason to expect a consistent historical allegory in it), and its art exists to debase everything associated with man--even its own "art" of dissimulation: narration by frustrating normal narrative expectations (see also 1979.4), and allusion (to Lucan, for example) that magnifies in order to bring about

greater depreciation. Butler was a rationalist, but the poem "presents the self-destruction" of reason; he was a misogynist but used his misogyny in the service of his misanthropy (see also 1976.4). Trulla, a slut, and the widow (who may be nothing more than a woman) are the only alternatives to the squalor and defeat represented by the men in the poem; the first, with her arms, the second, with her words, controls Hudibras. Butler, like Hobbes, postulates a state made by mothers rather than fathers, but he leaves his judgment on this matter obscure. The widow still shares in the "mess" that is humanity. Nevertheless, women are the figures of the goddess Iustitia in the Iron Age world of the poem. The two shorter passages in this book consider Butler's poetic language, comparing the two versions of "The Elephant in the Moon," and discuss his shorter satires, comparing the "Satyr upon the licentious age of Charles the 2nd . . ." with Rochester's satires.

6 SCOTT, PAULETTE MAIER. "Samuel Butler and Seventeenth-Century Thought." Ph.D. dissertation, Indiana University, 317 pp.
Traces Butler's relation to trends in seventeenth-century philosophy, religion, politics, science, and literature. Butler's theory of knowledge was empirical, though it left room for innate ideas and right reason. His religious thought accommodated the major principles of Anglicanism, with which his views on Catholicism and the Sects are also consistent. His character of "An Atheist" owes "a special debt" to John Tillotson. Though he was familiar with the writings of Harrington, Hobbes, and Machiavelli, Anglican polemics also helped to form many of his political views (approval of a strong state church, disapproval of toleration) and made him "partially reject" the ideal of a secular state. As his political thought was ambivalent, his scientific thought was transitional: he read both the mystical alchemist Thomas Vaughn and the literary members of the Royal Society, and though he attacked the latter on moral and religious grounds, he also shared some of their scientific optimism. Butler's literary opinions include several neoclassical ideas, but he disapproved of critical judgment based solely upon rules. See also DAI 34 (1974):7722A.

7 THORSON, JAMES L. "A Broadside by Samuel Butler (1612-1680)." BLR 9 (December):178-86.
Provides bibliographical description and a summary of the content of a Tory broadside entitled "The Priviledge of our Saints in the business of Perjury. Useful for Grand-Juries. By the Author of Hudibras" (London, 1681). The printer and compiler of the broadside (Butler died in 1680) was Benjamin Tooke, who simply reprinted 152 lines from the second canto of Part II and (for a dozen of those lines) the second canto of Part I of Hudibras to capitalize on the public interest in grand juries arising out of those (of Whig bias) that were meeting in the aftermath of the Popish plots. In this context, the words of the broadside

either ironically excuse jurors of their oaths, or, directly, warn them of the duplicity of Puritan witnesses.

1975

1 NEEL, JASPER PHILLIP. "'A Kind of Mungral Breed': The Allusive Method in Butler's Hudibras." Ph.D. dissertation, University of Tennessee, 200 pp.
    Studies Butler's satiric use of allusions to Don Quixote, the Faerie Queene, the Iliad, the Aeneid, and the Bible. Allusions to the first two works force the reader to compare the world of Hudibras to those of Quixote and Sir Guyon and to recognize the baseness and intemperance of the former. Allusions to the Iliad and the Aeneid serve a more general mock-heroic purpose; and those to the Bible set biblical heroes against pagan and Puritan heroes. See also DAI 36 (1975):3660-61A.

2 TOTTEN, CHARLES F. "Hypocrisy and Corruption in Four Characters of Samuel Butler." ELWIU 2 (Fall):164-70.
    Points out similarities in Butler's four longest and most inclusive characters in order to reveal a schematic purpose showing the spread of corruption throughout four levels of human experience: the corruption of normal social relations by the "Modern Politician," of spiritual relations between God and man by the "Hypocritical Nonconformist," of the intellectual relation between the mind and its productions by the "Small Poet," and of the relation between scientific procedure and truth, a "material corruption," by the "Hermetic Philosopher." Butler's satire reveals the fact that these four destroyers of civilization are the heroes of the culture. See also 1972.6.

3 WILDING, MICHAEL. "Flecknoe's Diarium: A Source for Hudibras." N&Q 220 (July):310-12.
    Finds a "possible" source for Hudibras in Richard Flecknoe's The Diarium, or Journall (1656), a plotless series of satiric observations of locales and characters encountered on a twelve-day journey through England in a manner and style "remarkably" like Butler's. The Diarium also burlesques epic structure, parodies the conventionally poetic description of the dawn and the invocation of the muse, and uses octosyllabic couplets, comic rhyme, and "broad" (or scatological) language, animal imagery, and proverb.

1976

1 LANDON, MICHAEL. "'The Learned Glynne and Maynard': Two Characters 'Dashed Out' of Samuel Butler's Hudibras." PAPS 120 (June):205-10.

Investigates Anthony à Wood's report that two couplets referring to Sir John Glynne and Sir John Maynard were deleted from the 1674 edition of Hudibras for fear of offending the two men "then living." According to Wood, the lines in question—"Did not the learned Glynne and Maynard / To make good subjects Traytors strain hard? / Was not the King by Proclamation / Declar'd a Rebel o'er all the Nation?"—belong in canto 2 of the First Part, around line 621. Because Maynard lived until 1690, the lines were never restored to the poem. But modern editors have continued to omit them in the text. The lines are judged authentic on the grounds that Wood received them from John Aubrey, who either heard them "from Butler's own lips, or else saw them in some early draft of Hudibras."

2 NELSON, NICOLAS H. "Astrology, Hudibras, and the Puritans." JHI 37 (July-September):521-36.

Sketches the main lines of a debate carried on in the 1650s between the judicial astrologers and their later radical sectarian defenders on the one hand and their Presbyterian critics on the other, the germ, "undoubtedly," of the debate between Hudibras and Sidrophel. The latter is not an allegory of the individual participants in the historical controversy (cf. 1929.1), but it does suggest the general arguments they employed (e.g., that astrology is unscientific) and the standard defense (which invoked Baconian concepts). Butler makes his own use of these arguments to satirize both Hudibras and Sidrophel, the debate between knight and astrologer extending that between (Presbyterian) knight and (sectarian) squire, and establishing the contentious character of the Puritan movement. An appendix to this essay supplies an annotated bibliography of 41 titles that constitute the debate over astrology.

*3 WALTER, JAMES F. "Satiric Effects of the Mock-Epic Form in Hudibras and The Dunciad." Innisfree 3:14-22.
    Cited in 1976 MLA International Bibliography.

4 WASSERMAN, GEORGE R. "Hudibras and Male Chauvinism." SEL 16:351-61.

Continues the argument (from 1973.6) that Hudibras is a satire on mankind: as Part I attacks rational pride by elevating animals over men, Parts II and III do so by elevating women over men, a satiric strategy that challenges the male chauvinistic identification of human reason with masculine reason. Hudibras defends the traditional fictions about the sexes, mistaking the shrew of the skimmington and the crafty widow for vulnerable heroines of romance; the latter's submissiveness, which conventionally permits the knight to display his superiority, is a trick to reveal his inferiority. (The widow is the satirist's accomplice in the poem.) Reduced to such ignomiy (Trulla earlier demonstrated the limits of the knight's physical prowess), Hudibras must resort to orthodox concepts of hierarchy to save his self-esteem, concepts that betray, however, his Republican principles: if domestic women have ceased to obey their natural betters, it is because political men have ceased to obey theirs. Butler was not a feminist; his notebook comments on women and marriage reflect the prejudices of his age. His apparent softness on the sex in Hudibras is a satirical pose, a technique for revealing not the virtues of women, but the pride of men.

5 _____. Samuel "Hudibras" Butler. Boston: Twayne Publishers, 142 pp.

Discusses Butler's thought--his general views on morality and society (see 1970.6) as well as those on government and religion--and his works--especially Hudibras and the prose characters--as expressions of that thought. History is therefore de-emphasized in the analysis of Hudibras, which is read as a satire on mankind, theriophilist in Part I, ironically feminist in Parts II and III (see 1973.6, 1976.4); the plot of the poem is internally rather than externally generated; its conclusion reduces the differences between Presbyterian knight and Independent squire (between ignorance and knavery) to an essential villany. Butler's prose characters also grow out of his moral assumptions; their method is reductive, revealing one or two faults as the motives of all wrongdoing. Analyses of "An Anabaptist" and "An Undeserving Favourite" suggest that character writing was less a form of moral exhortation than an intellectual exercise for Butler; his figures are less the expression of insights (as metaphysical conceits are) than the play of wit for its own sake. History enters Butler's satire, indirectly, as the experienced past and as the present that tradition normally replaces. If Hudibras manages to escape the narrowing partisanship of most of its imitations, it is because its overall point of view is retrospective; the defeat of Puritanism made ridiculing it fun. On the other hand, the poem repudiates the idea of the great poem. Hudibras displaces itself in the epic tradition and takes the tradition to pieces in order to reveal the real world it overlooks. Viewed thus, Butler becomes the first important literary "Modern."

1977

1 JAFFE, NORA CROW. The Poet Swift. Hanover: University Press of New England, pp. 33-40.

Examines parallels and resemblances in the thought and poetry of Butler and Swift, waiving any "clear debt" of the latter to the former. Though common sense was the "ultimate poetic standard" for both, there are significant differences in tone and technique. Butler is always milder (more humorous) than Swift. Though both draw their images from everyday life, Butler's are "ingenious" and "memorable," Swift's "pallid" and "forgettable" (except in his prose). Butler's tone is unvaryingly farcical, Swift's varied. Swift shared so many of Butler's dislikes, he must have picked up hints from him; but "he returned to posterity, with interest, the little that he borrowed."

2   VIETH, DAVID M. "Divided Consciousness: The Trauma and Triumph of Restoration Culture." <u>TSL</u> 22:46-62.
    Describes <u>Hudibras</u> as a structure of "reversible meaning," one of four literary responses to the cultural revolution of the mid-seventeenth century. The inadequacy of Butler's norm--"empirical common sense"--invites one to respond positively to delusion--to accept the examples of nothing as something. The process is further enacted in metaphors by the replacement of tenors by their vehicles, and by the tyranny of the concrete (rhyme) over the abstract (meaning).

1978

1   SELDEN, RAMAN. "Butler and Rochester: Low-Style Satire." In <u>English Verse Satire: 1590-1765</u>. London: George Allen & Unwin, pp. 89-92.
    Maintains that the rationalist, materialist, and skeptical thought of Hobbes, Bacon, and Glanvill produced the "low-style" satire of Butler and Rochester. Though Butler himself departs from the Augustan norm of rationality, deviations from that norm are the chief objects of his ridicule. His link with the neoclassical tradition is linguistic; the "bizarre linguistic surface" of <u>Hudibras</u> implies by contrast a norm of lucid speech. Man is expressed in his language, the abuse of which in the Restoration, as in the past, was an index of his low estate. See also 1984.3.

1979

1   BLOOM, EDWARD A., and LILLIAN D. <u>Satire's Persuasive Voice</u>. Ithaca: Cornell University Press, pp. 174-81.
    Finds, beneath the harshness of Butler's ridicule in <u>Hudibras</u>, something humanely restorative (see also 1974.3). The mode of the poem is nevertheless ambivalent: joviality (achieved by combining irony, hyperbole, and parody) disguising cruelty. A similar ambivalence is found in the hero's name: <u>hue de bras</u> ("hue of brass") suggesting a surface at odds with its reality.

2   DE QUEHEN, HUGH, ed. General introduction and textual introduction to <u>Samuel Butler: Prose Observations</u>. Oxford: Clarendon Press, pp. xvii-lx.
    Traces the history of Butler's manuscript prose observations in the surviving holograph manuscripts and in William Longueville's partial transcription of them in the "commonplace book"; reviews the various printings of these materials, includ-

ing the six selections ([sic], cf. 1948.1) printed in the London Magazine; and analyzes Butler's controlling ideas and their historical reference. The holograph materials were written between 1655 and 1677, with apparently some lapse in the early 1670s when Butler was turning his prose into verse satire. Observations on religion make up the largest part of the holograph and reveal Butler's rationalist tendencies. A list of writers drawn upon and identified in the Longueville commonplace book includes Tillotson, Stillingfleet, Parker, Taylor, and Hooker among the theologians. The collected material is often analogical in nature; examples of paradox and contradiction predominate. The textual introduction describes in detail the state of the manuscript material and presents the rationale for arranging the holograph folios for this edition (see 1928.4). See also 1972.2.

3 ENGLER, BALZ. "Hudibras and the Problem of Satirical Distance." ES 60 (August):436-43.

Argues that Hudibras lacks the satirical distance needed to lift the subject above its historical context, and that this shortcoming accounts for the rapid aging of the poem, evidence of which was Butler's need to supply explanatory notes to the 1674 edition of Parts I and II. Butler did not make consistent use of devices creating distance: the planes of reality and representation are too close to one another to allow for allegorical reading; the author's presence in the poem is that of a wit, not a distancing judge; the function of characters fluctuates between that of comic butt and that of author's mouthpiece; and the form of the poem is unsystematic. Because satire conflicts with burlesque, the poem cannot be enjoyed as a poem, but as a collection of maxims and an example of the triumphs and failures of satire.

4 SEIDEL, MICHAEL. "The Internecine Romance: Butler's Hudibras." In Satiric Inheritance: Rabelais to Sterne. Princeton: Princeton University Press, pp. 95-134.

Sets Hudibras within a theory of satire as a violation of narrative generation (see also 1974.5). If narrative works with "the accumulation of potential through issue" (Anchises's forecast of the future for Aeneas is the prototype), then satire is a questioning of this generation, and Hudibras--"the real subject" of which is represented by the widow's small inheritance, "the schismatic, divided, devalued 'estate' of the English historical scene"--is the record of the Restoration "internecine dispossession." The narrative imitates the schismatic history of the years 1640-60; Hudibras's wooing of the widow suggests the Presbyterian wooing of monarchy after the death of Cromwell. What prevents such a reading from turning the poem into allegory (see 1955.4) is the satiric strategy that undermines the value and meaning of the historical details. Interpretation itself becomes schismatic: "the madness of the mind's record." What Butler did with his narrative models--The Faerie Queene (II.ii) and Don

Quixote--illustrates satire's divorce of descent from continuity, a confusion of "moral and spatial notions of direction." In Spenser's account of Sir Huddibras, another family is divided: Perissa (excess) contends against her youngest sister Elissa (lack), and their respective lovers, reckless Sans-loy and blustering Sir Huddibras, oppose one another and Sir Guyon (moderation), who is allied to the middle sister Medina and who eventually restores order. In Butler's Hudibras, this chivalric potential miscarries: only discord survives; the widow (Butler's Elissa) and Sir Hudibras turn the rituals of romance into the settlements of war--"odde perverse antipathies," in Butler's words. From Don Quixote, Butler took a fable of monomania and extravagance, a generating principle of narrative itself; but whereas Quixote converts his fancy and returns to sanity, Hudibras still wanders in delusion at the end.

5 STAVES, SUSAN. Players' Scepters: Fictions of Authority in the Restoration. Lincoln: University of Nebraska Press, pp. 207-20.

Objects to the critical tendency (Jack [1952.1] and Seidel [1971.11] are specifically cited) to read Parts I and II of Hudibras as a general or philosophical satire, a strategy for ignoring Butler's commitment to older, undemocratic "fictions of authority." Hudibras is topical and doctrinaire: specifically, it ridicules the parliamentary side for breaking oaths, the traditional signs of obligation to authority, and treats the Royalists "encomiastically" for their faithfulness in keeping them. The widow's curious insistence, in Part II, that Hudibras vow to undergo a whipping, is another exposure of Puritan oath-breaking or, at best, mistaking words for things. But Butler's satire is confused in this case: we are expected both to laugh at men who ignore words for things and to share the poet's skeptical belief that only things are real. The theme of perjury continues even in the more contemporary Restoration satire of Part III, where faithlessness is shown to have infected even the fundamental social institutions of marriage and law. See also 1984.3.

1980

1 WHITE, ROBERT B., JR. "Gulliver, Sir Hudibras, and the Logicians." N&Q 225 (February):33.

Notes Butler's satirical use of the logical cliché juxtaposing man and horse as a precedent for its use by Swift in Gulliver's Travels and as support for R. S. Crane's interpretation of the fourth book of the Travels. See also 1973.6.

1981

1 COPE, KEVIN L. "The Infinite Perimeter: Human Nature and Ethical Mediation in Six Restoration Writers." Restoration 5 (Fall):58-75.

Considers Butler's place in the Restoration project of closing the gap created by earlier dualistic thought--that between mind and matter, the natural and supernatural. The problem for Butler, in this quest for a middle-ground, lay in restricting human activity too severely. The essential truths of nature and heaven, he believed, are within the reach of human reason; but reason is individual and therefore biased. The virtuosi in "The Elephant in the Moon" are blinded to the truth by prejudicial reason and enthusiasm. Butler's definition of human nature and of the limits of permissible knowledge is so narrow that it denies human access to man's legitimate links with nature and heaven. It remained for Dryden in "Religio Laici" to both "bound and expand the human world."

2 COUSINS, A. D. "The Idea of a 'Restoration' and the Verse Satires of Butler and Marvell." SoRA 14 (July):131-42.

Argues that for Butler the "Restoration" as the cultural myth invented by Dryden, Waller, and Sprat--the return of justice, order, learning, civility--never occurred. According to Butler's "Satyr upon the Licentious Age of Charles the Second," the new cavaliers recreated "the disordered puritan sensibility," institutionalizing vice as an art and a theology, and inverting natural law--a view that would be "unthinkable" in Hudibras (cf. 1973.6). Butler creates a countermyth that parodies the Augustan: civility in the new courtliness is demonic, "an aesthetic of vice stylizing moral disorder." In the couplet version of "The Elephant in the Moon," Sidrophel's Interregnum unreason has been institutionalized in the Royal Society, turning Sprat's praise of Charles's interest in science into an endorsement of hubris. The Society has not purified language, but debased it, turned it into a "canting Idiom," a phrase Royalists earlier used to criticize Puritan enthusiasm (see 1984.3). The "restoration" of learning distorts the Baconian ideal. The context for these views on Restoration morality and learning is Butler's "Satyr upon the Weakness and Misery of Man," which universalizes Puritan unreason. Although these satires are shaped by a Senecan distrust of illusion, they lack Seneca's faith in the restorative power of reason.

3 ROTHSTEIN, ERIC. In The Routledge History of English Poetry. Edited by R. A. Foakes. Vol. 3, Restoration and Eighteenth-Century Poetry: 1660-1780. Boston: Routledge & Kegan Paul, pp. 24-26.

Suggests that Hudibras be read not as a coherent narrative, but as a series of more or less separate episodes; its narrative exists "to provide showcases for self-display." Butler imposes the heroic on a "homely norm," common sense, a use that occurs rarely in later mock-heroic.

1982

1 DE QUEHEN, A. H. "An Account of Works Attributed to Samuel Butler." RES 33 (August):262-77.
   Makes a generally negative estimate of the authenticity of more than eighty works in verse and prose attributed to Butler since 1680. Those printed by Robert Thyer (mostly from Butler's holograph) in the Genuine Remains (1759) are accepted as genuine. Of the contents of the three volume Posthumous Works (1715), however, evidence against Butler's authorship or of authorship by another (e.g., John Birkenhead) is abundant. Mercurius Menippeus (also entitled "Memoirs of the Years 1649 and 50"), included in the Posthumous Works and accepted by Lamar as genuine, is here attributed to Thomas Winyard. Also accepted by Lamar, but not included in the Genuine Remains, is Mola Asinaria, which is here consigned to a "doubtful" status, pending identification of Anthony à Wood's source for the attribution to Butler. Dildoides seems more properly the work of "a court wit" (as a manuscript text, attributing it to Sedley, suggests); nor is anything recognizably Butler's found in The Rehearsal. Anderson's claim (1947.1) that Butler wrote The Transproser Rehears'd, The Character of the Rump, and The Censure of the Rota is also challenged: similarities between Butler's works and these--partial basis for Anderson's claim--are regarded as insignificant, and the summary of two of Parker's works allegedly by Butler is here identified as a transcription by William Longueville. The translation of "Cydippe to Acontius," published by Tonson in Ovid's Epistles (1680), may be Butler's, but its ascription depends on the good reputation of the publisher; it is also "reasonable to credit Butler with Lord Roos His Answer."

2 HORNE, WILLIAM C. "'Between th' Petticoat and Breeches': Sexual Warfare and the Marriage Debate in Hudibras." In Studies in Eighteenth Century Culture. Vol. 11, edited by Harry C. Payne. Madison: University of Wisconsin Press, pp. 133-46.
   Points out a dilemma in "the marriage debate" between Hudibras and the widow--the former defending marriage hypocritically, the latter attacking it out of fashionable cynicism; and attempts to understand the debate in the light of a shift in the conception of marriage away from the traditional patriarchal model to a contractual model. Butler's conception of the marriage debate may have been influenced by a "role-reversal play" like William Cavendish's The Triumphant Widow. Seen in this light, the widow is at once the voice of the satirist, an object of the satire, and a reflection of what was happening to marriage at the time. The

product of neither an "unreconstructed sexist" nor one "who-is-almost-a-feminist" (cf. 1976.4 and 1974.5, respectively), the behavior of the widow "follows its own vector of degeneration," demonstrating that women may be as tyrannical as men.

3   KORSHIN, PAUL J. Typologies in England: 1650-1820. Princeton: Princeton University Press, pp. 277-82.
    Regards Butler's attacks on mysticism in Hudibras and in the character of "An Hermetick Philosopher" as satire of the Renaissance tradition of mythography. Ralpho's mystical analogies are sometimes typological: for every point he makes against the "Antichristian Game" of bear-baiting, he can find a pagan custom that prefigures it. He argues that synods that persecute the foes of Presbyters are like the Romans who persecuted the Christians, and like the baiters who persecute bears: synods, then, are "mystical i.e., typological Bear-gardens." Hudibras typologizes the shrew in the skimmington as the Whore of Babylon (a postfiguration), or finds the latter a type of the former (a prefiguration). In Part III, Butler develops the idea of the Rump as an Egyptian hieroglyphic or type to which the various schemes of government proposed in 1658-59 are antitypes. Though Ralpho and Hudibras are of different religions, both are mad exegetes of the Bible.

4   WAGNER, JOSEPH B. "Hudibras and the Hermaphrodite." CLAJ 25 (March):359-64.
    Investigates Butler's use of the image of the hermaphrodite (the hermetic symbol of divine and prelapsarian perfection and completeness) to ridicule hermeticism, the new science, and the institution of marriage. Sir Hudibras unwittingly employs the image, along with the hermetic concepts of man-as-microcosm and universal correspondences, to prove to the widow that marriage is natural. Yoked together in the pillory, the knight and squire suggest the image again and allow the widow to redefine "hermaphrodite" (wedded man and woman) as a forced and unnatural union. See also 1973.5.

1983

1   HORNE, WILLIAM C. "Curiosity and Ridicule in Samuel Butler's Satire on Science." Restoration 7 (Spring):8-18.
    Surveys "micro" (e.g., 1929.1, 1969.1) and "macro" (e.g., 1933.1) criticism of Butler's satires on science in order to reconcile antithetical interpretations of his attitude: Baconian critic of the Royal Society virtuosos, or unqualified skeptic of scientific experimenters? Support for one or the other view seems to depend on which of the satires is considered, and efforts to extract a single intellectual position from them violates the rhetorical integrity of any one. The views are "complimentary," though the first "is the more accurate." "An Hero-

ical Epistle . . . to Sidrophel" scorns the value of certain
Royal Society experiments (see 1965.3), but does not disparage
the experimental method generally; neither does "An Occasional
Reflection on Dr. Charlton's Feeling a Dog's Pulse," which satirizes the Society's creation of a public image; and "The Elephant in the Moon," far from being anti-science, criticizes the
Society for not being Baconian in its experiments. Butler's
moral skepticism in the last of these satires (see 1972.5) is a
response to metaphysical philosophy, not scientific experiment.
His notebooks contain "at least six or seven New Science entries"
that suggest not mockery but "up-to-date curiosity," and the
"Satyr Upon the Royal Society" may have been abandoned because
his scientific curiosity triumphed over his sense of the ridiculous.

2 _____. "Hard Words in Hudibras." DUJ 75 (June):31-43.
Defines the phrase "hard words" (used in Hudibras and several of the prose characters) as (1) quarrelling ("hard words
. . . Set Folks together by the ears"); (2) Puritan cant (i.e.,
calling "Fire and Sword and Desolation, / A goodly-thorough-
Reformation"); (3) pedantic jargon, employed by rhetoricians,
lawyers or lovers; and (4) simply harsh-sounding words. Butler
not only maintains that linguistic violence leads to physical
violence; he employs "hard words" affectively in the poem to
produce an aesthetic violence on the reader, drawing out the
practice in extended passages of impenetrable density. The satirical attack on "hard words" has its origin in the Royalist anthology called Rump (see 1971.4-5); Butler worked this conventional topic of satire as a rich mine of metaphorical wit.

3 ROBINSON, KEN. "The Skepticism of Butler's Satire on Science:
Optimistic or Pessimistic?" Restoration 7 (Spring):1-7.
Maintains that Butler subscribed to an optimistic epistemol-
ogy, that his skepticism was chiefly an instrument of satire, and
that his satire of science--the argument is based on a reading of
the octosyllabic "Elephant in the Moon," corroborated by the
prose observations--is an attack on bad scientific method. Proper scientific method is normative in the poem; between the self-
interest of the virtuoso and the noninterest of the foot-boys is
the disinterested reporting of fact by the narrator (Butler).
The positives implied in all his satires of science are Baconian,
suggesting that skeptical care must be taken to correct the dis-
torted reflection of the world in the mirror-like mind. The
lines in "The Elephant in the Moon" (411-18) describing the
solitary path to truth are no exception; they are spoken not by
Butler (cf. 1972.5), but by a pseudoscientist who is more interested in singularity than in truth. Butler's analogical habit
of mind does not, then, necessarily commit him to an analogical
world view (cf. 1967.3 and 1979.2); it provided a "skeptical
weapon" for a nonskeptical end.

1984

1 EADE, J. C. The Forgotten Sky: A Guide to Astrology in English Literature. Oxford: Clarendon Press, pp. 215-16.
   Analyzes the astrological significance of Hogarth's illustration of Hudibras II,iii, entitled "Hudibras beats Sidrophel and his Man Whacum." Two astrological schemes are visible in the illustration, neither representing Sidrophel's summary in the poem (lines 991 ff.). The symbols on the larger scheme are random and fragmentary, a commentary, perhaps, on Sidrophel's proficiency. Those on the smaller scheme, which appear to indicate the opposition of Saturn to Venus, may be a gloomy comment on the occasion of Hudibras's visit to the astrologer: his attempt to win the widow. The illustration is reproduced.

2 NUSSBAUM, FELICITY A. "The Better Women: The Amazon Myth and Hudibras." In The Brink of All We Hate: English Satires on Women, 1660-1750. Lexington: University Press of Kentucky, pp. 43-56.
   Argues that Hudibras does not make a feminist statement (cf. 1974.5), although sex roles and sexual ambiguities are central to the poem. Though the Widow's deflation of Hudibras's sexist arrogance seems to merge with the satirist's, her views on woman's place in the world are extreme: rule by women, while superior to rule by men, "is not much to be preferred" (see also 1976.4-5). Butler associates ruling (or masculine) women with the Amazons, mythologized by antifeminists as monsters of nature. But the Amazons of Hudibras (Trulla and the shrew of the skimmington are two others) challenge the myth and force the reader to reconsider antifeminist texts.

3 SNIDER, ALVIN. "Babel Reversed: Samuel Butler's Hudibras and the Language of Things." Ph.D. dissertation, University of Chicago, 346 pp.
   Explores the nature and underlying assumptions of Butler's "language satire." Verbal shortcomings, Butler believed, are the fruits of our fallen reason, but abuses of logic and definition are of human origin and may be avoided. Proper use of language depends on the matching of thoughts and things and on the matching of words to thoughts. Hudibras and Ralph misunderstand these relationships, projecting "insubstantial" words and thoughts onto the world. In Hudibras, Butler politicizes the clarity of discourse issue and the dangers of casuistry (the deliberate exploitation of the gap between words and things) and "hard words." Butler in turn exploits the misuses of language to produce "an aesthetic of anti-style," a characteristic use of diction, figure, prosody, and rhyme that alerts the reader to "the ruins of Babel." See also 1978.1 and 1983.2.

Writings about the Earl of Rochester, 1680-1985

1680

1   BURNET, GILBERT. Some Passages of the Life and Death of the Right Honourable John Earl of Rochester. London: Richard Chiswel.
    Summarizes Rochester's own account of his past life and, at much greater length, the discussions on morality and on natural and revealed religion that led, in the final months of the poet's life, to his conversion to Christianity. Reprinted: 1972.5.

1685

1   WOLSELEY, ROBERT. Preface to Valentinian: A Tragedy. London: Timothy Goodwin.
    Vindicates and eulogizes the late poet's character, praises, generally, his poetry, and, in particular, defends it against Mulgrave's opinion that "Bawdry bare-fac'd" is "poor Pretence to Wit"--an absurd statement, it is argued, by any definition of wit. Reprinted: 1972.5.

1691

1   [RYMER, THOMAS.] "A Preface to the Reader." In Poems etc. on Several Occasions: With Valentinian, a Tragedy. London: Printed for Jacob Tonson.
    Praises Rochester as the improver of whatever he imitated or translated from Ovid, Lucretius, Seneca, Anacreon, and Boileau, even though he wanted their maturity and the disciplining authority and taste of their audiences. Reprinted: 1972.5.

1693

1   DENNIS, JOHN. Preface to Miscellanies in Verse and Prose. London: Printed for James Knapton.

Cites Rochester's adoption of Butler's burlesque manner in several poems as evidence that Boileau's criticism of burlesque did not extend to the English poet. The standard text is Edward Niles Hooker's edition of The Critical Works of John Dennis, vol. 1 (Baltimore: Johns Hopkins Press, 1939).

1707

1 BROWN, TOM. "A Short Essay on English Satire." In Works. Vol. 1. London, 1707, pp. 34-38.
  Compares Rochester and Dorset to one another and to Oldham, together the three "greatest Satirists of the English." Rochester's satiric performance is behind Dorset's. His wit, often profane, exposed persons rather than vices and "begat more crimes" than it corrected faults.

2 "The Memoirs of the Life and Character of the Late Earl of Rochester, in a Letter to the Duchess of Mazarine. By Mons. St Evrement." In The Miscellaneous Works of the Right Hon. the late Earls of Rochester and Roscommon. London: B. Bragge.
  Rates Rochester the Modern nearest the Ancients in satire and cautions against the reading of his "looser Songs," which beside their peculiar beauty have the power of alarming the fancy and rousing the blood and appetite. The letter is no longer ascribed to St. Evremond. Reprinted: 1972.5.

1713

1 GRAMMONT, ANTHONY HAMILTON, COMTE DE. Mémoires du comte de Grammont. Paris.
  Records many of Rochester's escapades at court, including the contretemps with Mary Hobart and Anne Temple, his banishment and interim residence in the city, and his intrigue with Elizabeth Barry. The narrative ends with his marriage to a "melancholy heiress." The English translation by Abel Boyer (frequently reprinted) appeared in 1714.

1733

1 AROUET, FRANÇOIS-MARIE [Voltaire]. "Of the Earl of Rochester and Mr. Waller" (Letter XXI). In Philosophical Letters. Translated by John Lockman. London.
  Displays Rochester's genius by comparing lines 72-95 of the "Satyr against Reason and Mankind" (in French translation) with corresponding lines in Boileau's Satire. The French edition (frequently reprinted) appeared in 1734.

1758

1 WALPOLE, HORACE. A Catalogue of the Royal and Noble Authors of England. Vol. 2. Strawberry Hill, pp. 37-42.

Condemns Rochester's poetry chiefly for its lack of "politeness"; it calls everything by its own name, the Restoration reaction to the use of scripture names in the preceding age. Indelicacy damages even satire. Reprinted: 1972.5.

1779

1 JOHNSON, SAMUEL. "Rochester." In The Works of the English Poets, With Prefaces, Biographical and Critical, by Samuel Johnson. 68 vols. in 58. London: Printed by H. Hughes for C. Bathurst et al., 1779-81. [Lives of the Poets.]

Maintains that Rochester's poems are read more for their author's reputation than for his genius. His songs are conventional, lacking nature and sentiment; the imitation of Horace is noteworthy for preserving the parallel with its original. "Upon Nothing" is his "strongest effort," though he was not the first to celebrate this subject: "Nihil," a poem by the sixteenth-century French poet Passerat, is quoted in full, and Boileau had used the word rien in the positive sense in which Rochester plays with it. Rochester's "buffoon conceit" is identified as the line "all men would be cowards if they durst" in the "Satyr against Reason and Mankind," which owes much to Boileau.

1820

1 WOOD, ANTHONY à. Athenae Oxonienses. Edited by Philip Bliss. Vol. 3. London: F. C. & J. Rivington et al., 1813-20, pp. 1228-34. Facsimile reprint. New York: Burt Franklin, 1967.

Supplies information on Rochester's life and education and provides a list of works attributed to him (some wrongly). Wolseley's preface to Valentinian (1685.1) is said to contain too many "high-flown surfeiting Encomiums."

1857

1 FORGUES, EMILE DAURAND. "John Wilmot, comte de Rochester." Revue des deux mondes 10 (August):822-62; 11 (September):144-87.

An essay in two parts, the first biographical, arguing that Rochester resisted the contamination of the court by turning its evil into a curse against itself; the second part is critical, an apology for his poems in terms of historical necessity (the anonymous lampoon, for instance, was the logical reaction to the Licensing Act of 1662). The poems--"The History of Insipids,"

"Timon," and "Tunbridge Wells" are particularly noticed--have primarily a historical value. Rochester, the best of the Restoration satirists, was only the Petronius, not the Juvenal, of his age (cf. 1927.3).

1863

1 TAINE, HIPPOLYTE ADOLPHE. Histoire de la littérature anglaise. Paris: Hachette, 1863-67.
   Condemns, relentlessly, Rochester as man and poet: his cowardly declining to duel was a display of skeptical principle; his writing is the very negation of poetry. The English translation by H. van Laun first appeared in 1871.

1871

1 CLARKE, CHARLES COWDEN. "On the Comic Writers of England." Gentleman's Magazine, n.s., 7 (November):693-95.
   Presents familiar information on Rochester, but observes that his reputation as a poet has been unduly tarnished by the misattribution to him of poems he would not have written. Lines from a Satire on the Times and "On Nothing" are quoted as illustration of his bold wit. Reprinted: 1972.5.

1881

1 BELJAME, ALEXANDRE. Le public et les hommes de lettres en Angleterre au dix-huitième siècle: 1660-1744. Paris, pp. 88-107. 2d ed., 1897.
   Focuses on Rochester's relations with Dryden--first as patron of the latter, then (in retaliation for Dryden's acceptance of Mulgrave's friendship) as patron of Dryden's playwright rivals, and finally as instigator of the Rose St. ambuscade. Rochester emerges as a spiteful and untrustworthy man. Translated: 1948.1.

1892

1 STREET, G. S. "Rochester." National Observer, 5 March.
   Finds Rochester's life (he was "a mass of contradictions") more interesting than his poetry; nevertheless, there has been "no cult of his memory." What recognition his poetry has received has been misplaced: Johnson's preference for "On Nothing" reflects merely his own modesty; the coarseness of his lampoons on Charles can be matched by many. His wit and good sense is most marked in his "least fastidious attempts."

1895

1. GARNETT, R[ICHARD]. "Poets Contemporary with Dryden." In The Age of Dryden. London: G. Bell & Sons, pp. 46-48.

    Comments, in passing, on the general insipidity of Rochester's amatory lyrics, while granting that "some of his songs are not devoid of merit." The epitaph on Charles II is probably by neither Rochester nor Buckingham.

1898

1. AUBREY, JOHN. "John Wilmot: Earl of Rochester." In "Brief Lives," chiefly of Contemporaries, set down by John Aubrey, between the Years 1669 & 1696. Edited by Andrew Clark. 2 vols. Oxford: Clarendon Press, 2:304.

    Familiar bits of information on Rochester's life and character recounted with characteristic personal force: e.g., "I remember I sawe him a Prisoner in the Tower. . . ." Reprinted in Aubrey's Brief Lives, ed. Oliver Lawson Dick (London: Secker & Warburg, 1950).

1899

1. ELTON, OLIVER. The Augustan Age. New York: Charles Scribner's Sons, pp. 233-36.

    Praises Rochester's lyrics which have more of the "incommunicable" than any poet's between Herrick and Burns. The philosophy of "Upon Nothing," applied to the times, is found in "The History of Insipids."

1903

1. COURTHOPE, W. J. A History of English Poetry. Vol. 3. London: Macmillan, pp. 355-77.

    Places Rochester's satire on a par with that of Dryden, Pope, and Byron and notes its strong reliance upon the philosophy of Hobbes.

2. LONGUEVILLE, THOMAS. Rochester and Other Literary Rakes of the Court of Charles II. with Some Account of Their Surroundings. London: Longmans, Green & Co., 375 pp.

    Presents Rochester as the genius of vice and frivolity at the court of Charles. The account is, admittedly, "a mass of discursive gossip," discursively treated, Rochester's escapades and associations being the excuse for further indulgent investigation. His poems, however, are simply an embarrassment to the author.

1912

1 WHIBLEY, CHARLES. "The Court Poets." In The Cambridge History of English Literature. Edited by A. W. Ward and A. R. Waller. Vol. 3. New York: G. P. Putnam's Sons, pp. 224-52.

Attempts to correct misunderstandings of Rochester the man--fostered largely by the witless and the injured--and of his poems--their general condemnation as well as particular judgments; his worst poems have been called the best (witness Johnson's praise of "Upon Nothing" [1779.1]). Rochester's superiority is found in his satires, though his lyrics are recognized as having no equal in his age. Farley-Hills (1972.5) regards this essay as the beginning of modern Rochester criticism.

1921

1 NICOLL, ALLARDYCE. "Dryden, Howard and Rochester." TLS, 13 January, p. 27.

Examining B.M. Add. MS 28,692, which contains copies of Lucina's Rape or The Tragedy of Valentinian and "A Scaen of Sir Robert Hoard's Play [The Conquest of China], written by the Earl of Rochester," Nicoll concludes: (1) the manuscript text of Valentinian suggests a date of composition and performance earlier than 1679, while the printed text suggests a revival of the play after the Union of Companies in 1682; and (2) deletions in the manuscript of certain passages in the printed text of the play indicate that the manuscript volume may be a transcript made for Rochester prior to 1680, reflecting the self-censorship resulting from his conversion, and suggesting that the "Scaen" is his. On the other hand, if these deletions reflect a later (post-Collier) sense of dramatic morality (and therefore indicate a later transcription of the manuscript), the "Scaen" may not be Rochester's, but Dryden's. See also 1926.3, 1937.8, 1956.2, and 1968.2.

1925

1 HAM, ROSWELL J. "Thomas Otway, Rochester, and Mrs. Barry." N&Q 149 (5 September):165-67.

Reviews information surrounding the identity of the "cruel and capricious mistress" of Otway's love letters, concluding that Mrs. Barry "can upon no account be easily dismissed" and that Rochester "may very well" have been an early lover of the actress and also the father of her child, born in 1677. Otway's letters (written after Rochester's death) refer to a living rival, however, identified here as Etherege. See also 1931.1 and 1974.6.

1926

1 HAYWARD, JOHN, ed. Textual and biographical introductions to Collected Works of John Wilmot, Earl of Rochester. London: Nonesuch Press, pp. xi-l.

Draws upon tradition and published sources of information (principally Gilbert Burnet's life, the Memoirs of Grammont and St. Evremond's letter to the duchess of Mazarin) for the life of Rochester, and reviews the textual history of his works. The edition that follows--the first twentieth-century attempt to collect Rochester's works--includes Valentinian, the scene for Robert Howard's play (but not Sodom), "Alexander Bendo's Advertisement," and letters to Savile, Mrs. Barry, and his family, as well as the lyrics and satires.

*2 PRINZ, JOHANNES, ed. Rochesteriana: Being Some Anecdotes Concerning John Wilmot, Earl of Rochester. Leipzig: Privately printed.

Cited in 1968.4.

3 SPRAGUE, ARTHUR COLBY. "Rochester's Valentinian." In Beaumont and Fletcher on the Restoration Stage. Cambridge, Mass.: Harvard University Press, pp. 165-78. Reprint. New York: Benjamin Bloom, 1965.

Argues that Rochester's alterations of Fletcher's play impart greater probability and unity of action at the cost of oversimplifying character: Rochester's Emperor, who "lapses into the monster," suggests "not infrequently" the reviser himself (cf. 1937.6-7); Lucina, "over-laid with sentiment and prudery," ceases to be real. Discrepancies between a manuscript version of the play, entitled Lucina's Rape, and the printed quarto are of little significance. The manuscript, however, retains more features of Fletcher's original than the latter, which--following Nicoll's conclusion (1921.1)--probably represents a stage copy. See also 1956.2 and 1968.2.

1927

1 ISAACS, J. "The Earl of Rochester's Grand Tour." RES 3 (January):75-76.

Documents Rochester's visit to Venice from a letter of Abraham Hill (dated 1 October 1664) and from Rochester's own signature in the register of visitors to the University of Padua.

2 PRINZ, JOHANNES. John Wilmot, Earl of Rochester: His Life and Writings. Palaestra, no. 154. Leipzig: Mayer & Müller, 460 pp.

Reconstructs the poet's life to show that the "man was better than his reputation." Specific attention is paid to Rochester's personality, to his career as a courtier, his importance as a literary patron, and, chiefly, as a writer of lyric, satire, pornography, drama, and letters. This pioneer study does not claim to be definitive but aims to encourage further investigation. It accordingly reprints Rochester's correspondence from the Harleian manuscripts in the British Museum and presents an extensive bibliography of the early editions and of modern historical, biographical, and critical studies. See also 1938.2.

3   WILLIAMSON, GEORGE. "The Restoration Petronius." University of California Chronicle 29:273-80.
   Characterizes Rochester as the Restoration Petronius, his life and works comprising the Satyricon of the period. This character is stamped most clearly on Rochester's satires. His edifying end, whether sincere or not, was his final satire, an "ignis fatuus of the mind." Cf. 1857.1.

1931

1   GREENE, GRAHAM. "Otway and Mrs. Barry." TLS, 16 April, p. 307.
   Casts doubt on the legendary quarrel between Rochester and Otway over the latter's advances to the actress Mrs. Barry. Since it is "far more probable" that "A Trial of the Poets for the Bays"--which contains an uncomplimentary reference to Otway-- was written by Buckingham than by Rochester (cf. 1931.3), and since Otway dedicated his Titus and Berenice (1677) to Rochester, "there is little evidence to show that there was any quarrel at all between the poets." See also 1925.1, 1933.1, 1946.3, 1963.2, and 1974.6.

2   HARRIS, BRICE. "'A Satyr on the Court Ladies.'" TLS, 20 August, p. 633.
   Claims to have found the fugitive "Satyr on the Court Ladies," attributed to Rochester by Prinz (1927.2), in a manuscript "Collection of Satirical Ballads and Poems in the Time of Charles II," in the Harvard Library. But the "Satyr" (beginning "Curse on those critics ignorant and vain") is not Rochester's: it praises Dryden's satirical skills, is stylistically marred, and is followed in the manuscript by an "Answer to the Foregoing Satyr" which does not mention Rochester but attributes the poem to Goodwin Wharton. See 1932.1 for another attempt to identify Rochester's "lost" satire, and 1973.1 for still another satire on the court ladies.

3   WALMSLEY, D. M. "'A Trial of the Poets.'" TLS, 28 May, p. 427.
   Points out that "A Trial of the Poets for the Bays," attributed to Buckingham by Greene (1931.1) and to Settle by Roswell Ham (in Otway and Lee [New Haven: Yale University Press, 1931]), is identical with "A Session of the Poets" and is ascribed to Rochester in Poems on Several Occasions. See also 1933.1, 1946.3, and 1963.2.

1932

1 BULLOUGH, GEOFFREY. "'A Satyr on the Court Ladies.'" TLS, 18 February, p. 112.

Suggests that a poem "On the Court Ladies" (beginning "Young galants o'th towne, leave off your whoreing I pray"), found in a manuscript "Collection of Severall Satyrs, Lampoons, Songs and other Poems" in the Edinburgh University Library, may be the lost "Satyr on the Court Ladies" attributed to Rochester by Prinz (1927.2). But Rochester, it is asserted, did not write the manuscript satire. See also 1931.2 and 1973.1.

2 HARRIS, BRICE. "Rochester's 'Remains' and an Old Manuscript." N&Q 163 (September):170-71.

Finds approximately twenty poems in the "Remains of the Right Honourable John Earl of Rochester" (1718) that also appear in an early manuscript; but doubts Hayward's conclusion (1926.1) that the "Remains" and Harleian MSS 6913-14 are identical, or the basis of the "spurious" Poetical Works of the Witty Lord, John Earl of Rochester (1761). The early manuscript volume may have been "a mere commonplace book of much later date into which the poems from the 'Remains' were copied."

1933

1 HAM, ROSWELL G. "The Authorship of 'A Session of the Poets' (1677)." RES 9 (July):319-22.

Answers Walmsley's objection (1931.3) to the attribution of "A Session of the Poets" (or "A Trial of the Poets for the Bays") to Settle with new corroborative evidence: the allusions to "Settle's misadventures on account of the Session" in the anonymous adaptation of Chamberlayne's Love's Victory (1677). See also 1946.3 and 1963.2.

1934

1 'ESPINASSE, PAUL G. "Rochester on Charles II." TLS, 1 November, p. 755.

Supplies an alternate first line ("Here lies the mutton-eating king") to the epigram/epitaph on Charles II. The suggestion was anticipated by Loane (1934.4), who attributed it to Voltaire. For additional comment on these lines, see 1934.2-3 and 10.

2 HAYWARD, JOHN. "Rochester on Charles II." TLS, 25 October, p. 735.

Noting that Rochester's lines on Charles II are not printed in the two editions of 1680 and 1691, which Powley (1934.10) had not seen, Hayward goes on to identify the two undated "Antwerpen" editions of Rochester in the British Museum.

3 LOANE, GEORGE G. "Rochester on Charles II." TLS, 4 October, p. 675.

Questions Powley's authority for substituting "the halting and rhymeless" line, "Here lives a Great and Mighty Monarch," in the epigram on Charles II, and suggests instead the line in Thomas Hearne's version: "We have a pritty witty king." See also Powley's response (1934.10) and Loane's rejoinder (1934.4).

4 _____. "Rochester on Charles II." TLS, 25 October, p. 735.

Observes that Thomas Hearne's record of the lines on Charles II (see 1934.10) is a year earlier than Powley's first source, 17 November, 1706, and that Hearne supplies the "occasion" for the lines: "his majestie's saying, he would leave everyone to his liberty in talking . . . and would not take what was said at al amiss."

5 NEEDHAM, FRANCIS, ed. Introductory note to A Collection of Poems by Several Hands. Welbeck Miscellany, no. 2. Bungay, Suffolk: Richard Clay & Sons, pp. v-vii.

Introduces a selection of verses culled from single sheets collected by Robert and Edward Harley, earls of Oxford. One of these, a New Years gift by Robert Whitehall to Rochester, contains "the only firsthand reference to Rochester's university life that has survived." Two Rochester poems from autograph drafts are included: one beginning "T'was a dispute 'twixt heav'n & Earth," and the other, "Could I but make my wishes insolent."

6 PINTO, VIVIAN DE SOLA. "An Unpublished Poem Attributed to Rochester." TLS, 22 November, p. 824.

Discusses a poem called "Faith and Reason," attributed to Rochester in a seventeenth-century source. The speaker in the poem (Thanour) "obviously represents Rochester's own opinions," "the difficulties of a mind that wants to believe but encounters overwhelming difficulties." See Pinto's retraction of this attribution (1934.7).

7 _____. "A Poem Attributed to Rochester." TLS, 6 December, p. 875.

Admits "jumping too hastily" to the conclusion that "Faith and Reason" was written by Rochester (1934.6), and reports that the poem is actually a continuation of Gondibert written by Davenant but not included in his printed works until 1673. See also 1934.8.

8 _____. "Rochester and the Deists." TLS, 13 December, p. 895.

Identifies Rochester as the addressee "Strephon" in three letters by the deist Charles Blount, printed in the latter's Miscellaneous Works (1695). The first of these (dated "Feb. 7th 1679 80") refers to Strephon's translation of a passage from Seneca, Rochester's version of the chorus from Troades. This connection between Rochester and a deist may account for John

Verney's mistaken attribution to Rochester of Davenant's "Faith and Reason" (see 1934.6-7). Blount's letters are more fully examined in 1935.6, where the reference to this article is misdated 6 December. See also 1964.1.

9 _____. "The Poetry of John Wilmot, Earl of Rochester." In *Essays by Various Hands: Being the Transactions of the Royal Society of Literature of the United Kingdom*. Edited by W. B. Maxwell. N.s. 13. London: Humphrey Milford, pp. 109-33.

Attempts to avoid the prejudiced caricatures of Rochester by pietists and profligates and to reevaluate his poetry in the light of Prinz's more authentic portrait (1927.2). Rochester was the only serious thinker among the Court Wits; his favorite theme was not so much pleasure as Hobbesian sensationalism, the inspiration of a song like "Love and Life." He experimented intellectually in Hobbes's "State of Nature," and followed his investigations unflinchingly to their misanthropic and skeptical conclusions. These attitudes inspire his social and political satires. Nevertheless, Rochester's poetry (like his life) was filled with contradictions, the product of a mind at war with itself. This is the first of Pinto's major biographical and critical statements on Rochester; for his full portrait of the poet, see 1935.6 and its revision, 1962.2.

10 POWLEY, EDWARD B. "Rochester on Charles II." *TLS*, 18 October, p. 715.

Replies to Loane's questioning (1934.3) of the authority for the line "Here lives a Great and Mighty Monarch" in the epigram (not, originally, an epitaph) on Charles II, citing the "earliest printed version" ("Posted on Whitehall-Gate") in *Miscellaneous Works of . . . Rochester and Roscommon* (1707). Two other first-line versions are supplied.

1935

1 BROOKS, HAROLD. "Attributions to Rochester." *TLS*, 9 May, p. 301.

Points out that "The Commons' Petition," an epigram attributed to Rochester, is a redaction of an anonymous "Madrigall on Justice," alluding to the Parliament," printed in *Rump: Or an Exact Collection of the Choycest Poems and Songs Relating to the Late Times* (1662). A second poem, "Upon the Author of the Play call'd Sodom," included in the "Antwerpen" edition of Rochester (1680), is "certainly by John Oldham."

2 _____. "When Did Dryden Write *MacFlecknoe*?--Some Additional Notes." *RES* 11 (January):74-78.

Notes that a couplet in "Rochester's Farewell"--"Lewd Messaline was but a Tipe of thee / Thou highest, last degree of

Letchery"--is a "clear debasement" of MacFlecknoe, lines 29-30: "Heywood and Shirley were but Types of thee / Thou last great Prophet of Tautology."

3 GREENE, GRAHAM. "Rochester and Lee." TLS, 2 November, p. 697.
   Supplies additional evidence for the identification of the Duke Nemours (a character in Nathaniel Lee's The Princess of Cleve) with Rochester. Nemours's words appear to have come from Rochester's adaptation of Fletcher's Valentinian. See also 1935.5 and 1976.4.

4 HARRIS, BRICE. "Dorset's Poem, 'On the Young Statesmen.'" TLS, 4 April, pp. 227-28.
   Argues against Rochester's authorship of "On the Young Statesmen." Between October 1679 and April 1680 ("practically the entire period during which the poem might have been written"), Rochester was too ill to have written the poem, and Burnet, who visited him weekly throughout this period and would "surely," therefore, have known of the duke's authorship, believed it was written by Buckingham. Moreover, the poem praises Hyde, a man Rochester "never admired." Dorset is the more likely author.

5 LAWRENCE, W. J. "Rochester and Lee." TLS, 9 November, p. 722.
   Comments on Greene's suggestion (1935.3) that Lee borrowed from Rochester's Valentinian for an allusion in The Princess of Cleve. The passage in question was more likely introduced into Lee's play when it was revised for revival, and probably came from the 1685 quarto of Valentinian.

6 PINTO, VIVIAN DE SOLA. Rochester: Portrait of a Restoration Poet. London: John Lane, Bodley Head, 316 pp.
   Surveys the social, intellectual, and spiritual influences that shaped Rochester's life and writing. These include Sir Andrew Balfour, with whom the adolescent Rochester toured France and Italy (and whose Letters Written to a Friend are here for the first time drawn upon for information); the king and court; Hobbes, whose materialist principles were initially the stimulus of a living experiment in sensual indulgence and the inspiration of some of his loveliest lyrics, but later became the cause of disillusioned cynicism and his bitterest satires; the freethinker Charles Blount (whose three letters to Rochester--that is "Strephon"--are a second new source of information); and the Latitudinarian Gilbert Burnet, whose ministrations brought the poet "into a settled Faith and Conversion." A restless explorer of experience, Rochester was driven by a quest for "high spiritual emotion." His life of pleasure--which was not without its moments of tenderness, affection (for his wife), and sincere friendship (with Henry Savile)--was a poor substitute for the demands of his nature, for what Sir Henry Blount called the "Divinum Aliquid," the "divine element in the world." "Only through reli-

gion could he attain to such an experience." For a review of this book by a French critic, see 1937.5. See also 1962.2 for an updated version.

7 WILKINSON, C. H. "Lord Rochester." TLS, 11 July, p. 448.
Notes that some nineteen poems by, or attributed to, Rochester--a number of them containing additional lines and numerous differences from the editions of 1680 and 1685--are printed in The Triumph of Wit, or, Ingenuity display'd in its Perfection, Being the newest and most usefull Academy (1688). The texts of these poems do not derive "wholly" from either of the already existing editions. Records as well Narcissus Luttrell's dating of a number of broadsides.

*8 WILLIAMS, CHARLES. Rochester. London: Arthur Barker.
Cited in 1968.4.

1936

1 DE BEER, E. S. "John Wilmot, Earl of Rochester: A Conversation and a Speech." N&Q 170 (June):420.
Disputes the attribution to Rochester of a recorded conversation with Charles II and a speech given in Parliament. The former is part of an imaginary correspondence between Waller and St. Evremond; the latter was delivered by Laurence Hyde, "the future Earl of Rochester of a new creation."

2 WHITEFIELD, FRANCIS. Beast in View: A Study of the Earl of Rochester's Poetry. Harvard Honors Theses in English, no. 9. Cambridge, Mass.: Harvard University Press, 75 pp.
Describes and evaluates particular qualities of Rochester's lyrics, translations, imitations, and satires. The "beast" in the poet's view is the "Thrice happy" beast whose irrational nature he could never attain. It is because of this failure, however, "that his work merits discussion."

1937

1 CROCKER, S. F. "Rochester's Satire against Mankind: A Study of Certain Aspects of the Background." West Virginia University Studies: III. Philological Papers 2 (May):57-73.
Challenging the authority of similarities between Rochester's Satire and Boileau's "Satire VIII" by citing parallels of thought between the former and Montaigne's Apologie de Raimond Sebond, Crocker concludes that Rochester's denigration of mankind "belongs to the common stock of antirationalistic expressions" (including La Rochefoucauld's Maximes), not to Boileau in particular; that (with the exception of Des Barreaux) the French libertine poets

contributed little to this body of skeptical thought; and that of all the material consulted Rochester's Satire "most closely resembles" Montaigne's Apologie. For other views on Rochester's originality or indebtedness in the Satyr, see 1943.1, 1956.3, 1958.2, and 1969.2. See also 1960.2 and 1973.6.

2 DALE, DONALD A. "Antwerp Editions of Rochester." N&Q 172 (20 February):137.
   Surveys the locations in England and Copenhagen of copies of the Antwerp editions and requests more information about them and their supposed dates. See also 1937.3-4, 1938.2, 1939.4, and 1947.2.

3 _____. "Antwerpen Editions of Rochester." N&Q 172 (20 March): 206-7.
   Brings together available information on the Antwerp editions, querying the date 1684 assigned to one of the two British Museum copies. (The second British Museum copy, assigned the date 1685, may be a reissue of the original 1680 text.) See also 1937.4, 1938.2, 1947.2, and 1950.2.

4 _____. "Antwerpen Editions of Rochester." N&Q 172 (8 May):332.
   Adds several bits of information to his earlier queries on the Antwerp editions. The fugitive copy belonging to the duke of Bridgewater (see 1937.2) is now in the Huntington Library in California. Pepys' copy of Rochester's poems--designated "Rochester's Life" (see 1937.3)--is described: it is actually two books bound together, the 1680 Antwerp edition of the poems and Burnet's account of the earl's life. See also 1938.2, 1939.1, and 1950.2.

5 LEGOUIS, PIERRE. "Rochester et sa reputation." EA 1:53-69.
   Reexamines Rochester's character and the incidents in his life in order to negotiate between the claims of modern apologists (the studies of Pinto [1935.6] and Williams [1935.8] occasion this review article) and those of their less sympathetic predecessors (e.g., Taine [1863.1]). From evidence in Rochester's correspondence, there is more to exonerate than condemn him; as a husband, the worst that may be said is that he was typical of his class: unfaithful but charming. Focusing on the particularly unsavory experiences in Rochester's life--e.g., the duel with Mulgrave and the general question of Rochester's courage--the English biographers have been overly solicitous, finding justifications for his acts that would not have occurred even to Rochester. The German, Prinz (1927.2), excused Rochester's conduct in the duel by invoking the code of chivalry; but this is "too commonplace" for the English biographers. Hayward (1926.1), Pinto, and Williams compete in finesse to turn the disagreeable incident to Rochester's glory. For Pinto, the abortive duel was an illustration of Rochester's sense of humor; Williams argues that Rochester reduced the whole affair to an absurdity. Rochester's part in the brawl at Epsom and in the Rose Alley affair is similarly whitewashed by

these biographers. He as much as admitted his guilt in a letter to Savile. To set the story straight, it is necessary only to attend to chronology: Rochester did not become seriously interested in politics near the end of his life (see 1936.1). Pinto's account of the initial religious discussions between Rochester and Burnet sticks closer to the facts than does Taine's or Beljame's, who regarded the conversion as "imperfect"; but Pinto tones down the egoism of the later talks. In general, Pinto's view of Rochester as a daring intellectual explorer should leave one incredulous. See also 1966.1 and 1969.3.

6 WILSON, J. HAROLD. "Rochester's Valentinian and Heroic Sentiment." ELH 4:265-73.
   Argues that changes in the characters of Valentinian, Lucina, and Maximus attempt to incorporate the contemporary theme of heroic sentiment which dramatizes the conflict between spiritual love and physical passion, and that Rochester appropriated this sentiment from Fletcher's source for the play, d'Urfe's L'astrée. See also 1926.3, 1937.7, and 1956.2.

7 _____. "Satiric Elements in Rochester's Valentinian." PQ 16 (January):41-48.
   Interprets Rochester's additions to and alterations of Fletcher's play as evidence of an intention to satirize Charles II in the character of emperor Valentinian. Since these variations occur in speeches of the character Maximus and since parallel sentiments appear in Rochester's nondramatic satire, the "philosophical-minded favorite" of Valentinian reflects Rochester's personality. See also 1926.3 and 1937.6.

8 _____. "The Dating of Rochester's 'Scaen.'" RES 13 (October): 455-58.
   Infers from an allusion to Rochester's improved state of health in Howard's partially dated letter to the former that Rochester's scene for Howard's The Conquest of China by the Tarters was written in July 1678, not 1672--after, that is, not before the production of Settle's unsuccessful play of the same title. See also 1921.1 and 1979.8.

1938

1 BROOKS, HAROLD F. "The Date of Rochester's 'Timon.'" N&Q 174 (28 May):384-85.
   Narrows the date of the composition of "Timon" to the spring (between March and May) of 1674. See also 1963.2.

2 GRAY, PHILIP. "Rochester's Poems on Several Occasions: New Light on the Dated and Undated Editions, 1680." Library, 4th ser., 19 (September):185-97.

Supplements and corrects Prinz's bibliographical description of Rochester's Poems on Several Occasions (1927.2), distinguishing five editions--two dated 1680 "at Antwerp" (variants in the title pages indicating that one is a "separate edition or issue"); two undated, said to be "Printed at Antwerpen" (one of them probably set up from one of the dated "Antwerp" editions, the other possibly its reissue); and a third undated edition ("Printed at Antwerpen") of 136 pages rather than 152 pages. Three copies of the dated issues are located in English and American libraries. Dale (1937.4) mentions a fourth copy, and Pinto (1939.4) locates and describes two others. See also 1937.2-3 and 1950.2.

1939

1 DALE, DONALD. "The 1680 'Antwerp' Edition of Rochester's Poems." Library, 4th ser., 20:105-6.
   Points out that Pepys's copy of "Rochester's Life" (see 1937.4) is actually "two books bound together"--the dated "Antwerp" edition of the Poems and Burnet's life of the poet, thus dispelling the belief that Pepys had falsely titled the volume because he was ashamed to own it.

2 HUNTLEY, FRANK LIVINGSTONE. "Dryden, Rochester, and the Eighth Satire of Juvenal." PQ 18 (July):269-84.
   Analyzes Dryden's preface to All for Love (1678) as a satire on Rochester inspired by Juvenal's eighth satire on true and false nobility. This opposition of the true and the false also determines the aim of the preface as literary criticism--the vindication of the talented professional poet-critic against the powerful privileged dilettante--and allows Dryden to make several veiled references to Rochester's character. Rochester's relations with Dryden are also examined in 1939.5 and 1961.1.

3 MURDOCK, KENNETH B. "'A Very Profane Wit.'" In The Sun at Noon: Three Biographical Sketches. New York: Macmillan Co., pp. 269-306.
   Interprets Rochester's life as the quest for an object of faith, some general principle "more potent than the promptings of flesh and proof against the vicissitudes of earth." He did not find this "sun at noon." The creed by which he lived--that the sensual is the key to all values--did not provide it: there were times when not feeling was the truest joy; his interest in questions about the soul shows that materialism did not satisfy him. Yet it was through "instinctive feelings" (evoked by the poetry of Isaiah's fifty-third chapter) that he finally surrendered to what he had been pursuing.

4 PINTO, VIVIAN DE SOLA. "The 1680 'Antwerp' Edition of Rochester's Poems." Library, 4th ser., 20:105.

Describes an unnoticed copy of the dated "Antwerp" edition of Rochester's Poems on Several Occasions. See 1938.2 for the location of three other copies of this edition.

5 WILSON, HAROLD. "Rochester, Dryden and the Rose-Street Affair." RES 15 (July):294-301.
   Disputes Pinto's acceptance (1935.6) of Rochester's complicity in the cudgeling of Dryden on 18 December 1679 by showing that Rochester's "Black Will" letter (which alludes to the vexation of a "certain Poet") could not have been written after the spring of 1678, when its recipient Savile began an eighteen-month tour of diplomatic duty in Paris. Other evidence indicates that it was written in the spring or early summer of 1676. Although it is likely that the poet mentioned in this letter is Dryden, and the cause of his vexation Rochester's "An Allusion to Horace," there is no reason to believe that Dryden retaliated with "An Essay upon Satyr," the supposed motivation of Rochester's alleged act of revenge. See Pinto's rejoinder (1940.2).

6 _____. "Two Poems Ascribed to Rochester." MLN 54 (June):458-60.
   Rejects Rochester's authorship of two poems beginning "Since Death on all Lays his Impartial Hand" and "Fruition was the Question in Debate," both printed by Hayward (1926.1). The first is, with minor textual variants, identical with Etherege's "The Libertine"; the second, "a turgid paraphrase" of Etherege's poem by that title, is too clumsy to be Rochester's work. For more on the second poem, see 1963.1.

1940

1 DUNCAN, RONALD. "Rochester." Townsman 3, no. 12:14-21.
   Attempts to combat certain critical prejudices against Rochester's poetry, recommending that it should be read aloud, the songs sung (though, in the case of "Love a Woman! You're an Ass," not by a tenor or alto). The phallic songs, which have a "natural vitality," are not pornographic. Rochester's satires are neither trivial in subject nor petty in manner; they have contributed to the English tradition of social satire, to the conversational idiom of Pope and the satiric portraits of Crabbe. Rochester's poetry (unlike Cowley's and Dryden's) is not made from other poetry; its reckless independence reflects the poet's aristocratic status.

2 PINTO, VIVIAN DE SOLA. "Rochester, Dryden and the Duchess of Portsmouth." RES 16, no. 62 (April):177-78.
   Disagrees with Wilson's dismissal (1939.5) of the duchess of Portsmouth's role in the Rose Alley ambuscade. She is "the real instigator of the outrage": Wood (in his "Life of Buckingham")

connects her with it; Luttrell corroborates his statement; and she is attacked, in "An Essay upon Satyr," in "far more" than a "bare reference" as Wilson maintained.

1941

1   WILSON, J. HAROLD. "Rochester's 'Buffoon Conceit.'" MLN 56 (May):372-73.
    Identifies the "buffoon conceit" mentioned in Sir Carr Scroope's "In Defense of Satire" as the six-line "extempore" printed by Prinz (1926.2) under the title "Spoken to a Post-boy, 1674." Its original may be the fourteen-line poem entitled "Earle of Rochester's Conference with a Post Boy, 1674" included in a manuscript volume entitled "A Choice Collection of Songs, etc." The speaker's claim here to have left his "Life's Defender Dead" ("certainly a reference to the affair at Epsom") may be recognized in Scroope's charge that Rochester could "put off" the betrayal of "His brave Companion . . . with some Buffoone Conceit." See also 1962.2, 1963.2, and, for an argument against Scroope's authorship of "In Defense of Satire," 1970.1.

2   _____, ed. Introduction to The Rochester-Savile Letters: 1671-1680. Columbus: Ohio State University Press, pp. 1-28.
    Reviews the careers of Rochester and Savile as background to this collection of 33 letters. Rochester's correspondence, complete, has been edited by Treglown (1980.7).

1942

1   "Rochester and Dr. Bendo." TLS, 13 June, p. 300.
    Summarizes the contents of Thomas Alcock's copy of the Bill of Dr. Bendo. Alcock, a servant of Rochester's and a collaborator in his impersonation of the mountebank, made the copy as a gift to the earl's eldest daughter, Ann, in 1687. This version of the Bill is the source for the story of Rochester/Bendo's secondary disguise as a "grave matron" called into consultation on female complaints too delicate for the doctor's ears. For further discussion of Bendo's Bill, see 1962.2 and 1974.6.

2   LEVIN, HARRY. Introduction to A Satyr Against Mankind and Other Poems. Poets of the Year. Norfolk, Conn.: New Directions, pp. 3-8.
    As an introduction to a selection of Rochester's poems, Levin emphasizes the paradoxes in the poet's life and thought: he was the "most shameless scandal-monger and the most desperate moralist" of the period; his professions of hedonism are undercut by expressions of insipidity and impotence; the only subject he could wholeheartedly praise was nothing: Stoic skepticism was

was the only creed he could believe in. Despite the concreteness and immediacy of his themes, his language is abstract: unlike Donne, who spoke familiarly of philosophical matters, Rochester spoke philosophically about vulgar ones.

1943

1 MOORE, JOHN F. "The Originality of Rochester's 'Satyr Against Mankind.'" PMLA 58 (June):393-401.
Defines an "eclectic originality" in Rochester's "Satyr." Boileau's "Satire VIII" probably inspired the initial satirical impulse and determined the rhetorical structure of the "Satyr." But Rochester's independence of Boileau appears in more important area: in the (Hobbesian) reduction of human motivation to fear and in the (Epicurean) insistence upon sensory experience in "right Reason." Attention to similarities of imagery in the two satires suggests that Rochester's language is closer to that of certain earlier writers (e.g., Plutarch, Menander, Lucretius) than to Boileau's. For other views on Rochester's originality or indebtedness in the "Satyr," see 1937.1, 1958.2, and 1969.2.

2 WILSON, J. HAROLD. "Rochester's Marriage." RES 19 (October): 399-403.
Explains why Rochester attempted to abduct Elizabeth Mallet in 1665 and how their marriage eventually came about in 1667. Rochester had not yet acquired the reputation of a libertine, nor is there evidence of Elizabeth's deep piety (cf. 1927.2). Rochester was "simply not a good match"--young, having little income, and no prospects. The abduction occurred "not improbably" with the lady's consent; but her family, anxious to drive a hard bargain with any suitor, would have opposed the marriage. How, then, did the marriage come about? Rochester's estate was no better when he married Elizabeth in 1667. By then, however, she had found her family's choices unsatisfactory, realized that Rochester loved her (and she him), and that her guardians were merely using her for their own advantage.

1944

1 WILSON, J. HAROLD. "Rochester: An Overlooked Poem." N&Q 187 (12 August):79.
Argues that Rochester wrote the poem beginning "Fling this useless Book away," attributed to him by Tom Brown. (The "Book" is a lady's prayer book in which the lines are putatively inscribed.) The poem is an imitation (with additions) of two lyrics by Malherbe, first printed in 1615.

1946

1 BAINE, RODNEY M. "Rochester or Fishbourne: A Question of Authorship." RES 22 (July):201-6.

Supplies biographical information on Christopher (not John) Fishbourne, strengthening the likelihood that he, not Rochester, was the author of Sodom. Fishbourne, the nephew of the architect Wren and author of the first St. Cecilia's Day ode, served in Flanders in 1678 and may have left behind a copy of the farce, the so-called "Hague" copy. Attribution to Fishbourne is dismissed by Adlard (1974.1).

2 BRUSER, FREDELLE. "Disproportion: A Study in the Work of John Wilmot, Earl of Rochester." University of Toronto Quarterly 15 (April):384-96.

Considers Rochester the man and his work in terms of the distance that separates a vision of the unattainable from reality. Psychologically, this disproportion consists in the gap between desire and the means of satisfying it, intellectually in that between thought and action. Aesthetically, disproportion appears as a tension between form and content, convention and personal emotion.

3 WILSON, J[OHN] HAROLD. "Rochester's 'A Session of the Poets.'" RES 22 (April):109-16.

Argues against Ham's attribution (1933.1) of "A Session of the Poets" to Elkanah Settle and for its inclusion in the Rochester canon (Rochester having had "at least the major hand in its composition"). Since most of the plays alluded to in the "Session" were performed before the end of 1676, the satire was probably written at that time and is therefore not the "libell" sent to Will's coffeehouse in October 1677 to which Henry Savile referred in his letter to Rochester in November of that year. Settle's denial of having composed the "Session," then, should be accepted at face value: hence the cruel portrayal of him in the satire (and the less severe criticism of his enemy, Thomas Shadwell). In general, the "Session" vilifies professional, not gentlemen poets; its tone is consistent with Rochester's expressed attitudes toward poets of the day; its meter and style are those of his "Signor Dildo." It is "quite possible" that the satire was produced by a group of Court Wits, meeting perhaps at Rochester's retreat, Woodstock. The name "Newport" is identified as Francis ("Frank") Newport, a profane wit who might well have been present at such a gathering. See also 1931.1, 3 and 1963.2.

1947

1 THORPE, JAMES. "Authenticity of 'The Wish' as a Rochester Poem." MLN 62 (April):267-68.

Presents evidence that Rochester did not write the song beginning "Oh, that I could by some chymic art," printed in Hayward (1926.1) as "The Wish." The poem appeared, under the title "Insatiate Desire," in the second part of Merry Drollery, published in 1661, when Rochester was only fourteen years old.

2 _____. "The Earliest Edition of Rochester's Poems." Princeton University Library Chronicle 8:172-76.
   Describes a copy of Poems on Several Occasions (Antwerp) recently acquired by Princeton University Library, cites the location of two other copies (see 1937.2-4, 1938.2, and 1939.4), and hints at the bibliographical project that will culminate in Thorpe's introduction to the facsimile edition of Rochester's Poems (1950.2).

1948

1 BELJAME, ALEXANDRE. Men of Letters and the English Public in the Eighteenth Century: 1660-1744, Dryden, Addison, Pope. Edited by Bonamy Dobree. Translated by E. O. Lorimer. London: Kegan Paul, Trench, Trubner, pp. 88-107.
   A translation of 1881.1.

2 WILSON, JOHN HAROLD. The Court Wits of the Restoration: An Introduction. Princeton: Princeton University Press, 270 pp. Reprint. New York: Octagon Books, 1967.
   Provides a unified view of the human and literary activities of the wits at the court of Charles II, assuming that, since "each [of the wits], to some degree at least, spoke for the group as much as for himself . . . they can be seen best as individuals if they are seen first as a cohesive group." Of the fourteen members of this "inner circle," Rochester, who bore the newest title, was the most handsome, the most poetically gifted, and, along with Buckingham, the most sinful--though his reputation in the last category has been exaggerated. His chief distinction as a poet rests upon satire, in which he exploited his peculiar gift of hitting upon and popularizing descriptive epithets for his targets.

1949

1 BROOKS, HAROLD F. "The 'Imitation' in English Poetry, Especially in Formal Satire, Before the Age of Pope." RES 25 (April): 124-40.
   Traces the development of the "imitation" in its relations to both formal satire and to translation, paraphrase, and related forms of textual reproduction. Boileau's importance in this evolution is central; nevertheless, as early as Wyatt, English for-

mal satire made use of the technique of imitation, and most of the features for which the French satirist is granted priority are also found in two of Thomas Sprat's satires, one of which was written before Boileau's. Rochester unites the French and English traditions: in the "Satyr against Reason and Mankind" and especially in "Timon," he very freely imitates Boileau's third and eighth satires, much as Boileau had freely imitated his Latin models. On the other hand, the "Allusion to Horace" follows the English model of Sprat, a paraphrase that is also a translation, following its original passage by passage (cf. 1972.13). This example became the model for Augustan imitations. See also Davies's consideration of Rochester's "Satyr" as an imitation of Boileau (1969.2), and Righter (1967.3) for an interpretation of Rochester's imitations as instances of a characteristic play with identity.

1950

*1 LANE, JANE. "Court Rake: The Second Earl of Rochester: 1647-1680." In Puritan, Rake, and Squire. London: Evans.
Cited in 1968.4.

2 THORPE, JAMES, ed. Introduction and Appendices to Rochester's Poems on Several Occasions. Princeton Studies in English, no. 30. Princeton University Press, pp. ix-xxxviii, 153-91.
Discusses the bibliographical circumstances surrounding the 1680 editions of Rochester's poems and analyzes their interrelations to determine the copy-text for this photographic facsimile edition. Ten distinct editions of Poems on Several Occasions are differentiated (four, of 152 pages, bearing the imprint "Antwerp 1680," four of the same length, undated, bearing the imprint "Antwerpen," and two, of 136 pages, similarly imprinted and dateless). Two lost editions are further postulated--and, given the popularity of the book, there is a likelihood of still others. The Huntington Library copy, in the first of these groups, is determined the earliest and, therefore, chosen copy-text. Of the sixty-one poems in the volume, thirteen "can be demonstrated with a fair degree of certainty not to be Rochester's"; his authorship of another eleven may at least be questioned. The remaining thirty-seven poems, regarded as "the core of the Rochester canon," appear among those printed in, roughly, the first half of the volume, leading to the conclusion that the compiler began with authentic works and filled out the collection with miscellaneous materials of doubtful authorship. On specific poems in the 1680 editions believed not to be by Rochester or doubtfully ascribed to him there, see 1931.3, 1933.1, 1935.1, 1946.3, and 1963.2. On editions and copies of the 1680 text, see 1935.7, 1937.2-4, 1938.2, 1939.1, 4, 1947.2, 1953.5, and 1956.4.

1951

1 SMITH, HAROLD WENDELL. "'Reason' and the Restoration Ethos." Scrutiny 18 (Autumn):118-36.
   Defining the Restoration ethos in terms of the change, in society and religion, from a static order protecting and protected by the Old Monarchy to a state of dynamic flux advanced by (and in turn maintaining) Puritan theology and bourgeois commercial enterprise, Smith argues that strong criticism of abstract reason together with espousal of the sensory and the natural in the writings of Sprat, Dryden, Rochester, and Butler represent their reactions to this historical phenomenon. Paradoxically, it is the intellectual "flight beyond material sense" (in Rochester's words) that leads to both the "deep mysteries" of Puritanism (antirationalism) and, in the form of the mental science of capitalist economics, to the very material effects of the rise of the bourgeoisie upon the old order. Rochester's opinion of intellectualism in the "Satyr against Reason and Mankind" is identical, notwithstanding his literary differences, with that of Dryden (cf. 1961.1) and, though more crudely primitivist, that of Sprat; indeed, his part in the Rose Alley affair is his version of Sprat's "inviolable correspondence between the hand and the brain"--the action that prevents impertinence of thought.

2 THORPE, JAMES. "New Manuscripts of Sodom." PULC 13:40-41.
   Describes Princeton Library's newly acquired manuscript volume containing two previously unrecorded manuscripts of Sodom. One is a five-act version of the play, generally similar to the Hamburg manuscript, the other a much shorter three-act version, the third act differing markedly from the former version. For more detailed discussion of the relation of these manuscript versions to other manuscripts of the play, see 1976.2 and 1977.1, and for another "find" in the manuscript, 1974.3.

3 VIETH, DAVID M. "Rochester and Cowley." TLS, 12 October, p. 645.
   Attributes to Cowley a four-line verse fragment (beginning "Is there a man yee gods whome I doe hate") in one of Rochester's letters to his wife, and asks for further study of Cowley's influence on Rochester. The authority for the attribution to Cowley is the word "Cow" written in the margin of the manuscript letter.

1952

1 BABLER, C. F., and EDITOR. "The Second and Later Bottles." N&Q 197 (August):389-90.
   Points out that Rochester's use of the term "bottle" (to mean the quantity of wine held by a bottle) is the earliest example by thirteen years of the three parallel forms cited in the OED.

2   HOGAN, PATRICK G. "Rochester: A Metaphysical Restoration Rake." Abstract of paper read before the South Central Modern Language Association, October 1951. SCN 10:22.
   Finds the presence of metaphysical qualities ("Metaphysical shudder, combination of thought and image, sensuality, common diction, & universal outlook") in the "less scurrilous" poems of Rochester. The similarities between "Absent from thee I languish still" and Donne's "A Valediction Forbidding Mourning" are cited as evidence.

1953

1   [HANSON, LAURENCE]. "A Rochester Poem." BLR 4:183-84.
   Provides the date 1679 for the folio printing of Rochester's A Letter from Artemiza in the Town, to Chloe in the Country and describes another "apparently unrecorded" 1679 edition of the poem, said to be "a better text . . . than any other printed version."

2   PADEN, W. D. "Rochester's Satyr." Books and Libraries at the University of Kansas 1, no. 3:8-11.
   Argues that the 1679 folio leaflet of the Satyr against Reason and Mankind (recently acquired by the University of Kansas Library) is a better text of the poem than that of the 1680 edition of Rochester's Poems and suggests that it may have been the source, with some editorial correction, of the 1691 edition of the poems. The absence in the 1679 folio of the 51-line "epilogue" included in the 1680 text of the poem may indicate that the folio derived from an early manuscript of the "Satyr" that circulated before the completion of the poem. For more on the epilogue of the Satyr, see 1971.4.

3   PINTO, VIVIAN DE SOLA. "John Wilmot, Earl of Rochester, and the Right Veine of Satire." In Essays and Studies. Edited by Geoffrey Bullough. English Association, n.s. 6. London: John Murray, pp. 56-70.
   Traces the "right veine of satire" to the "dialectic bent" of Rochester's mind, which allowed him to understand both the excellences and the weaknesses of an aristocratic culture, to view relations between the sexes from both male and female standpoints, to admit the claims of both mind and body, and to speak, in the early poems, as the hedonistic "Aesthetic Hero" and, in the later ones, as the selfless "Religious Hero" (cf. 1953.4). For another interpretation of Marvell's phrase, "right veine of satire," see 1960.2. Reprinted: 1962.3.

4   _____, ed. Introduction to Poems by John Wilmot, Earl of Rochester. Muses' Library. London: Routledge & Kegan Paul, pp. xv-l.

Reproduces, in less detail, the "portrait" of Rochester as a "daring and original explorer of reality" (see 1935.6 and, for later expressions of this view, 1962.2 and 1966.1). At the same time, Rochester's life is seen as a labor of self-integration and an attempt to come to terms with the new mathematical universe. The simple transformation of "Aesthetic Hero" into "Religious Hero" (see 1953.3) is complicated by a medial phase of "Ethical Hero," the disillusioned and penetrating observer of the satires. The second edition of this text is slightly revised (see 1964.7).

5 TODD, WILLIAM B. "The 1680 Editions of Rochester's Poems with Notes on Earlier Texts." PBSA 47:43-58.
   Argues that the Pforzheimer copy of Rochester's Poems--not, as Thorpe believed, the Huntington copy (see 1950.2)--is the most authoritative of the 1680 editions. This edition most closely approximates a postulated archetypal text (its supposed immediate source) reconstructed from a collation of 55 critical readings believed not to have descended from the 1680 editions and therefore preserving readings anterior to those in the editions. See 1956.4 and 1963.2 for the use of a similar editorial method that arrives at a different conclusion.

6 VIETH, DAVID M. "A New Song by Rochester." TLS, 6 November, p. 716.
   Argues for the inclusion in the Rochester canon of a lyric ("Tell mee noe more of Constancy") overlooked by Pinto (1953.4) and all previous editors. The poem, "one of the finest lyrics of the later seventeenth century," is reproduced here in both manuscript (Bod. MS Don. b.8) and printed (A New Collection of the Choicest Songs [1676]) versions, the latter providing a limiting date for its composition. The attribution is made on internal evidence and on the authority of the compiler of the manuscript miscellany. The poem is included in subsequent editions of Rochester's poems (see, e.g., 1964.7). For additional comment on this song, see 1954.1, 3.

7 _____. "John Oldham, the Wits and A Satyr Against Virtue." PQ 32 (January):90-93.
   Presents evidence (dated 1677) from an unnoticed manuscript of Oldham's "A Satyr Against Vertue" suggesting that Rochester's acquaintance with Oldham may have begun in the spring of 1677/8.

1954

1 EMSLIE, MACDONALD. "A New Song by Rochester." TLS, 26 February, p. 137.
   Produces a third text of the lyric "Tell me no more of constancy" (see 1953.6) from the manuscript of Edward Lowe, and, because of the popularity of the "through-composed" (durchkom-

poniert) song in the third decade of the seventeenth century, advises against attempting to deduce the musical setting of this song from the lyric alone (cf. 1954.3). Otherwise, the Lowe text offers more support than opposition to Mackie's suggested readings of the song.

2 LEGOUIS, PIERRE. "Three Notes on Rochester's Poems." MLN 69 (November):502-6.

Corrects and amplifies Pinto's annotation of three of Rochester's poems (1953.4). (1) In "Rochester's Farewell," the name Frazier (line 42), identified by Pinto as "the well-known court physician," is here identified as a woman, Carey (or Carry) Fraser of Durris, and thus the wife Charles Mordaunt (line 37) fled by joining the expeditionary force sent to Tangier. (2) Pinto's identification of the epithet "Bardash S----y" (line 33) as "Shrewsbury" (that is, Francis Talbot) in "A Satyr" ("Must I with patience ever silent sit") is also rejected. Since Francis Talbot was killed in 1668, and since the poem makes reference to the Rose Alley Ambuscade of 1679, the Shrewsbury in question is probably Charles Talbot, Francis's son, a more likely candidate for the role of "Bardash"--that is, "catamite." (3) In the satirical hit at Samuel Parker ("Bayes") in "Tunbridge-Wells" (lines 63-74), the word "Importance" is used not merely as a lexical parody of the archdeacon, but in Marvell's sense of the word--that is, "a female." Thus "Bayes, with Importance comfortable" may be a reference to Parker and his wife. See also 1973.3 and, for an instance of Marvell's borrowing from Rochester, 1972.3. For further comment on Marvell's expression in "Tunbridge-Wells," see 1963.2.

3 MAKIE, J. L. "A New Song by Rochester." TLS, 19 February, p. 121.

Points out at least three places where Vieth's choices among variant readings in the two available texts of Rochester's "Against Constancy" (1953.6) may be contradicted on the textual principle that "one should prefer the more difficult reading": "cold age" (line 3) is better than "old age"; "or" (line 5) "is not necessarily a misprint for 'on'"; "for" (line 20) is better than "to." The "weaknesses" (but not mistakes) of the printed version are due to its adaptation as a text for singing; the "mistakes" of the manuscript version are due to faulty memory. See also 1954.1.

4 NORMAN, CHARLES. Rake Rochester. New York: Crown Publishers, 210 pp.

Provides a popular version of Rochester's life and times.

5 PINTO, VIVIAN DE SOLA. "A Poem Attributed to Rochester." TLS, 5 November, p. 705.

Attributes to Rochester a poem entitled "A Young Gentleman, desirous to be a Minister of State, thus pretends to qualifie himself," and dates its composition (on internal evidence) at some time between the spring of 1675 and the summer of 1677. The admittedly "doubtful authority" on which the claim is made is the attribution of the poem to Rochester in two manuscript miscellanies (A Collection of Poems and Lampoons &c. Not yet Printed [71A in the University of Nottingham Library] and Harl. 7315). For further exchanges on this poem, see 1955.4 and 1955.3.

1955

1 HARTMANN, CYRIL HUGHES. "Rochester's Marriage." History Today 5 (December):840-49.

Retells the familiar story of Rochester's marriage to Elizabeth Malet (see 1943.2). From beginning to end there is evidence of the husband and wife's mutual love, though Lady Rochester's long-suffering patience was strengthened, it is suggested, by her Catholicism (on the obscure motives of which, see 1941.2, 1962.2, and 1963.2). On the speech against the Exclusion Bill, allegedly delivered by Rochester in the House of Commons, see 1936.1.

2 JEROME, JUDSON BLAIR. "Rochester and the Generation of Wit." Ph.D. dissertation, Ohio State University, 170 pp.

Uses Rochester's life and works as a means of access to the idea of wit, which in turn is the means of access to the character of Restoration literature. Rochester presents his poetic (the world be hanged; I will write my own laws) in "An Epistolary Essay from M. G. to O. B." (cf. 1963.2), and his definition of wit (free intelligence in search of truth) in "A Letter from Artemisa in the Town . . ."; truth, according to this view, "is always ugly . . . but must be experienced at all costs." For the wit as for the scientist of the day, this search for truth was conceived of in opposition to tradition, law, and morality. But if nothing but sense experience is worthwhile, the ethic of the wits is doomed to failure, for sense is uncertain, painful, and unsatisfying. The failure is revealed in "The Imperfect Enjoyment." See also DA 15 (1955):1233-34.

3 PINTO, VIVIAN DE SOLA. "Rochester and 'A Young Gentleman.'" TLS, 7 October, p. 589.

Dismisses Vieth's arguments against ascribing "A Young Gentleman &c." to Rochester (see 1954.5 and 1955.4) as unconvincing because based upon internal evidence. The wit of Rochester and his friends, it is suggested, transcended both friendship and political allegiance. Moreover, the style of the lampoon is that of the street-ballad, which aimed at vigour, not polish, as Vieth seems to expect.

4 VIETH, DAVID M. "Rochester and 'A Young Gentleman.'" TLS, 23 September, p. 557.

Argues, on internal evidence, against Pinto's attribution to Rochester of the lampoon "A Young Gentleman, &c." (1954.5). The strong uncritical attack upon supporters of the County party in the lampoon presupposes a strong advocate of the policies of the Court party which Rochester, who generally remained aloof from political factions, was not. Moreover, two of the satirical targets in the lampoon, Buckingham and Halifax, the brother of Henry Saville, were men with whom Rochester was on friendly terms. Finally, the style of the lampoon bears little relation to Rochester's. The ascription which Pinto accepts is judged "unfounded," since the manuscripts which authorize it merely reprint the ascription from the printed text of 1689. For Pinto's reply, see 1955.3.

1956

1 DUCLOS, PAUL-CHARLES. "John Wilmot, 2º comte de Rochester." Revue des langues vivantes 22:241-56.

Assembles available information on the life and times of Rochester as a context for several of his poems. "Nihilism" is too strong a word for Rochester's philosophy; "Upon Nothing" is less a philosophic celebration of nothing than the "cry of a heart" that has discovered the futility of everything human. "The Maim'd Debauchee," a superior poem, is an expression of the ailing poet himself.

2 HOOK, LUCYLE. "The Publication Date of Rochester's Valentinian." HLQ 19:401-7.

Argues, from Luttrell's correction of the date of his copy of Mulgrave's An Essay upon Poetry, that Rochester's Valentinian was printed at the end of 1684, not 1685. The Essay is the final shot in the fracas that began with the aborted feud between Rochester and Mulgrave and climaxed in the circulation in manuscript of Mulgrave's An Essay upon Satyr and in Rochester's action in the Rose-Alley Ambuscade and several poetic attacks. Mulgrave's retaliation in An Essay upon Poetry, printed in 1682, was answered by Rochester's friend, Robert Wolseley, in the preface to the first edition of Valentinian, dated 1685. Hindmarsh, the publisher of An Essay upon Poetry, seized this occasion to print a new title page for the Essay, dated 1685. Luttrell's correction of this date to "1684: 6. Dec." therefore pushes back the publication of Valentinian to an earlier date, possibly as early as November 1684, the date of its listing in the Term Catalogue. See 1921.1, 1926.3, and 1968.2.

3 PINTO, VIVIAN DE SOLA. "Rochester and Salvator Rosa." English Miscellany 7:19-24.

Speculates that, on his grand tour, Rochester may have met the Italian painter-poet Salvator Rosa and read a copy of his fourth satire, La Guerra. It is suggested that Timon's speech in the opening of the satire may be echoed in the opening of Rochester's "Satyr against Reason and Mankind." The latter's "Upon Nothing" may also owe something to Rosa.

4   VIETH, DAVID M. "The Text of Rochester and the Editions of 1680." PBSA 50:243-63.
    Argues that a previously unrecorded manuscript miscellany (the "Yale MS") preserves a text anterior to any of the 1680 editions of Rochester's Poems and that it belongs to a family of manuscripts another of which served as the copy-text for the first of these editions. Comparison of seventy-six variants exhibited by the Huntington and Pforzheimer copies of the 1680 editions with the readings of the Yale MS and with readings in a large number of separate texts of the poems and in the remaining 1680 editions leads to two conclusions: (1) that both the Huntington and the Pforzheimer editions derive from manuscript sources; and (2) that only the Huntington derived entirely from these sources, the Pforzheimer having consulted them for only "a few readings." Further collation of these materials restores priority to the Huntington copy of the 1680 editions (see 1950.2), not the Pforzheimer copy (see 1953.2). See also 1963.2.

5   _____. "Two Rochester Songs." N&Q 201 (August):338-39.
    Comments on the authenticity of two poems ascribed to Rochester by Tonson in Examen Poeticum (1693)--"A Song" (beginning "Insulting Beauty, you mispend") and "Another Song in Imitation of Sir John Eaton's Songs" (beginning "Too late, alas! I must confess"). Rochester's authorship of the second is "virtually certain" since it appears in his hand in the Portland MS. However this version of the poem begins "Att last you'l force mee to confess," a fact which caused it to be printed in several early miscellanies as an additional stanza to Rochester's song beginning "While on those lovely looks I gaze." The earliest of these printings, A New Collection of the Choicest Songs, licensed 28 April 1676, provides a limiting date for the composition of the poem (see also 1963.2 and 1968.4). The authenticity of the first song ("Insulting Beauty . . .") rests solely upon the general reliability of Tonson's ascriptions.

1957

*1 BERLIND, BRUCE P. "Studies in Rochester and his Circle." Ph.D. dissertation, Johns Hopkins University.
    Cited in 1973.4.

2   PINTO, VIVIAN DE SOLA. "John Wilmot, Earl of Rochester." In From Dryden to Johnson. Pelican Guide to English Literature, edited by Boris Ford, vol. 4. Harmondsworth: Penguin Books, pp. 142-55.

Resketches the portrait of Rochester as an explorer of reality (see 1935.6), one who dared reject, as lifeless and repressive, the "new orthodoxy based on the Cartesian-Newtonian world picture." For an Augustan view of Rochester, see 1963.2. See also 1953.3,4.

3   VIETH, DAVID M. "Poems by 'My Lord R.': Rochester versus Radclyffe." PMLA 72 (September):612-19.
    Identifies "Lord R"--the author of seven poems long ascribed to Rochester--as Edward Radclyffe, best known as the recipient of Dryden's dedication to Examen Poeticum (1693). The poems in question are: "Song" ("While in Divine Panthea's Charming Eyes"), "A Song" ("Pity, Fair Sapho, One That Dies"), "A Paean, or Song of Triumph, on the Translation and Apotheosis of King Charles the Second," "Out of Horace," "Cornelius Gallus Imitated. A Lyrick," "Apollo's Grief, for Having Kill'd Hyacinth by Accident. In Imitation of Ovid," and "Song" ("Where Is He Gone Whom I Adore"). See also 1963.2.

1958

1   BURTON, K. M. P. "John Wilmot, Earl of Rochester (1648-80)." In Restoration Literature. London: Hutchinson & Co., pp. 135-39.
    Comments, generally, on the "Satyr against Reason and Mankind." Although Rochester deprecates reason from an Epicurean standpoint, the "Satyr" does not praise sensuous delight.

2   FUJIMURA, THOMAS H. "Rochester's 'Satyr Against Mankind': An Analysis." SP 55:576-90.
    Argues that an appreciation of the "Satyr" depends upon our awareness of the relationship of its parts and our recognition of what in these is uniquely Rochester's. There is little of the latter in the first part of the "Satyr" (to line 112), a statement of the familiar criticism of speculative reason as opposed to "right reason" (i.e., reason grounded in sense experience and directed toward the practical ends necessary for happiness). Rochester's voice is first heard in the second part (lines 124-73), a "savage" indictment of man's moral depravity based upon the exposure of fear as the dominant motive of his actions. This emphasis upon fear and the "more or less absolute" moral standards that implicitly underlie it mark the independence of Rochester's ethic from the Hobbesian epistemology of the first part. The concluding epilogue does not recant or mitigate this moral criticism (cf. 1935.6), but ironically underlines it. For other views of Rochester's originality or indebtedness for the "Satyr," see 1937.1, 1943.1, and 1969.2. See also 1973.11.

3   VIETH, DAVID M. "Etherege's 'Man of Mode' and Rochester's 'Artemisa to Cloe.'" N&Q 5 (November):473-74.

Draws attention to the expression of four ideas in Etherege's play and Rochester's poems (both written at about the same time): (1) folly is the product of art and education; (2) women prefer fools to wits as lovers; (3) wits pry too deeply into secrets better left alone; and (4) fools are easily deceived and happy in the deception. See 1963.2 for additional evidence of Rochester's relation to Etherege.

4 _____. "Rochester's 'Scepter' Lampoon on Charles II." PQ 37 (October):424-32.

Cites six manuscript ascriptions to Rochester (all of them possessing independent authority) of the "Scepter" lampoon (beginning "In th' isle of Britain long since famous grown"). Both external evidence, provided by the manuscript copies, and internal evidence favor a date of composition "after the early months of 1674 and before the end of 1675"; the manuscripts also strengthen the possibility that this is the poem for which Rochester was banished from court and "turn'd Mountebank" (cf. 1941.2). Thus the poem may be regarded as an "essential" biographical document.

1959

1 AUFFRET, JEAN. "Rochester's Farewell." EA 12 (April-June): 142-50.

In French. Finds at least two hands in the poem: Rochester's, "very probably," in lines 1-36 and 55-63 and "perhaps" in lines 154-77, and that of a second party in lines 37-54 and 64-110. It is impossible to assign an author for the remainder of the poem. Since the lines attributed to Rochester suggest nothing of his impending spiritual change (dated 19 June 1680) and since they cannot have been written before 1 June (cf. 1953.4), the only possible conclusion concerning his conversion is that it was indeed sudden.

2 VIETH, DAVID M. "Order of Contents as Evidence of Authorship: Rochester's Poems of 1680." PBSA 53:293-308.

Argues that the ascriptions and order of poems in the lost copy-text of the Huntington edition of the 1680 Poems are best preserved in the Yale MS (see 1956.4), and serve as a means of authenticating specific poems. When the twenty-three ascriptions in the manuscript (only two of which are "probably incorrect") attribute to other authors poems ascribed on external evidence to Rochester (e.g., "A Session of the Poets"), they serve to discredit that evidence (see e.g., 1931.3 and 1946.3). The order of the poems in the manuscript also clarifies the organization of the archetype of the manuscript and the lost copy-text assumed to be the ancestor of the 1680 editions: it now appears not only that the contents of these editions fall, as Thorpe suggested (1950.2), into two groups--the first consisting mostly of Rochester's works, the second of works by other poets--but that the "Rochester half" of this division may be divided again--first, into a group of satires and translations, and second, into a group of songs, many of which have been assigned to Rochester on "very flimsy evidence." The position of the songs in the manuscript "furnishes a much-needed warrant that they are probably genuine." A table comparing the presumed order of the archetype of the Yale MS (with the ascriptions of the latter) and the contents of the 1680 editions is provided. See also 1963.2. Reprinted: 1966.2.

1960

1   HOOK, LUCYLE. "Something More About Rochester." MLN 75 (June): 478-85.

   Presents information, found in the letters of Godfrey Thacker, concerning four poems "generally attributed" to Rochester: "The Debauchee" (attributed to Buckhurst, but satirizing Rochester), "A Ramble in St. James's Park," "On the Women about Town," and "The Dispute" ("Betwixt Father Patrick and His Highness of Late"). Thacker's letter of 20 March 1672/3 supplies limiting dates for the first three poems (15 April 1673), and a limiting date and twelve new lines for the fourth. A detail in the earlier letter is interpreted differently in 1964.6.

2   MAIN, C. F. "The Right Vein of Rochester's Satyr." In Essays in Literary History Presented to J. Milton French. Edited by Rudolf Kirk and C. F. Main. New Brunswick: Rutgers University Press, pp. 93-112. Reprint. New York: Russell & Russell, 1965.

   Analyzes Rochester's "Satyr against Reason and Mankind" as an example (the first in English, it is claimed) of formal verse satire, a structure that balances denunciation of a particular vice with commendation of its opposite virtue. Formal satire focuses upon a single object; it does not break into distinct parts (cf. 1958.2). The satirical object of the "Satyr" is pride (not reason), pride in learning and accomplishment. The partial retraction of this attack at the end of the poem is a formal convention of the genre, not a concession to criticisms by the first readers (cf. 1953.4). Neither is the commendation of humility Rochester's personal credo; the speaker of the poem is a persona, another convention, as is also the interrupting adversarius. Because of the wholly rhetorical nature of the persona, the views expressed in the "Satyr" cannot be simply identified with those of existing philosophical sources. The convention of the satirical persona obliges him to disturb his audience. Thus, the satirist forestalls the pious accusation that he is a Hobbist by deliberately associating himself with that philosopher's alleged materialism and by turning on the audience the accusation they would turn on him: the image of reasoning man as an "Engine."

Similarly, the concept of "right reason" that the satirist endorses associates him with the libertine characters of popular drama (e.g., Shadwell's Don John, Otway's Oeidamia, and Rochester's own Marcellina), thus preempting the concept of its humanist value. The positive doctrine of the "Satyr" combines Hobbesian naturalism with "tinctures of epicureanism and liberalism"; the standard it sets for mankind is modest, but mankind still falls short of it. See 1971.5 for another view of Rochester's formal satire, and, for a different interpretation of the phrase "right veine of satire," 1953.3.

3 PALMER, MELVIN DELMAR. "The Identity of 'M. G.' and 'O. B.' in Rochester's 'An Epistolary Essay from M. G. to O. B. Upon Their Mutual Poems.'" MLN 75 (December):644-47.

Argues against interpreting the poem as an expression of Rochester's attitude toward Mulgrave and recommends altering the initials to "M. C." (Martin Clifford) and "D. B." (the duke of Buckingham) on the authority of a note in the Bodleian copy of the 1691 edition of Rochester's poems and of Pope's alteration of his copy of this edition. The poem is an "ironic epistolary satire" in which Clifford, one of Buckingham's literary collaborators, exposes himself to ridicule, by complaining to the nobleman that his part in the collaborations has not been recognized. See 1963.2 for another interpretation of the poem as ironic satire. See also 1966.1, 3.

4 PINTO, VIVIAN DE SOLA. "Libertines and Puritans: A Note on Some Lyrics of the Late Seventeenth and Early Eighteenth Centuries." N&Q 205 (June):224-26.

Suggests two unexpected echoes of Rochester's love lyrics in Watts' hymn "Our God, our Help in Ages past." Watts, in the opening lines ("A thousand Ages in thy Sight / Are like an Evening gone"), "was surely thinking" of two of Rochester's opening lines --"An Age, in her Embraces past, / Would seem a Winters Day"--not only reproducing their rhythm, but importing the word "Ages" which is found in neither the A. V. nor Prayer Book version of the ninetieth psalm that is paraphrased in the hymn. Another echo of Rochester—repeating the figures of flying and dreaming in the lyric beginning "All my past life is mine no more"--occurs with the reference to the Sons of time ("They fly forgotten as a Dream") in the seventh stanza of the hymn. See 1962.1 for another indication of Puritan familiarity with a poem of Rochester's.

5 VIETH, DAVID M. "A Textual Paradox: Rochester's 'To a Lady in a Letter.'" PBSA 54:147-62.

Establishes the relationship between three versions of a Rochester song: version A, "How happy Chloris (were they free)"; version B, in Rochester's hand, preserved in the Portland MS; version C, "Such perfect Blisse fair Chloris, wee." The holograph text is an intermediate state in the process of revision; version A is the earliest text; C, the earliest printed of the versions (in a miscellany dated 1676), was evidently the last written version and therefore the best choice for a copy-text. Most editors, however, have printed this version from Tonson's bowdlerized texts. "To a Lady" is here reprinted using the Harvard MS Eng. 636 F as a copy-text with emendations based upon variants in the three earliest printings of version C. See also 1963.2. The text of the poem printed in the Complete Poems (1968.4) changes "his" (1.15) to "its," but according to Patterson (1981.5) Vieth has returned to the reading in the text printed here.

1961

1 PINTO, VIVIAN DE SOLA. "Rochester and Dryden." Renaissance and Modern Studies 5:29-48.
  Attempts to balance the traditional subordination of Rochester to Dryden in literary history by postulating a symbiosis between the aristocratic amateur and the industrious professional, an ambiguous relationship, part attraction, part antagonism. Rochester's criticism of Dryden is "fair enough"; it attacks his imitation of the Court Wits, but it also recognizes his genius. On the other hand, though Dryden did not take kindly to Rochester's criticism, he was forcibly affected by the personality and poetry of the earl in what is termed "the second start" in his career, which began with the writing of MacFlecknoe. Thereafter, "a questioning spirit" is found in Dryden's writing. In Aurengzebe, for instance, there is a "vision of emptiness" reminiscent of "A Satyr against Reason and Mankind." Similarly, "Upon Nothing" and "The Maim'd Debauchee" are marked by a humor of "'holy nonsense'"--a way of overcoming the horror of emptiness by making fun of it--that descends to Dryden's MacFlecknoe and then to Pope's The Dunciad. Rochester and Dryden are both major, though imperfect, poets (cf. 1957.1) and "must be regarded as the first real Augustan poets." On the question of Rochester's Augustan character, see also 1961.6, 1963.2, and 1966.1.

2 VIETH, DAVID M. "An Unsuspected Cancel in Tonson's 1691 'Rochester.'" PBSA 55:130-33.
  Confirms for the most part the conjectural readings of a text of Rochester's "To a Lady in a Letter" (see 1960.5) by comparing a canceled and an uncanceled text of the poem in Tonson's 1691 edition of Rochester's Poems. This evidence qualifies the earlier conclusions only at lines 15 and 24. (For the textus receptus, see 1968.4.) The cancel also provides proof of Tonson's bowdlerization of Rochester's poems. See also 1963.2.

3 WILLIAMSON, GEORGE. The Proper Wit of Poetry. Chicago: University of Chicago Press, pp. 125-30.
  Places Rochester with Dryden (one another's complement) at the end of "the line of wit" in the seventeenth century--but as examples of Augustan, not Restoration wit (cf. 1966.1). The

force of Rochester's wit comes from a new ethical basis: pain--
the certainty of sense and hence a test of falseness, of fear--
which leads, in "Upon Nothing," with a religious efficacy to truth.
In, "The Maim'd Debauchee" and the "Satyr against Reason and Mankind,"
we find "a new form of wit," the inverting of values and
the treatment of this inversion in heroic style. See 1963.2 for
other examples of the mock heroic in Rochester.

1962

1 GRABO, NORMAN. "The Profligate and the Puritan." N&Q 207 (October):392-93.
   Provides evidence of the transplantation of Rochester's "Upon Nothing," to seventeenth-century New England. An incomplete and garbled version of the poem is preserved in the commonplace book of a prominent Boston judge, John Saffin (1632-1710). The faulty nature of this text and the absence of any evidence that Rochester's writings were distributed in New England suggest oral transmission of the poem. For another indication that Rochester's work was known by a Puritan, see 1960.4.

2 PINTO, VIVIAN DE SOLA. Enthusiast in Wit: A Portrait of John Wilmot, Earl of Rochester 1647-1680. Lincoln: University of Nebraska Press, 268 pp.
   Reproduces the main outlines of the portrait first presented in Rochester: Portrait of a Restoration Poet (1935.6), incorporating much of the biographical and bibliographical scholarship of the intervening twenty-five years to correct and supplement the earlier book. Rochester is now characterized as "the Byron," not "the Marlowe" of the Restoration.

3 _____. "John Wilmot, Earl of Rochester, and the Right Veine of Satire." In Seventeenth-Century English Poetry: Modern Essays in Criticism. Edited by William R. Keast. New York: Oxford University Press, pp. 359-74.
   Reprinted from 1953.3.

*4 QUAINTANCE, RICHARD E. "Passion and Reason in Restoration Love Poetry." Ph.D. dissertation, Yale University.
    Cited in 1973.4. See 1963.1.

1963

1 QUAINTANCE, RICHARD E. "French Sources of the Restoration 'Imperfect Enjoyment' Poem." PQ 42 (April):190-99.
   Brings together ten examples--five French (the latest published in 1660) and five English (all produced during the Restoration)--of a minor commonplace of the seventeenth-century love lyric: "the imperfect enjoyment." Though Rochester's poem by

that title (beginning "Naked she lay, claspt in my longing Arms) is one of these, its relation to the French model by Rémy Belleau is "slight and tenuous"; "The Disappointment," a poem printed in the 1680 editions of Rochester's poems, is probably a free translation by Aphra Behn of part of another attributed to "Cantenac." A third of the English examples, "Fruition was the Question in Debate," also ascribed to Rochester, is probably not his either (see 1939.6). This essay is based on the author's Ph.D. dissertation (1962.4). See also O'Neill's attempt (1977.3) to arrange the five English poems in an order of composition.

2 VIETH, DAVID M. Attribution in Restoration Poetry: A Study of Rochester's "Poems" of 1680. Yale Studies in English, edited by Benjamin Christie Nangle, no. 153. New Haven: Yale University Press, 537 pp.

Confronts bibliographical, historical, and biographical problems involved in establishing the texts and authenticating the canon of Rochester's poems. Much of the textual material has appeared before (see e.g., 1956.4 and 1959.2). In addition, the 1680 editions are set in the context of later editions of Rochester's poems (until 1761), and eleven "special studies" take up the problems of authenticating specific poems. These studies include: (1) An analysis of the structure of the "Heroical Epistle in Answer to Ephelia" as a satire in which the speaker—not Rochester (see, e.g., 1927.2 and 1935.6), but Mulgrave—ironically exposes his own pride, thus providing the prototype for the structure and persona (MulGrave) of the "Epistolary Essay from M. G. to O. B. upon Their Mutual Poems" ("O. B." possibly referring to "Old Bays" or Dryden, and "their Mutual Poems" to "An Essay upon Satyr"), and a conjectuctural date of late November or early December 1679 for its composition. For other identifications of the titular initials, see 1950.2 and 1960.3. For the initial reaction to this Augustan reading of Rochester, see 1966.1; see also 1966.3. (2) An examination of evidence bearing on the authorship and dates of four "linked" satires ("An Allusion to Horace," "In Defence of Satyr," "On the Suppos'd Author of a Late Poem in Defence of Satyr," and "The Answer") to reestablish the validity (cf. 1953.4) of the traditional ascriptions of the first and third poems to Rochester and the second and fourth to Scroope. See also 1939.5 and 1941.1; cf. 1970.1 (3) A survey of lampoons on Rochester, demonstrating the failure of most to foster a convincing mythical image (Oldham's Satyr against Vertue and Scroope's "Answer" are the exceptions—as is, most notably, Rochester's lampoon on himself, "To the Post Boy"). For more on the last (the text of which is here for the first time printed "in full"), see 1941.1, 1967.3, and 1980.3. (For an unnoticed lampoon on Rochester, see 1981.7). (4) Examination of the contents of the Portland MS (see 1934.5), arguing for Lady Rochester's authorship of the seven poems in her hand, and pointing out certain weaknesses in Pinto's treatment of the manuscript (see 1953.4, 1962.2, 1956.4, 1960.5, and 1973.9). The "blustring

Bard" satirized in the epigram beginning "To forme a Plott" (one of the texts in Rochester's hand) is identified here as Otway. (5) A consideration of relations between the "Song" ("I cannot change as others do"), ascribed to Scroope in the Yale MS and said to be addressed to Cary Frazier, and the "Mock Song" ("I swive as well as others do"), attributed here to Rochester as part of his quarrel with Scroope. (6) Removal from the Rochester canon of four "linked" hudibrastic epistles (appearing in the section of the 1680 editions containing poems by miscellaneous authors), with evidence that they were written by Buckhurst and Etherege (see 1950.2). (7) A review of the life and occasional writings of Colonel Edmund Ashton (1643?-95) to whom is attributed one of three linked lampoons on Edward Howard (that beginning "As when a Bully, draws his Sword") ascribed to Rochester in the 1680 editions. Another of the lampoons ("Come on ye Critticks! find one fault who dare") is attributed to Sackville; the author of the third ("Thou damn'd Antipodes to common sense") is uncertain. To Ashton is also attributed a prologue ("Gentle Reproofs have long been try'd in vain") which was later attached to Rochester. (8) Reexamination of the evidence for authorship and date of "Timon" (see 1938.1) and "Tunbridge Wells" (see 1954.2) in order to provide firmer basis for attribution to Rochester. See also 1973.3. (9) A reconsideration of the authorship of "A Session of the Poets" that finds little support for Wilson's attribution to Rochester (1946.3), somewhat more for Ham's attribution to Settle (1933.1) or some unknown author. See also 1931.1, 3. (10) A reexamination of problems underlying five linked satires in the Yale MS: "Ephelia to Bajazet," "A Very Heroical Epistle in Answer to Ephelia," "On Poet Ninny," "My Lord All-Pride," and "A Familiar Epistle to Mr. Julian Secretary of the Muses," arguing that Poet Ninny is Scroope, not Howard, that "On Poet Ninny" is Rochester's "lost" lampoon on Scroope (see 1948.2), and thus suggesting that the satirical targets of all but the first poem constitute a pattern of attack and counterattack between Mulgrave and Scroope, but written, with the further exception of the last poem, by Rochester. The traditional ascription of the first poem to Etherege is retained here; the last is doubtfully attributed to Buckingham. On the possible relation between Rochester and Etherege, see 1958.3. (11) A review of contradictory evidence concerning Rochester's authorship of "On Rome's Pardons," the final poem in the 1680 editions, but not included in the Yale MS. The poem is ascribed to Rochester in two manuscripts independent of the 1680 editions; yet Rochester's poems express little anti-Catholic sentiment. This book also includes a comprehensive list of early texts of the sixty-one poems printed in the 1680 editions, together with available information on their authorship (superseding Thorpe [1950.2, appendix C]), and checklists of relevant manuscripts and printed sources of the poems. The fruit of this study is Vieth's edition of The Complete Poems (1968.4).

1964

1 ALLEN, DON CAMERON. "The Atheist Redeemed: Blount, Oldham, Rochester." In Doubt's Boundless Sea: Skepticism and Faith in the Renaissance. Baltimore: Johns Hopkins Press, pp. 186-223.

Treats Rochester's "atheism" as his effort, after 1678, "to believe something." Hobbes himself was a "religious eccentric rather than an atheist." Blount, Rochester's deistic "dark angel," attempted to convert him to a "philosopher's religion," but his conversion by Burnet (his "bright angel") was genuine. Indeed, Burnet's record of it (summarized here) is one of the rare examples of a truly "happy-miserable end" offered by history to "atheist hunters." See also 1934.8, 9, 1935.6, 1962.2, and 1974.6.

2 BERMAN, RONALD. "Rochester and the Defeat of the Senses." KR 26 (Spring):354-68.

Interprets Rochester as a paradoxical moralist for whom lust is virtue, while action committed without that lawless desire—in "cold blood"—is vice or "philosophical error." His heroes, like Baudelaire's, embrace one form of decadence in order to reveal "an even uglier possibility": the dehumanization of "feeling nothing." "Failure of the senses is Rochester's great obsession." The sexuality of the poems is "loveless and rarely erotic"; nevertheless, "the capacity to feel," is their great theme—that is what distinguishes them from pornography. Cf. 1974.1.

3 GIDDEY, ERNEST. "Rochester, poète baroque (1647-1680)." EdL, ser. 2, 7:155-64.

Points out similarities between Rochester's love poems and those of the French baroque poets, emphasizing Rochester's essentially serious view of life. Rochester is said to have reached the final stage of the baroque, reunion with the metaphysical poets, transcending the attractions and agitations of the world.

4 GRAVES, WALLACE. "The Uses of Rhetoric in the Nadir of English Morals." Western Speech 28 (Spring):97-105.

Argues that in Sodom, Rochester used the formal devices of ethos, pathos, and, to a lesser extent, logos to further "the cause of appearances, opinion and pleasure," thus radically modifying the traditional moral purposes of rhetoric and reversing the nonrhetorical character of much seventeenth-century English drama.

5 MONCADA, ERNEST J. "The Source of an Epigram Attributed to Rochester." N&Q 209 (March):95-96.

Finds a possible source for the obscene lines "Written under Nelly's Picture" (beginning "She was so exquisite a whore") in a

Spanish epigram recorded in a letter by James Howell in 1622, and published in his second book of letters in 1647.

6 PINTO, VIVIAN DE SOLA. "Godfrey Thacker and Sir Charles Sedley." N&Q 209 (March):94-95.

Interprets Thacker's letter to the earl of Huntington (dated 20 March 1672/3) as referring not to Rochester's cruel treatment of his wife (see 1960.1), but to Sedley's treatment of his wife, and to her madness and subsequent institutionalizing.

7 _____, ed. Introduction to Poems by John Wilmot, Earl of Rochester. Muses' Library. 2d. ed. Cambridge, Mass.: Harvard University Press, pp. xv-l.

Reprints, virtually unchanged, the introduction to the first edition (1953.4). One poem (beginning "Tell mee noe more of Constancy") is added to the group doubtfully ascribed to Rochester (see also 1953.6 and 1954.3), and some new material is incorporated into the commentary.

8 PINTO, VIVIAN DE SOLA. "English Literature 1660-1800: A Current Bibliography." PQ 43 (July):381-84.

Contends, in this review of 1963.2, that Vieth's conjectured date (1679) for Rochester's "Epistolary Essay," is unsupported by "real evidence," arguing not only for the traditional early date, but for Rochester's narration in his own person.

1965

1 ELLIS, FRANK H. "John Freke and The History of Insipids." PQ 44 (October):472-83.

Presents evidence that John Freke of Strickland, a Republican militant, was committed for high treason as the author of "The History of Insipids." Anthony à Wood noted the incident. Cf. 1970.4.

2 PINTO, VIVIAN DE SOLA, ed. "John Wilmot, Earl of Rochester;" with Introduction; and Conclusion to The Restoration Court Poets: John Wilmot, Earl of Rochester, Charles Sackville, Earl of Dorset, Sir Charles Sedley, Sir George Etherege. Writers and Their Work, no. 186. London: Longmans, Green, pp. 7-13, 13-21, 39-40.

Sets the distinctive features of Rochester's love songs and satires against the background of Restoration court poetry and, more generally, the polite tradition deriving, through Waller and Cowley, from Jonson. Compared to the writing of Dorset, Sedley, and Etherege, Rochester's exhibits a finer sense of the relation of phrase and form and is more philosophical. It is marked by an intense perception of the effects of the new materialism on the world and by the creative use of the poet's reading. Rochester is called "the first poet to use the Augustan method of 'imitation'" (see 1949.1). For more extensive comment along these lines, see 1935.6 and 1962.2.

1966

1 ERSKINE-HILL, HOWARD. "Rochester: Augustan or Explorer?" In Renaissance and Modern Essays: Presented to Vivian de Sola Pinto in Celebration of His Seventieth Birthday. Edited by C. R. Hibbard. New York: Barnes & Noble, Inc., pp. 51-64.

Argues against Vieth's view of Rochester (1963.2) as "a complete Augustan"--that is, one whose satiric judgments presuppose a system of stable values--and for Pinto's view of him (1935.6, 1957.2, and 1962.2) as an explorer of the "Perplexity of endless Thought." Examination of "A Satyr against Reason and Mankind" provides no evidence of acceptance of hierarchical principle, and the "almost empty" world of this poem is even more pointedly expressed in the imitation of Seneca's Troades and "Upon Nothing," the last of which uses irony in its praise of a "mock-positive-deity" (but not systematically) to imply a belief in God's creation as the opposite of Uncreation (cf. 1971.6). Rochester's inconsistent irony is the literary form of his metaphysical uncommittedness and the principal means of his satiric explorations. Its effect, in "A Very Heroical Epistle," is a balancing of the reader's critical detachment "against a chance to identify with the speaker," and, in the "Epistolary Essay from M. G. to O. B.," a blending of "the egoistic with the acceptable, so that each modifies the reader's reaction to the other." See 1937.5 for an early reaction to Pinto's view of Rochester, and 1961.3 for an earlier expression of Vieth's. The latter view is rearticulated in 1968.4 and defended (against Erskine-Hill) in 1969.3.

2 VIETH, DAVID M. "Order of Contents as Evidence of Authorship: Rochester's Poems of 1680." In Evidence for Authorship: Essays on Problems of Attribution. Edited by David V. Erdman and Ephim G. Fogel. Ithaca: Cornell University Press, pp. 256-72.
Reprint of 1959.2.

3 _____. "Pope and Rochester: An Unnoticed Borrowing." N&Q 211 (December):457-58.

Notes that the line "But ever writ, as none e'er writ before," in a "Prologue, Design'd for Mr. Durfy's Last Play" (1713), attributed to Pope, is borrowed from Rochester's "An Epistolary Essay from M. G. to O. B." Pope's use of the line in the context of an ironic approval of writing without regard to the Ancients reenforces Vieth's argument (1963.2) that "An Epistolary Essay" is spoken by a persona who unwittingly damns himself. Pope's familiarity with the line suggests that the technique may have contributed to his own practice in the Dunciad. See also 1960.3 and 1966.1.

1967

1 BENDER, ROBERT M. "Wilmot: A Satire against Mankind." In *Master Poems of the English Language*. Edited by Oscar Williams. New York: Washington Square Press, pp. 247-50.

Comments on "the unrelenting savagery" of Rochester's attack in the "Satyr." The ending of the extended version of the poem is not a conditional recantation (see, e.g., 1962.2), but the ultimate expression of "hopelessness" about mankind. For Hobbes, there was a redeeming brevity to the "nasty and brutish" human condition; for Rochester, it is not only "wrong," but "long."

2 DANIELSSON, BROR, and VIETH, DAVID M., eds. Introduction and notes to *The Gyldenstolpe Manuscript Miscellany of Poems by John Wilmot, Earl of Rochester, and Other Restoration Authors*. Stockholm Studies in English, no. 17 (Acta Universitatis Stockholmiensis). Stockholm: Almqvist & Wiksell, pp. xiii-xxvii, 315-73.

Supplies information on the provenance and physical features of the Gyldenstolpe manuscript miscellany "evidently compiled in England in late summer of 1680" and now preserved in the Royal Library, Stockholm, as MS Vu. 69. The miscellany consists of 65 poems, 43 of them included in the Rochester editions of 1680; a large portion of it also survives in Portland MS PwV 40 in the library of the University of Nottingham. The notes provide information on the authors and dates of the poems with references to previous scholarship and lists of other texts, both early and modern.

3 RIGHTER, ANNE. "John Wilmot, Earl of Rochester." *Proceedings of the British Academy* 53:47-69.

Interprets Rochester and his work as the most brilliant example of the seventeenth-century tendency to confound antithesis with identity. Thus, "The Post Boy"--Rochester's only instance of self-mythologizing in his own voice--simultaneously magnifies and deflates both its subject and the orthodox values by which it is judged. More typically, Rochester is mythologized by an "other" of his own creation, a disguise like Dr. Bendo or a role that contradicts the "normal" self. His poems make use of a wide variety of impersonations, including impersonations of women, as in the "Letter from Artemesia" and the "Song of a Young Lady to Her Ancient Lover." His contribution to the developing genre of the imitation is a similar exercise in transforming an original into its opposite or, as the technique appears in "To His Mistress," in determining the point at which Quarles's expression of abasement before God merges with the lover's despairing cry to his mistress. Rochester pushes the technique to its limit in the song "All my past Life is mine no more," a poem that works its way to a conventional defense of inconstancy that is, by that very process, transformed into an expression of the sense of existence outside duration. Reversal is frequent in the movement of Rochester's verse; individual lines and stanzas flow--syntactically and semantically--backward as well as forward, forcing the reader to decide whether the two halves of a parallel construction are appositive or opposite, whether in fact the construction involves real equivalence. "Upon Nothing" is the consummate instance of meeting of opposites and the relinquishing of identities; the very formal existence of the poem is called into question by its own premise: Nothing is best.

1968

1 HAYMAN, JOHN. "An Image of the Sultan in Waller's 'Of Love' and 'A Very Heroical Epistle in Answer to Ephelia.'" N&Q 213 (October):38-81.

   Defends Vieth's attribution of the "Heroical Epistle" to Rochester (1963.2) on the grounds that the poem echoes a passage of Waller's, a poet Rochester admired. The passage in question, from "Of Love," compares the supposed political tyranny exercised by English women; the "Epistle," in turn, describes the freedom of the sultan in his harem as a happiness denied English lovers.

2 HOOK, LUCYLE. "The Rape of Europe by Jupiter." In On Stage and Off: Eight Essays in English Literature. Edited by John W. Ehrstine, John R. Elwood and Robert C. McLean. Pullman: Washington State University Press, pp. 56-62.

   Argues that a hitherto unnoticed masque, The Rape of Europa by Jupiter, was written for the 1694 revival of Valentinian, and, on this assumption, takes full notice of the musical elements in the play and the strong feminine orientation Rochester gave to Fletcher's "male-centered" tragedy. The earlier 1684 production of the play made dramatic use of a masque (by Sir Francis Fane) together with songs and dances both to foreshadow and to cover the elapsed time of the rape of Lucina. The Rape of Europa in the place of Fane's masque would represent symbolically on stage what was happening offstage. The music of the later masque was composed by John Eccles, and if, as seems likely, the libretto was written by Peter Anthony Motteaux, The Rape of Europa may have been the "try-out piece" for the team that went on to establish opera as an independent genre in the second decade of the eighteenth century. For evidence of an earlier production of Valentinian, see 1921.1. See also 1956.2.

3 PAULSON, KRISTOFFER FRIMANN. "A Subject of Debate: A Reevaluation of the Major Satires of John Wilmot, Second Earl of Rochester." Ph.D. dissertation, University of California, Davis, 277 pp.

   Demonstrates, in close readings of "Timon," "A Letter from Artemisa . . . to Chloe," "A Satyr against Reason and Mankind," and "Upon Nothing," that Rochester's satires do not express his own views or speak in his own voice, but (in the first three poems) create personae that speak in dramatic dialogues. The would-be wits of the first poem attempt to praise, but ironically condemn contemporary drama; the philosophy and language of the fine lady in the second are later echoed by the hack writer in Swift's Tale of a Tub; and the "Satyr" is a formal debate on the subject of Walter Charleton's The Immortality of the Human Soul--Charleton being the model for Rochester's "formal Band, and Beard." See also DA 29 (1969):2223A and Paulson's later article on the "Satyr" (1971.4). For more on the personae of Rochester's poems, see 1967.3.

4 VIETH, DAVID M., ed. Introduction to The Complete Poems of John Wilmot, Earl of Rochester. New Haven: Yale University Press, pp. xvii-lxix.
Sets forth the editorial principles on which this edition is based and supplies biographical information and a critical perspective for understanding Rochester's poems. Three important claims are made about Rochester's work: it strove for immediacy of experience in thought as well as in sensual gratification; it developed a technique of combining discontinuous planes of experience (see 1972.12), its chief contribution to the emerging literary sensibility; and it created, at its best, a structural openness, a refusal to privilege any one voice of a poem (cf. 1966.1). Rochester attained his greatest power in the work produced in 1674 and 1675, drawing elements from both contemporary drama and, through Boileau, from the Roman satirists; thereafter a decline in quality is noticeable. For an exhaustive treatment of the problems of establishing the texts of Rochester's poems, see 1963.2.

1969

1 BROOKS, HAROLD F. "A Satyricall Shrub." TLS, 11 December, p. 1426.
Finds the source of most of an eight-line "Rodomontade" ("Trust not that thing called woman"), possibly by Rochester (see 1968.4), in Jonson's "A Satyricall Shrub." See also 1978.1.

2 DAVIES, PAUL C. "Rochester and Boileau: A Reconsideration." CL 21:398-55.
Dismisses the arguments of Crocker (1937.1) and Moore (1943.1) that Boileau's influence on Rochester's "Satyr against Reason and Mankind" has been exaggerated, arguing instead that the "Satyr" is "'an imitation [of Boileau's Satire VIII] of the freest possible type'" (see also 1949.1). The structure of Rochester's "Satyr" is not "cumulative" but "dialectical," not a sequence of arguments one or another of which may be identified as Rochester's or Montaigne's (and hence not Boileau's), but a rhetorical device for placing in perspective the opening libertine attack upon reason. In view of this "more meditated . . .

more artful" aspect of the "Satyr," it seems not unreasonable to regard its verbal echoes of Boileau as evidence of his influence on the work.

3 _____. "Rochester: Augustan and Explorer." DUJ, n.s., 30 (March):59-64.
Sides with Vieth (1963.2) rather than Erskine-Hill (1966.1) on the question of whether Rochester's poetry is a reflection of a stable world order (that is, the Augustan world), or a restless investigation of thought--an "exploration," to use the term that prompted this debate (see 1935.6). Rochester was not "a poet of unbelief"; his skeptical turn of mind would have prevented his becoming a "perfect Hobbist" or a perfect sensualist. The denunciations in "A Satyr against Reason and Mankind" are not expressions of Rochester's attitudes, but a rhetorical strategy designed to deflate an exaggeratedly exalted view of man. The distinction itself between "Augustan" and "explorer" is unsatisfactory: a stable world order may define An Essay on Man, but not Gulliver's Travels; moreover, it is possible to read The Dunciad as an exploration of the idea of folly. Rochester's Augustanism is finally reasserted in a consideration of the similarities, in technique and general assumptions, between "A Letter from Artemisa . . . to Chloe" and the work of Swift. Rochester and Swift are both skeptical, ironic, and subversive; yet good sense, restraint, and decorum are implicit in their work. Each is simply more concerned with the exposure of folly than with the recommendation of sense. See also 1974.2.

4 GRIFFIN, DUSTIN HADLEY. "Rochester's Poems: A Critical Study." Ph.D. dissertation, Yale University, 451 pp.
Provides a critical account of the poems to show that Rochester is a poet of skepticism. The libertine speakers of his poems are theatrical extensions of the author, though he frequently ridicules the libertine posture. This dissertation is the basis of 1973.4. See also DAI 31 (1970):1276A.

5 THOMAS, D. S. "Prosecutions of Sodom: or the Quintessence of Debauchery, and Poems on Several Occasions by the E of R, 1689-90 and 1693." Library, 5th ser., 24:51-55.
Investigates prosecutions for publishing obscene material in the Court of King's Bench and the Guildhall between the 1680s and Edmund Curll's case in 1725-28, and maintains that the precedent for severe penalties for this charge was the fine of twenty pounds leveled against Benjamin Crayle in 1690 for the publication of Sodom. In 1693, the publisher, Elizabeth Lathan, was fined and imprisoned for publishing Rochester's Poems, and so likely was the case to go against the printer Hill in his indictment for publishing the same work that he fled abroad. For an argument against Rochester's authorship of Sodom, see 1946.1.

6 THORPE, PETER. "The Nonstructure of Augustan Verse." PLL 5 (Summer):235-51.

Discusses "A Satyr against Reason and Mankind" as an example of poetic effectiveness that violates the "Augustan" insistence upon "design" or structure. The nonstructure of the "Satyr" is not that of the "satura"; it consists in "an apparent indecision about style," the antagonism between enjambed Donnean couplets, and--even more pronounced--between "strung-out" images and concise images. Several possible causes of this discontinuity are suggested: use of the couplet, the popularity of Horace, the conception of metaphor as ornament, the tendency to rebel against restraint, and the appeal to rhetorical acceptance of digression. See also 1972.12.

7 WEINBROT, HOWARD D. The Formal Strain: Studies in Augustan Imitation and Satire. Chicago: University of Chicago Press, pp. 40-49, 82-83.

Differentiates between imitations produced by Oldham, Rochester, and Pope, Johnson's examples of a "kind of middle composition between translation and original design." Oldham's imitation of Boileau's eighth satire and Rochester's "Satyr against Reason and Mankind" are viewed here as terminal bands in a spectrum: the first, a "virtual translation" according to conservative British practice, the second, a "virtual rejection" of the original in the manner of Boileau himself (see 1949.1). Indeed, Rochester's poem is so different from Boileau's (see 1943.1 and 1969.2) that Oldham may have felt no need to justify repeating Rochester's precedent.

1970

1 DAVIES, PAUL C. "Who Wrote 'In Defence of Satyr'?" EA 23, no. 4:410-14.

Argues that the internal evidence against Rochester's authorship of "In Defence of Satyr" and for Scroope's is not as strong as Vieth (1963.2) concludes. The irony that emanates from the authorial "I" in line 45 makes it possible to believe that Rochester could also expose himself to criticism in lines 48-59, lines that "certainly" refer to him and to the Epsom affair. Indeed, the satire in these and subsequent lines (assuming that Rochester is the author) is less severe on the libertine they describe than on the society that lionizes him, accepting his "Buffoone Conceit" but condemning his remedial satire. The ironic design of the poem dramatizes two distinct aspects of the speaker: the libertine and the satirist; insofar as society accepts the former and rejects the latter, the "Defence" makes a strong criticism of Restoration morality. There is no evidence of this force in Scroope's writing.

2 FIELD, P. J. C. "Dryden and Rochester." N&Q 225 (July):259-60.

Argues that the opening lines of Dryden's Religio Laici may have their source in lines 12-24 of Rochester's "Satyr against Reason and Mankind." That Dryden would turn Rochester's "ignis fatuus" into a welcome beam to "wandring Travellers" (however dim it might be in contrast to the sun of revelation) may be a serious reproof of the earl.

3 KNIGHT, CHARLES A. "The Paradox of Reason: Argument in Rochester's 'Satyr against Mankind.'" MLR 65:254-60.

Argues that Rochester's fierce attack on human nature in the "Satyr" should be read in the light of its complex rhetorical structure and its playful tone, a reflection of the poet's penchant for imposture. At the center of the poem stands a paradox: that any reasoned denunciation of mankind and reason must itself exemplify what it denounces. The poem, then, is a comic development of the speaker's initial distress that he cannot be other than he is. The speaker's use of reason in the argument—a form of logical play that includes argument by analogy and from unexamined assumptions, and the blurring of logical distinctions—is of course itself unjustifiable and inconsistent; but from the point of view of the argument—that man's goal is happiness and that honesty and virtue are not conducive to that end—this use of reason is justified by the speaker's motivation: self-interest.

4 PINTO, VIVIAN DE SOLA. "'The History of Insipids': Rochester, Freke, and Marvell." MLR 65 (January):11-15.

Rejects attribution of "The History" to both Freke (see 1965.1) and Marvell, arguing that it be returned to the Rochester canon. The dismissal of charges of high treason against Freke is a stronger argument against his authorship than for it; and Rochester was quite capable of writing in the popular street-ballad style of the poem. Moreover, the tone of "The History" argues for an author both intimately acquainted with the king and interested in the naval wars with Holland. The Marvellian qualities of "The History" may indicate that Rochester, in his disillusionment with Charles in 1675-76, was influenced by the principles of the leading pamphleteer.

1971

1 CLARKE, REGINALD DENNIS. "Rochester's Satire." Ph.D. dissertation, University of Washington, 179 pp.

Argues that Rochester as a satirist is as conventional in his values as Swift or any of his contemporaries—that is, that he is essentially a moralist (his obscenity is a rhetorical device used to sharpen effects and to shock the reader). What is peculiar to his satire is its form, parody, and its mode, a dialectic that usually resolves conflict and ends in some semblance of order. Four basic conflicts provide Rochester's themes: lust versus love; false versus right reason; pride versus humility; and hypocrisy versus integrity. See also DAI 32 (1972):2677A.

*2 IGLESIAS, JOHN H., JR. "Panegyrics upon Vice: Contexts of Rochester's Transvaluative Satire." Ph.D. dissertation, Johns Hopkins University.
    Cited in 1976.11.

3 PAULSON, KRISTOFFER F. "Pun Intended: Rochester's Upon Nothing." ELN 9 (December):118-21.
    Finds a submerged pun--"T-W'at? (twat)"--in the final words of line 6 of the poem: "Then all proceeded from the great united --What?" The imagery of generation and birth continues in the third stanza, forming an extended metaphor. Rochester's wit here is explained as the incongruity of expressing an "abstract absolute" in terms of a concrete personification.

4 _____. "The Reverend Edward Stillingfleet and the 'Epilogue' to Rochester's A Satyr against Reason and Mankind." PQ 50 (October):657-63.
    Argues that Edward Stillingfleet's criticism of the "Satyr" (the poem of 173 lines) in a sermon preached 24 February 1674/5 prompted Rochester's retaliation in the "epilogue" to the poem (lines 174-221), a satirical reflection of the sermon and its author. Though Stillingfleet mentioned neither Rochester nor the "Satyr" by name in the sermon, he attacked sensual indulgence, the denigration of man as a rational creature, mockery of conventional morality, and misanthropy. On the other hand, in three of the most authoritative early manuscript texts of the "Satyr," the phrase "Stillingfleet's replies" occurs as an example of the "very reason" the satirist despises. Fear of possible repercussions, it is argued, caused the printer of the first published text of the poem (1679) to interpolate "Sibbes' soliloquies" for this reading and, further, to suppress the epilogue. See also 1972.7 for more on the epilogue of the "Satyr."

5 POWERS, DORIS C. English Formal Satire: Elizabethan to Augustan. De Proprietatibus Litterorum, edited by C. H. Van Schoonveld, no. 19. The Hague: Mouton, pp. 13-25, 198-202.
    Considers Rochester's place in the history of formal satire, a genre distinguished by its effort to duplicate the effect of thought verbalized as it forms (cf. 1960.2), and analyzes his use of such formal devices as the opening response to a stimulus, the interlocutor, and the implied location of the conversation in "An Allusion to Horace" and, especially, "A Satyr Against Reason and Mankind." Even though, in the "Satyr," there is little sense of extempore speech, there is still, as the more formal, stilted language of the interlocutor points up, an effect of "living dialogue." Rochester's "Satirist" speaks the "loose" style of baroque speech which avoids measured parallelism, makes only loose

connections between statements, and frequently employs parenthetical expression and mild grammatical confusion. Other features of formal satire illustrated by the "Satyr" include the use of generalizing techniques and a conventional tone. Rochester's contribution to this genre is the elaboration of dramatic form. The "formal Band and Beard" is not just a means of externalizing the satirist's thoughts; as a secondary stimulus, he causes the satirist to refine his thoughts, thereby strengthening the illusion of spontaneity.

6 SILVERMAN, STUART. "Upon Rochester's 'Upon Nothing.'" EnlE 2 (Fall-Winter):190-200.

Explicates "Upon Nothing," describing the movement of the poem not only as an opposition between two metaphysical absolutes —"Nothing" and "Being" (or "Something")—but as an equivocation upon the ontological and logical senses of each of these terms. Upper- and lower-case initials differentiate the two senses, and an emendation of the 1680 "Antwerp" text (stanza 14) is suggested in this connection. Cf. 1966.1.

7 WILCOXON, REBA GRAY. "The Philosophy and Rhetoric of Sex in the Poems of John Wilmot, Earl of Rochester." Ph.D. dissertation, Vanderbilt University, 377 pp.

Argues that sexuality in Rochester's poems is both a vehicle for satirizing self-deception and social folly and a symbol of the senses as a source of knowledge. Rochester's hedonism is ethical in that it draws distinctions of better and worse among pleasures. As seen in "The Imperfect Enjoyment" (see also 1975.8), his obscenity is not pornographic, since it implies an ideal relationship in which there is mutual concern and affection. See DAI 32 (1972):6397A.

1972

1 DAVIES, PAUL C. "Restoration Liberalism." EIC 22 (July):226-38.

Redefines the Restoration wits' irreverent criticism of authority as a spontaneous though unformulated liberalism. Given this point of view, "moral bankruptcy" does not describe the state of Rochester's mind, but a prevalent theme in his writing; the emperor's death at the end of Valentinian indicates that "there is a justice that transcends the personality of the sovereign." The positive liberalism that underlies the wits' cynicism connects them with the Augustan satirists. See 1973.12 for a criticism of this view and the exchange that followed it, 1974.2, 11.

2 DONALDSON, IAN. "Adonis and His Horse." N&Q 217 (April):123-25.

Cites the four concluding lines of Rochester's "Tunbridge Wells" as an example of the logical commonplace that human rationality is best observed by comparing it to equine instinct, and discusses the significance of this idea in Shakespeare's Venus and Adonis.

3 DUNCAN-JONES, E. E. "Marvell's Quotation from Rochester." N&Q 217 (May):176-77.
   Points out Marvell's quotation, in a pamphlet called Mr. Smirke or the Divine in Mode (1676), of the concluding couplet of Rochester's "Satyr against Mankind" (the early version of 173 lines, which had circulated in manuscript since early 1676). Marvell uses the quotation to suggest that his subject Frances Turner--a clergyman--was a reader of the profane wit. For an instance of Rochester's borrowing from Marvell, see 1954.2. See also 1973.3.

4 FABRICANT, CAROLE. "John Wilmot, Earl of Rochester: A Study of the Artist as Role Player." Ph.D. dissertation, John Hopkins University, 280 pp.
   Argues that Rochester's outlook was "fundamentally antithetical" to that of his Augustan successors. His world is nebulous, theirs ordered in a fixed hierarchy. The norms of his satire embody ambiguity and change; his ideal is the actor, whose protean function he himself undertook in his own life. Conservative neoclassicism was both a "vehement reaction" against and an "artful transformation" of this outlook. See DAI 33 (1973):6352A.

5 FARLEY-HILLS, DAVID, ed. Introduction to Rochester: The Critical Heritage. Critical Heritage Series, edited by B. C. Southam. New York: Barnes & Noble, pp. 1-26.
   Traces the course of critical commentary on Rochester from the seventeenth to the twentieth centuries, noticing how little of it confronts the poetry as poetry until Whibley's essay on "The Court Poets" in CHEL (1912), regarded here as the beginning of modern Rochester criticism. Four periods of critical opinion are distinguished: (1) seventeenth-century partisanship--extravagant praise or excessive blame, with occasional insights (e.g., Oldham's use of Rochester's own technique of impersonation as a vehicle for attacking the Earl's immorality); (2) early eighteenth-century interest (after a brief decline during the prudish reigns of William and Mary), evidence of which appears in quotations from and allusions to Rochester's poems (e.g., Moll Flanders's quotations from "Artemisia"); (3) a period of moral condemnation (1750-1850) that confused the character of the man with the quality of his poetry (noticeable even in Johnson's sympathetic judgment); and (4) a period of moral tolerance that gradually sanctioned an unprejudiced criticism of the poetry (and, for the first time, a preference for Rochester's lyrics). Though Rochester's reputation as a poet has come into its own in the twentieth century, "there is still no outstanding critical assessment" of the poetry. Rather, modern critics have tended to emphasize one aspect of it at the expense of another: thus Pinto, preferring

those emotional elements in which the poet seems to be "speaking in his own person," gives a "romantic" Rochester; on the other hand, Vieth, who "has done more than any other critic to free the poetry from the shadow of the poet," ignores the personal element in the poems.

6 LOVE, HAROLD, ed. "Rochester and the Traditions of Satire." In Restoration Liberature: Critical Approaches. London: Methuen & Co., pp. 145-75.

Argues that Rochester crossed a native satirical tradition with the classical tradition of satire to "perfect a stance from which he could draw on the resources of both traditions." The former is the tradition of the couplet lampoon, a loose aggregation of satiric epigrams subordinating serious moral purpose to the angry abuse of personal enemies and thus revealing as much about the speaker as about his recognizable victims; the latter is the generalized or public voice of collective values. "Tunbridge Wells"--with its informal rhythm, idiomatic language, and indecency, its immediate sense of the speaker, and the preponderance of direct denunciation over ironic presentation--illustrates Rochester's early work in the lampoon tradition. Even here, though, he begins to transcend its limitations by satirizing general types of vice rather than individual victims. Rochester's combination of the two traditions is demonstrated in "Timon," a translation from the neoclassical mode of Boileau into the native mode. The result is a new satiric mode, "a humanized lampoon," in which the satirist still functions as exposer rather than reformer, but is able to provide a "wider range of responses to human realities" than was possible in either tradition. In "A Letter from Artemisia," the two modes appear in discrete coexistence, the classical in Artemisia's measured assertion of humanist values, the native in the fine lady's partisan libertine doctrine of survival in a Hobbesian world: the poem is as much about the two satiric traditions (voices of both sides of the satirist) as about the opposing ethical positions. In "An Epistolary Essay," the classical triumphs over the native mode; the poet takes precedence over the persona. The latter's words are expected to provoke a critical reaction; the lampoon manner has become parody, a "characteristically Augustan" manner. See also 1963.2 and 1969.3 on Rochester's Augustan quality.

7 PAULSON, KRISTOFFER F. "A Question of Copy-Text: Rochester's 'A Satyr Against Reason and Mankind.'" N&Q 19 (May):177-78.

Questions Vieth's choice of copy-text (Bodlian MS) for lines 174-221 (the "Epilogue") of the "Satyr" in The Complete Poems (1968.4) because it omits four lines after line 197. (The omitted passage, lines 197-200, may be found in Pinto's edition [1953.4, 1964.7], Thorpe's facsimile of the 1680 Poems [1950.2], and Danielsson and Vieth's facsimile of the Gildenstolpe MS [1967.2]. These lines (a careless omission by the scribe of the Bodlian MS, it is maintained) should be included in a definitive text of the "Satyr." See also 1971.4 for more on the epilogue of the "Satyr."

8 _____. "The 'Dog-Drawn Bitch' of Rochester's Ramble." Satire Newsletter 10 (Fall):28-29.

Disagrees with Vieth's annotation, in The Complete Poems (1968.4), of the concluding simile in "A Ramble in St. James's Park": "she [Corinna] whines like a dog-drawn bitch." The image describes a coupled bitch dragged by a dog that is pelted with stones.

9 SELDEN, R. "Rochester, Lee and Juvenal." N&Q 19 (January):27.

Argues that Nathaniel Lee's description of Hannibal in Sophonisba is indebted to Juvenal's tenth satire, and that Rochester's sarcastic allusion to the play in "An Allusion to Horace" (lines 37-40) depends for its witty point upon this primary reference. Whereas Juvenal's Hannibal is punished by becoming a standard theme for schoolboys' compositions, Rochester's Lee is returned to the whipping schoolmaster, Busby.

10 SILVERMAN, STUART. "Rochester's 'The Maim'd Debauchee': A Poem to Rival Marvell." EnlE 3:208-16.

Provides a close reading of Rochester's poem to illustrate that it rivals "all but a handfull" of Marvell's. The virtuosity of the former consists in the artful development of its effects: its judicious narration by an impersonalized narrator (the first-person subject uses constructions associated with the third-person); its focus upon essence (of sensuality) rather than act; and its careful movement to a climax (in the next-to-last stanza). The narrator's impotence is an "ingenious paradox," not an unnatural condition that prevents his satisfaction (as in "The Imperfect Enjoyment"), but a shelter behind which he can experience vicariously--"a source of strength." Passion that opposes will, reason that opposes sense: the overexploiting of any faculty is a dominant motif in Rochester's work. At the structural center of the poem is the figure of the voyeur, appearing in various forms: the admiral, the debauchee, the narrator, the ghost of the latter's departed vice, but each exhibiting the structural feature of "two participants and one outsider."

11 THORPE, PETER. "'No Metaphor Swell'd High': The Relative Unimportance of Imagery or Figurative Language in Augustan Poetry." TSLL 13 (Winter):593-612.

Argues that current critical interest in imagery and figurative language is misplaced in the study of Augustan poetry, which de-emphasized and even avoided imagery. Rochester's "Satyr against Reason and Mankind" is cited as a transitional instance of the movement from the rich figuration of earlier seventeenth-century poetry to the restraint of Augustan poetry. With its opening images of man as a "vain animal" and of speculative reason as an "ignis fatuus" and an "engine" "huddled in dirt," the "Satyr" promises elaborate imagery but fails to deliver it in the "plain style" that follows them.

12   VIETH, DAVID M. "Towards an Anti-Aristotelian Poetic: Rochester's Satyr Against Mankind and Artemisia to Chloe, With Notes on Swift's Tale of a Tub and Gulliver's Travels." Lang&S 5: 123-45.
    Argues that knowledge of an anti-Aristotelian poetic (one that contradicts the autonomy, coherence, and unity of Aristotelian poetics and that deliberately cultivates discontinuity) is indispensible for interpreting Rochester's "Satyr" and "A Letter from Artemisia." The discontinuity of the "Satyr" (signaled in the two terms of the full title--"Reason" and "Mankind") appears in the oft-noticed division of the poem into two parts (see, e.g., 1958.2, but cf. 1960.2), here described as libertine and Hobbesian; the first presents "an attainable positive standard," enjoyment of physical appetite guided by "right reason," the second an unattainable standard, a morality of necessity to which depraved man cannot rise. The effect of this contradictory structure is "Rochesterian irony" (see 1968.4) that involves the reader as co-producer and contributes thereby to four ways of reading the "Satyr": as imitation of Boileau's Satire VIII (e.g., 1949.1); as pastiche of borrowings from Montaigne, Hobbes, and La Rochefoucauld (e.g., 1937.1); as formal satire (e.g., 1971.5); and as dramatic poem (e.g., 1970.3). None of these generally Aristotelian approaches to the "Satyr" is able completely to comprehend it. The anti-Aristotelian discontinuities of "Artemisia to Chloe" consist in the succession of mutually qualifying characters of the poem, in an "ideological split" between two approaches to experience, and in its "concentric structure," a system of exposition that proceeds by a sequence of balanced postponements and resumptions around a thematic center (speculation about the interaction of human identity with impersonal nature). The procedure generates complexity for its own sake and may (as in A Tale of a Tub) produce a discourse about nothing at all. Cf. 1969.6.

13   WEINBROT, HOWARD D. "The 'Allusion to Horace': Rochester's Imitative Mode." SP 69:348-68.
    Disagrees with Brooks's judgment (1949.1) that the "Allusion" belongs to "the English line of imitations that were also translations," arguing instead that Rochester here practiced "an extremely free" form of imitation, extending to an entire poem the meaning of "allusion"--a new creation that must be read against an old creation. The work to which Rochester's poem alludes, Horace's Satire, I, 10, justifies Horace's earlier (Satire, I, 4) criticism of the poet Lucilius against his pedagogical defenders by skillfully forming an alliance with the former and attacking the latter as Lucilius's enemies, since they would perpetuate what he, in a more correct age, would abandon.

Rochester's departure from this model is significant; he attacks Dryden, the modern equivalent of Lucilius, either directly or by ironically praising him (cf. 1948.2 and 1962.2). Horace's Satire clarifies the "Allusion" by providing its background, but it provides little more. Rochester's title hints at a relationship that the poem does not fulfill (cf. 1968.4).

14 _____. "The Swelling Volume: the Apocalyptic Satire of Rochester's Letter from Artemisia in the Town to Chloe in the Country." Studies in the Literary Imagination 5, no. 2:19-37.

Interprets the "Letter from Artemisia" as an "apocalyptic" or "revelatory" satire, one that reveals a terrible situation to begin with and prophesies the destruction to come: Artemisia's reluctant beginning promises to become a "swelling volume" as her own values collapse, and the poem "takes on a quality of rapidly spreading evil." Drawn into the fallen world she describes, Artemisia forgets the chastity and heroism associated with her name. She would offer Chloe a picture of "that lost thing, love," but, in creating the Fine Lady, communicates a fashionable and unsatisfying lust, symbolized in the latter's embrace of her monkey. In her turn, the Fine Lady "creates" Corinna, whose career of whoredom, revenge, and murder completely inverts the original intention. But Artemisia does not only surrender her original values in adopting the Lady's; she promises a sequel to her letter, thus helping to propagate her "values." Artemisia has ceased being critical; only Rochester continues to be so. The "Letter," then, is more pessimistic than the formal "Satyr against Reason and Mankind": the speaker of the latter preserves his anger and his values before his interlocutor; Artemisia loses both and succumbs to the values of hers. The "proper analogues" of the "Letter" (though it may be even grimmer than these) are A Tale of a Tub and The Dunciad. For a contrasting view of the "Letter" as Rochester's most positive vision, see 1976.3.

1973

1 BROOKS, ELMER L. "An Unpublished Restoration Satire on the Court Ladies." ELN 10 (March):201-8.

Reprints a poem ("On the Court Ladyes," written about 1664, possibly by an Oxonian named Robert Clarke) from a Collection of Manuscript Poetry (in the Duke University Library). The poem, which chronicles the scandals of known and unknown women associated with Charles's court, may be based on gossip recounted by Rochester to former schoolmates at Wadham College, or is perhaps an effort by the young earl himself, corrupted by oral transmission. See also 1931.2 and 1932.1.

2 CLARK, JOHN R. "Satiric Singing: An Example from Rochester." EngR 24 (Fall):16-20.

Interprets Rochester's "Song of a Young Lady to Her Ancient Lover" as a satire, the strategy of which is contradiction: the formalities of conventional love lyric, the avowed romantic sentiments of the lady, the very figure of the singer, all belie themselves. The "satire, quite literally, assaults on every hand . . . love itself."

3   DAVISON, DENNIS. "Marvell's Quotation from Rochester." N&Q 218 (October):394-95.
Replies to Duncan-Jones (1972.3), arguing that Rochester's phrase "comfortable importance," used as a comic reference to Samuel Parker's wife in "Tunbridge Wells," and borrowed from Marvell's The Rehearsal Transprosed (see 1954.2), had become a common comic name for a woman by 1678, when Dryden used it in this sense in Limberham. Vieth (1963.2) cited Rochester's borrowing to date the composition of "Tunbridge Wells" during "the spring of 1674," a year earlier than is assumed here. (Vieth's date is also questioned in 1973.7.)

4   GRIFFIN, DUSTIN H. Satires against Man: The Poems of Rochester. Berkeley: University of California Press, 335 pp.
Takes neither Pinto's view of Rochester as a "spiritual explorer" (1962.2) nor Vieth's view of him as an Augustan (1963.2), but views him as a product of the Restoration, a doubter in search of certainty. Not even libertinism provided the security Rochester sought: "Timon," "The Maimed Debauchee," and the "Epistolary Essay" are never consistently serious; they invite the reader to admire and sympathize as well as deplore. The libertine lover's obscenity is moral; it attacks mindless lust (frequently in women), but also depicts the lover as "a prey to the uncertainties of love." Poems like "The Imperfect Enjoyment" and "Absent from thee . . ." combine compulsive sexual promiscuity and concern with impotence. (An Oedipal explanation is offered.) Narcissism, maternal attachment, and psychic impotence suggest that Rochester was an "impotent Don Juan," possibly explaining his quarrelsomeness, alcoholism, and hypochondria (cf. 1975.3). "Artemisia to Chloe" reveals an analogous impotence: failure to bridge the gap between ideal love and actual behavior. The "Satyr against Reason and Mankind" is a Restoration, not an Augustan poem; it presents a mind unable to find a firm moral basis. Notwithstanding its formal structure, it moves in a curiously "nervous . . . ebb and flow," presenting and withdrawing possibilities that prevent the straightforward progress of the argument. "Upon Nothing" is "profoundly un-Augustan": it is not a pure mock-panegyric in which all praise is intended as condemnation; rather, it argues that nothing (contrary to the views of philosophers and poets) is something, and that what the world regards as something is nothing. Rochester's closest affinities are with the writers of the Restoration comic stage. (Dryden's middle-class aspiration to the heroic and surrender to authority are inimical to Rochester; cf. 1961.1.)

5 JOHNSON, JOSEPH A. "'An Allusion to Horace': The Poetics of John Wilmot, Earl of Rochester." DUJ 35 (December):52-59.

Maintains that the "Allusion" is not a personal lampoon of Rochester's literary enemies, but a statement of consistent artistic principles. Central to these is an insistence upon restraint in wit (where fancy and judgment must enliven and temper one another), in comedy (where Rochester "may be advocating a Jonsonian comedy of humors"), and in the lyric (which must avoid both "verbosity and loudness"). Love (1972.6) also regards the "Allusion" as an attempt to transcend the limitations of the lampoon.

6 JOHNSON, RONALD WAYNE. "'Humanity's Our Worst Disease': Rochester's Satiric Strategy." Ph.D. dissertation, University of Oregon, 137 pp.

Explores three areas of Rochester's satire: (1) his anticipation of Swift in parodying popular literature, (2) his manipulation of the satiric persona, and (3) his use of rhetoric and drama in the "Satyr against Reason and Mankind." Rochester's Alexander Bendo's Bill, a satiric imitation of conventional quack advertisements, established the precedent for eighteenth-century parodies of subliterary genres for satiric purposes. Swift's Bickerstaff "Predictions" and similar parodies by Sedley and Tom Brown illustrate the practice. Rochester's early poems (e.g., "Fair Chloris in a pigsty lay" and "Signor Dildo") depend upon burlesque for their satiric effects. A group of later poems ("A Ramble in St. James's Park," "The Imperfect Enjoyment," "Timon," "Tunbridge Wells") makes the persona a satirist who calls attention to his own inflated rhetoric and invents characters who mock themselves. The personae of Rochester's latest satires (e.g., "A Letter from Artemisia") are themselves the object of irony. Rochester's "Satyr" employs both the rhetorical persona and the dramatic illusion of debate. But the skillful rhetorician does not escape the rational folly he describes. His rhetoric ends in a "bleak ironic vision"; he affirms nothing. See DAI 34 (1974):5916A. See also 1975.2.

7 JORDAN, ROBERT. "The First Printing of Rochester's 'Tunbridge Wells.'" ELN 10 (June):267-70.

Notes a 1674 printing of "Tunbridge Wells" in Richard Mead's Proteus Redivivus. Vieth (1963.2) cites 1697 as the date of the first printing of the poem "under Rochester's name" and, on the basis of lines that echo Marvell's The Rehearsal Transpros'd (part 2), dates the composition of his version of the poem no earlier than the beginning of 1674. The absence of these lines in Head's version may indicate that they are a later addition to the text and, therefore, of little value in dating the composition. Vieth (1976.11) gives 1675 as the date of Proteus Redivivus. See also 1973.3.

8 MURPHY, JOHN A. "Rochester as Sabinus." N&Q 218 (May):176-77.
    Argues that the name "Sabinus," in Sedley's poem by that title, was a contemporary nickname of Rochester's. Like the original Sabinus (one who replied to three of Ovid's letters from heroines), Rochester composed several poems that answer a woman's complaint. Such an interpretation illuminates the cryptic title of Rochester's holograph poem "Sab: Lost"--the colon signifying an abbreviation of Rochester's nickname, and the poem going on to describe "a love affair Rochester lost to a '. . . heavy thing . . . .'" (See 1962.2 for an interpretation of this fragment as dramatic dialogue and 1963.2 for criticism of this view.) "Sabinus" is also used with likely reference to Rochester in Radcliffe's "The Ramble."

9 ROBINSON, K. E. "Rochester and Hobbes and the Irony of a Satyr against Reason and Mankind." In The Yearbook of English Studies. Edited by T. J. B. Spencer. Vol. 3. Modern Humanities Research Association, pp. 108-19.
    Argues that irony in the "Satyr" presupposes two mutually exclusive answers to the question of Rochester's Hobbism: (1) that the poem reflects not only the author's early Hobbesian discipleship, but his subsequent disillusion with it (see 1953.3), and (2) that it reveals the formative influence of Hobbism upon Rochester's ultimately more pessimistic philosophy (see 1958.2). Rochester does employ a materialist ethic and epistemology in the poem; he departs from it only in emphasizing the power of fear in human affairs. In Hobbes, fear is held in check by society's acceptance of a monarch; but Rochester's disillusion with his own monarch caused him to omit this essential element of Hobbist order, and without it, the poet's world became the state of war his master's philosophy was designed to prevent. Recognizing the disease of mankind, then, but unable to apply the cure for it, Rochester must include the materialist thinker (himself) along with the rationalist in his criticism of reason. The extent of this emotional reaction against materialism is impossible to measure, but it injects irony into the terminology of those parts of the philosophy Rochester accepted (e.g., the "reforming will" of "right reason" upon desire). This irony does not, however, govern the epilogue: the absence of virtuous men merely measures the degree of Rochester's disillusion. Obviously, this argument circumvents Vieth (1963.2, 1968.4, and 1972.12) and Davies's (1969.3) strictures against making inferences about Rochester from the statements of the narrator of the poem; nevertheless, cf. 1980.8.

10 _____. "Rochester and Shadwell." N&Q 218 (May):177.
    Notes an echo of Rochester's "Satyr against Reason and Mankind" (lines 127-38) in Shadwell's The History of Timon of Athens, the Manhater (December 1677 or January 1677/8). Since there is some question about the credibility of an attack on Shadwell by Rochester at the end of 1676 (see 1946.3 and 1963.2 for two views

of the matter), the very ambiguity of Shadwell's intention in the allusion to Rochester (is it "gratuitous, complimentary or polemic"?) may make it an important piece of evidence on relations between the two writers.

11 TREGLOWN, JEREMY. "The Satirical Inversion of Some English Sources in Rochester's Poetry." RES 24:42-48.

Supplies sources, travestied by inversion, for eight passages in Rochester's poems: (1) Rochester's "Leave this gaudy gilded stage" offers a sexual alternative ("love's theatre, the bed") to "Come leave the loathed Stage" in Jonson's "Ode to Himselfe." (2) "Love bade me hope, and I obeyed" ("Woman's Honour") inverts the sense of Herbert's "Love bade me welcome: yet my soul drew back" ("Love III"). (3) "Tell me no more of constancy" ("Against Constancy") contemptuously applies a conventional opening of idealistic love poems—e.g., King's "Tell mee no more how faire shee is." (4) The argument against the real existence of the past and future in "Love and Life" comes from Hobbes's Leviathan, I, iii; that for the reality of the "livelong minute" of sensual pleasure echoes the "Eternal Now" in Cowley's Davideis, I, and other Christian descriptions of heaven. (5) The phrase "magazines of joys" with which sexual activity is rewarded in "The Advice" derives from the language of "courtly adoration" adopted by the character Puntarvolvo in Jonson's Every Man Out of His Humor and by Lord Herbert of Cherbury. Rochester's "magazines" are connected to a reference to foreign trade related, perhaps, to Cowley's rich West-Indian "mine" in The Mistress. (6) The "easy steps" by which we "rise / Through all the joys on earth to those above" in "Written in a Lady's Prayer Book" may have their origin in Crashaw's title, Steps to the Temple, and Adam's words to Raphael in Paradise Lost (book 5). (7) The theriophilic sentiment with which "Tunbridge Wells" concludes echoes Sternhold's rendering of Psalm 8. (8) Rochester's references, in the "Satyr against Reason and Mankind," to Patrick's Pilgrim and to Ingelo divert attention from his use of the first as a model for the journey of the follower of reason and of the second for the inverted argument that knowing nothing is best. See also 1973.4. For Rochester's allusions to Davenant and others, see 1976.9.

12 WEITZMAN, ARTHUR J. "Who Were the Restoration Liberals?" EIC 23 (April):200-6.

Argues that Davies's characterization of the Restoration wits as liberals (1972.1) is perverse and simplistic. Far from being liberal (in the classic sense of equalitarian), the satiric criticism written by the wits is aristocratic, aimed at persons who "don't know their place." Rochester's satire is "almost never medicinal," the explanation, perhaps, why Charles abided it. The criticism written by true liberals was not so privileged. See Davies's rejoinder to this argument (1974.2) and Weitzman's reply (1974.11).

1974

1 ADLARD, JOHN, ed. Introduction to The Debt to Pleasure: John Wilmot, Earl of Rochester, in the Eyes of His Contemporaries and in His Own Poetry and Prose. Cheadle Hulme, England: Carcanet Press, pp. 7-18.

Interprets Rochester's response to the Restoration intellectual milieu (especially to Hobbes and Lucretius) in the light of the twentieth-century psychologist Wilhelm Reich's description of the "cultured human" as a three-layered "living structure": (1) a surface mask that covers up, (2) the Freudian unconscious--thus "the artifact of a sex-negating culture"--and (3) a ground of "natural sociality and sexuality." Rochester's conversion, an uncharacteristic act (see 1967.3), amounts to an acceptance of the artificial surface mask as a divine ordinance; but his poetry characteristically explodes this surface in order to confront the empty horrors of the second level and thereby expresses "'his spontaneous enjoyment of work' and a 'capacity for love'" (cf. 1964.2). Sodom, which may have been a diversion for Rochester while at work on Valentinian, illustrates this rejection of taboos. The "composite biography" which follows consists of extracts from the writings of Rochester and his contemporaries.

2 DAVIES, PAUL C. "Who Were the Restoration Liberals?" EC 24 (April):213-16.

Defends his thesis that Restoration satire is a laughing sort of liberalism (see 1972.1 and Weitzman's objections [1973.12]) by clarifying the sense in which the word liberal is intended: not that of being favorably disposed to constitutional changes tending in the direction of democracy, but, more generally, that of being open-minded to new ideas. Two objections are specifically answered: (1) Restoration satire generally (and dramatic comedy particularly) attempts to subvert, not reenforce, traditional notions of status; a critic like Collier was disturbed by the freedom with which title was ridiculed on the stage; and (2) the antiliberal view of the wits rests upon outmoded views of the period and its writers. Weitzman's view of Rochester's "Satyr" as a nihilist rationalization of "voluptuousness" (Johnson's word) is "erroneous" (cf. 1960.2 and 1969.3). See 1974.11 for Weitzman's reply.

3 EDWARDS, A.S.G. "Rochester's 'Impromptu on Louis XIV." N&Q 219 (November):418-19.

Supplies evidence of the probable source of Rochester's "Impromptu" (beginning "Lorraine you stole; by fraud you got Burgundy") from a manuscript commonplace book of the late 1670s (Princeton MS AM 14401--described by Thorpe [1951.2]). This volume contains the Latin distich "Una Dies Lotheros, Burgundos Hebdomas una" (said to be the occasion of Rochester's parody), and is followed by another headed "Resp.": "In Lotheros raptu Burgundos fraude petisti / In Batavos emptu fur cito lusor agit."

4 FABRICANT, CAROLE. "Rochester's World of Imperfect Enjoyment." JEGP 73:338-50.

Argues that the libertine ideal of unlimited sensuality and exaltation of the world and the body are undercut in Rochester's poetry by a revulsion against the worldly and the sensual. Although the poems often distinguish between false passion (sex as mental abstraction) and genuine passion (sex involving the living substance of body), the body is characteristically shown to be incapable of matching the vitality of genuine passion. "Sex inevitably winds up back in the realm of mind." It becomes a vicarious indulgence in "The Disabled Debauchee" (where sexual fantasy dramatizes Hobbes's notion of imagination as "decaying sense") and a facsimile of the real thing in the "old blear eyes" of the host's wife in "Timon." The separateness of represented parts of the body in "The Imperfect Enjoyment," the "Song of a Young Lady to Her Ancient Lover," and "A Satyr on Charles II" emphasizes the inability of the body to function as a whole, reducing the natural act to a farcical mechanical exertion. Rochester extends Descartes's view of animals as machines to a view of man as "the ultimate machine" (see 1964.2): hence the interchangeability of the Fine Lady's "necessary thing" and her monkey in "A Letter from Artemisia." Poems by Etherege, Buckhurst, Wycherly, and Behn on the theme of "The Imperfect Enjoyment" differ radically from Rochester's version, in which impotence epitomizes this revulsion of sexuality and becomes a metaphor of the failure to fulfill human desire. (See 1963.1 and 1975.8.)

5 FARLEY-HILLS, DAVID. "John Wilmot, Earl of Rochester: Lyric, Burlesque and Minor Satire" and "Rochester: The Major Satires." In The Benevolence of Laughter: Comic Poetry of the Commonwealth and Restoration. Totowa, N.J.: Rowman & Littlefield, pp. 132-55, 156-83.

Considers Rochester's comic oeuvre as three phases of development: (1) light poems that play with conventional forms and ideas, (2) burlesques that express a deepening sense of the chaos of experience, and (3) satires that attempt, through laughter, to impose order on this chaos. Convention, in the poems of the first phase, guarantees comic detachment, increased (in a poem like "A Young Lady to Her Ancient Lover") by the use of personae. This need for comic distance conflicts with the poet's personal involvement in the situations of the second phase poems ("The Ramble in St. James' Park" or "The Imperfect Enjoyment," for example), producing self-satire. Rochester's relation to the heroes of the satires is more oblique. In "Tunbridge Wells," the persona's feelings are viewed critically by the poet, who demonstrates a superior detachment by imposing a hierarchy of values from outside the absurd world of the poem. The "Satyr against Reason and Mankind" (classified as a dramatic monologue) achieves comic detachment by means of a logical argument that shows the absurdity of its own logic (see also 1970.3). In "Artemisia to Chloe," structure again qualifies comedy. Here

Rochester judges Artemisia as she judges the Fine Lady. The structure of enclosed narratives equates comedy with civilization and thus completes the movement from the complete detachment of "The Disabled Debauchee" to a comedy of feeling and attachment. See also 1969.3.

6 GREENE, GRAHAM. Lord Rochester's Monkey. New York: Viking Press, 231 pp.
Presents a forty-year-old biography of Rochester, suppressed in 1934 because of the possibility of prosecution for publishing obscene material. The account proceeds chronologically to Rochester's marriage, where, because of the uncertainty of dates (the book makes little use of subsequent scholarship) it focuses upon specific aspects of his life and times: Rochester's strange relationship to the king; his relationship to Mrs. Barry (see also 1925.1 and 1931.1), to his wife, and to Dryden and other writers; his conversion and death. Rochester's character is interpreted as the expression of the splenetic disillusion and boredom of a postwar generation and of the antagonistic tendencies of the Cavalier and the Puritan, inherited from his father and mother. He was "a spoiled Puritan" aware of the "cracks in the universe of Hobbes." This psychological tension is the source not only of his best poetry, but of his own doubts in his disbelief, seen, for example, in the "half-truths" of Alexander Bendo's "Advertisement," and in his behavior, alternately, in health and sickness. For a detailed criticism of the book, pointing out invalidations caused by interpretations of poems no longer attributed to Rochester, see Vieth, PQ 54 (Fall 1975):1026-28; see also 1975.3.

7 JOHNSON, JAMES WILLIAM. "'My dearest sonne': Letters from the Countess of Rochester to the Earl of Lichfield." University of Rochester Library Bulletin 28:24-32.
Provides biographical context for twenty-one holograph letters from Rochester's mother to Edward Henry Lee (a grandson on her first husband's side), to Edward's wife (a bastard daughter of Charles II and Lady Castlemain, a cousin of the writer's), and to his mother. The countess is revealed as a wily and determined manager of the estates and affairs of two complex families, shrewd enough to use both her Puritan and Royalist connections to secure her fortune. Retaining a "special love" for the children of her first husband, Francis Henry Lee, and disapproving of Rochester's libertinism as well as his wife, she managed to obtain for young Edward Henry those benefits of his father that had been consigned to Rochester, thus virtually disinheriting the latter's son, Charles. The countess's letters, written in 1685-86, provide glimpses of "the intricacies of seventeenth century law," the "backstairs politicking" of James II's reign, and of Rochester's three daughters, whose upbringing she undertook in 1681. The letters now belong to the Rush Rhees Library of the

University of Rochester. The countess's letters to Rochester have been published by Treglown (1980.6).

8   MC VEAGH, JOHN. "Rochester and Defoe: A Study in Influence." SEL 14 (Summer):327-41.
    Argues that Defoe's enthusiastic references to Rochester (reckoned at between fifty and sixty in number--more than to any other writer) are a conscious appreciation of Rochester's criticism of Charles II's immoral court, an emotional affinity with his "audacious paradoxicality," and perhaps an unconscious attachment to his perception "that all spiritual effort is worthless." The second of these relations is illustrated by Defoe's citations of the "Letter from Artemisia," the "Epistolary Essay," and "Upon Nothing"; the third by his ambivalent response to the "Satyr against Reason and Mankind," the libertine principles of which he would have rejected while having to admit the justness of their application to human behavior. Defoe and Rochester agree on "practical truths": that human aims are illusory, that men are fools, that knavery is self-defense, virtue the surface of cowardice. Alongside Defoe's predominating commitment to rationalist thought stands the rational skepticism of rationalism deriving (as his allusions indicate) from Rochester. Defoe's similarly double view of human nature is also attributed to Rochester. Part 2 of Robinson Crusoe, for instance, depicts man as reasonable, capable of goodness, and genuinely religious; but part 3 contradicts this view, asserts that men are crueler than animals, and quotes lines 127-38 of the "Satyr" to cap the argument. Defoe assents to both the ideal and the cynical observation; faith and skepticism gain alternate control: Rochester's appeal for Defoe is the cause of this conflict. Indeed, the irreconcilable influence of Rochester seriously weakens the argument of Jure Divino. Finally, those glimpses of human insecurity in Colonel Jacques and Captain Singleton owe something to Rochester.

9   MINER, EARL. The Restoration Mode from Milton to Dryden. Princeton: Princeton University Press, pp. 373-76, 380-86, 412-22.
    Locates Restoration satire within the bounds of libertine lyric and Christian epic, and sets the limits of the first with Rochester's discovery of pleasure in pain (in a poem like "The Mistress") and his discovery of knowledge in nothing (in "Upon Nothing"). These limits describe another sequence: sensation requires constant stimulation, and creates, therefore, a continual quest for originality. Hence the exploitation of literary convention (as in "Fair Chloris in a pigsty lay") and the self-destruction of the lyric mode (as in the "perverted couplet-sonnet" "To the Postboy"). Rochester "had spiritually to come to nothing before anything positive could result." Something like this paradoxical exchange of the immaterial for the physical

may, as much as the efforts of Bishop Burnet, account for Rochester's conversion. His reputation as a satirist rests, rightly, on the "Satyr against Reason and Mankind," the most libertine of his satires. But many of his poems are satiric by fits; the "Allusion to Horace," for instance, "gains much of its force from not being wholly committed to satire."

10 MOEHLMANN, JOHN FREDERICK. "A Concordance to the Complete Poems of John Wilmot, Earl of Rochester, with an Introductory Essay on His Use of Language." Ph.D. dissertation, University of Tennessee, 384 pp.

Lists "every significant word" of every poem in Vieth's edition of Rochester (including those only "possibly" by him). The introduction examines four elements of Rochester's language: diction, allusions, rhetoric, rhyme--each said to be "intimately associated" with Rochester's view of the universe and his created world. See DAI 35 (1975):5356A. See 1979.3 for the published concordance.

11 WEITZMAN, ARTHUR J. "Who Were the Restoration Liberals?" EIC 24:323-24.

Uses Davies's evidence of the liberal atmosphere of the Restoration (1974.2) to argue the reverse. Davies's quotation from Maidwell's The Loving Enemies (cited as an indication that satire was regarded as anything but "trivial") only points out the repressiveness (illiberality) of the age. Similarly, it is argued, his quotation from Collier, cited to suggest the seriousness with which theatrical satire was regarded, "merely affirms the snobbery of Restoration society." See 1972.1 and 1973.12 for the discussion that preceded this exchange.

12 WILCOXON, REBA. "Rochester's Philosophical Premises: A Case for Consistency." ECS 8:183-201.

Finding Rochester's philosophical premises a mutually supporting blend of Pyrrhonist, Epicurean, and empiricist views, Wilcoxon demonstrates their coexistence in his poems--early and late (the translations from De Rerum Natura and "Troades"), satirical ("Upon Nothing" and "A Satyr against Reason and Mankind"), and lyrical ("Love and Life"). To these premises may be traced his rejection of the concept of Providence and the Christian system of personal rewards and punishments, his distrust of a priori reasoning and preference for knowledge based upon sense experience, and his insistence upon pleasure as the basis of happiness. Read against this philosophical background, "Upon Nothing" is seen as a new-science criticism of rationalism (cf. 1962.2) and a mockery of orthodox personifications of God (though not a denial of His existence). "A Satyr against Reason and Mankind" criticizes the misuse of reason in abstraction; ethically, Rochester's voluntarism counters Hobbes's behaviorism; he is an ethical, not a psychological hedonist, and distinguishes, as does Epicurus, between the good and the right (see also 1976.5).

Hobbes enters the "Satyr" through his reliance upon the senses (see 1958.2), though the poem's emphasis upon fear also reflects the Epicurean ideal of ataraxia, imperturbability, the absence of which in Rochester's life is here offered as "the source of his art." "Love and Life" plays with the Epicurean-Hobbist notion that truth is limited to sense impressions and hence to that which is psychologically present.

1975

1 ERICKSON, DON LOWELL. "'The Progress of Dulness': Imagery of 'Nothing' and Negation in the Satires of Rochester, Dryden, Swift, and Pope." Ph.D. dissertation, Washington University, 298 pp.

   Takes Rochester's "Upon Nothing" as the starting point of a progression of satirical investigations of certain negative absolutes, the series culminating with "Dulness" (a functional cognate for "Nothing") in the final version of Pope's Dunciad. This study elaborates upon and claims to correct Vieth's view of the poem as the "nearly archetypal expression" of "the inverted world of Augustan satire": it was indeed the model for later satirists; but because Rochester's skepticism was nihilistic and blasphemous, his followers worked to appropriate his "central strategy" to more ethically approved ends. Dryden (in MacFlecknoe) used Rochester's strategy to demonstrate the impotence and emptiness of bad art; Swift (in Tale of a Tub) pretends to practice such an art. See DAI 36 (1975):2217-18A.

2 JOHNSON, RONALD W. "Rhetoric and Drama in Rochester's 'Satyr against Reason and Mankind." SEL 15 (Summer):365-73.

   Argues that the "Satyr" is constructed on rhetorical and dramatic principles that allow Rochester to deal with his readers' resentment at being included in the satire--simultaneously to mock and entertain them (cf. 1972.12 and 1980.8). Rhetorically, the poem contains the parts of a declamation: First, an exordium (lines 1-7) setting forth the persona's impossible thesis, one that alienates him from his readers at the same time that it awakens an awareness of his own humanity. Part 2--the narration of the facts (lines 8-45)--conveys the same ironic complexity: man's ridiculous and pathetic attempt to follow his reason and the persona's critical and sympathetic presentation. (The dramatic movement of the narration--the movement, that is, of its main character, man--also evokes pathos; it is the movement of the tragic hero.) In part 3--the argument between the persona and the cleric (lines 46-167)--the persona himself becomes a pathetic character. His very success guarantees his failure, for the means of his rhetorical triumph--the "righting" of reason-- implies his ethical culpability. Rochester's right reason is pragmatic as well as empirical; in a world of knaves, then, the surest way to attain one's end is through knavery. The reader has been following an ignis fatuus in following the persona; he has been led to his own sea of doubt just as the narrator arrives at his all-too-human denouement. This ambivalent or "reflexively ironic persona" is also found in the "Disabled Debauchee" and "To the Postboy," and wherever irony has a particularly broad scope. The epilogue of the "Satyr" is also ambivalent; it explains the purpose of the whole as an attack on a part of mankind, but indicts all mankind. The exceptional just courtier or faithful churchman who would seem to qualify this inclusiveness "differs more from man, than man from beast"--i.e., cannot be a man at all.

3 JONES, R. T. "Lord Rochester's Mother." EIC 25 (October):444-51.

Finds fault with Griffin's psychoanalytic (1973.4) and Greene's biographical (1974.6) interpretations of Rochester's poems. Psychoanalysis--a tool for uncovering the hidden--is inappropriate for Rochester's uninhibited treatment of sexual themes; it is a technique for evading the poems themselves in order to identify a Don Juan syndrome in the poet. Rochester was not obsessed with sexual promiscuity and inadequacy; his poems are about these things. Greene misreads the poems to fit his hypotheses about Rochester's life; his readings reveal an insensitivity to the "teasing tones" of Rochester's poems. For this, Farley-Hills (1974.5) is recommended.

4 MUNKER, DONNA F. "The Paultry Burlesque Stile: Seventeenth-Century Poetry and Augustan 'Low-Seriousness.'" SCN 33 (Spring-Summer):14-22.

Maintains that the native tradition of vernacular four-stress satire (the "paultry" style) fulfilled a need that heroic couplet satire could not supply--dealing with ordinary and immediate social experience, and considers Rochester (and Swift) as making the "most significant post-Restoration attempt to expand this potential" to support the heavier intellectual burden of Horatian colloquial verse. Rochester's "The Mistress" is examined as an instance of this effort. The poem postulates a conventional "love's paradox" in order to demonstrate two others: that "sincere" love is best known by adhering to literary convention; and that such adherence demonstrates the insincerity (i.e., the wittiness) of the poet.

5 O'NEILL, JOHN H. "Sexuality, Deviance, and Moral Character in the Personal Satire of the Restoration." ECLife 2:16-19.

Examines the implications of sexual insults in Restoration personal satire or lampoon, including several examples by Rochester. Sexual insult involves questions of choice: the masturbatory choice of self and solitude over society (in "Signior Dildo") or the duchess's preference for porters and carmen over Churchill and Jermyn (in "Quoth the Duchess of Cleveland to Counselor Knight"). The latter choice exposes the inadequacies of the rejected sexual partner as well as the lust of the chooser; conversely, Cary Frazier's rejection of dildoes implies the impotence of her suitor Carr Scroope. In the "Heroical Epistle in Answer to Ephelia," Mulgrave is accused of indulging in fantasy, the masculine equivalent of masturbation (an exclusively feminine habit in the lampoon).

6 PROBYN, CLIVE T. "A New Draft of Rochester's 'Disabled Debauchee.'" Scriblerian 8 (Autumn):1-4.

Reprints a manuscript version of the poem from William Doble's commonplace book—now Bodelian MS (Don. f.29. fol. 23v) —possibly an earlier text than Bodl. MS Don. b. 8, dated 1672-73. The draft consists of nine stanzas; beneath the numeral "10," a note appears: "A Stanza wanting." No mention is made of the two additional stanzas of the twelve stanza version. Errata in this transcription are noted in 1977.5.

7 ROBINSON, K. E. "A Glance at Rochester in Thomas Durfey's 'Madam Fickle.'" N&Q 220 (June):264-65.

Points out a correspondence between Lord Bellamore's instigation of a tavern brawl, in Durfey's Madam Fickle (V.ii) and Rochester's rumored role in the Epsom Wells brawl. Bellamore's excuse for leaving the scene (as the constable and watch arrive) is the "fear of a disappointment with my Corinna," which recalls the Corinna of Rochester's "The Disappointment" (or "The Imperfect Enjoyment"). Durfey's animadversion to Rochester here might explain the reference to Madam Fickle in "A Session of the Poets," if that satire is Rochester's.

8 WILCOXON, REBA. "Pornography, Obscenity, and Rochester's 'The Imperfect Enjoyment.'" SEL 15 (Summer):275-90.

Argues that "The Imperfect Enjoyment" is not pornography (that is, "verbal signs of stimulated sexual organs without exploration of emotional responses, personality, or values") and that its obscenity is defensible on historic and aesthetic grounds. Metaphor, the mock-heroic, and parody of Platonic idealism in Rochester's poem create an aesthetic distance (see 1974.5) that is absent in pornography. The reader of the poem is engaged intellectually and emotionally, reminded of the traditional character of the theme in classical and seventeenth-century writers. Hedonistic as its speaker means to be, his words include an ethical norm, "Love," against which pure sensuality and sexuality are viewed as inadequate. Rochester's obscene language is a rhetoric of realism (see 1976.13) giving direct access to the poet's world through the only source of knowledge, the senses. While the poem laments the unfulfillment of one kind of sexual relationship, it attacks another, the purely selfish gratification of lust. The obscenity of the poem is an "ethical command for a relationship in which sex is necessary but not sufficient." See also 1973.4 and 1974.4.

1976

1 ADLARD, JOHN. "Plain-Dealing's Downfall." N&Q 221 (December): 559.

Points out that the poem "Plain Dealing's Downfall" (included in Pinto's edition of Rochester's poems) is principally connected not to the Suffering servant of Isaiah 53 (see 1964.7), but to the proverb "Plain dealing is a jewel, but they that use it die beggars."

2 EDWARDS, A. S. G. "Libertine Literature in Restoration England: Princeton MS AM 14401." BC 25 (Autumn):354-76.

Examines two manuscript versions of Sodom contained in a manuscript miscellany in the Princeton Library (see 1951.2): a five-act version (recorded in other manuscripts) that focuses on the issue of sexual aberration; and a unique and (after the first part of act 2) "completely different" three-act version that focuses on the issue of sexual promiscuity and thus brings the action more within the range of "normal" human relations. These differences are accounted for by the assumption of a second hand, working independently from an incomplete text and creating its own denouement, an hypothesis that is supported by the inclusion in the short version of the "Dramatic Personae" of the long version, even though one of the listed characters does not appear in the former at all. Comparison of the Princeton five-act version of Sodom with six other manuscript texts of the play leads to the conclusion that the former may be "the most authoritative single text" we possess, its "best, and probably the earliest, copy." Carver (1979.1) refines this argument; see also 1977.1.

3 FABRICANT, CAROL. "The Writer as Hero and Whore: Rochester's 'Letter from Artemisia to Chloe.'" ELWIU 3 (Fall):152-66.

Interprets the "Letter from Artemisia" as Rochester's "most positive vision" insofar as it reveals Artemisia's creative and redemptive potential as a practicing satirist (cf. 1972.14). Rochester identifies with the female persona of the poem who becomes normative for him because she rejects the claim to a transcendent moral authority and refuses to accept her perception of the world as objective truth, inconsistencies that have called upon her the censure of other critics (e.g., Vieth [1972.12]). Artemisia's letter, which dares to transcend conventional patterns in order to do justice to the subversive energies of the writer, is dangerous, particularly for a woman. Her formulation of the ideal of love cannot be regarded as a position from which she unfortunately strays, or which betrays her self-righteousness; it is a statement "fraught with ambiguity and ironic qualification"; similarly, those qualities she shares with the Fine Lady make her more rather than less attractive, at the same time that her own more comprehensive vision subsumes the Lady's views and makes them exemplify her negative comments on society. Artemisia does not deny her own sexuality; she expresses it in terms of her "androgynous and compulsive literary energies." As she is able to overcome the limitations of her own existence through her identification with the Fine Lady, Rochester himself managed to transcend the confinements of his society by identifying with her. In his own letters, he plays the roles of both Artemisia and Chloe, depending on whether they are written from Whitehall or Adderbury.

4 HUME, ROBERT C. "The Satiric Design of Nat-Lee's The Princess of Cleve." JEGP 75 (January-April):117-38.

Interprets the character Nemours as a personal attack (obviously moral, but latently political) on Rochester. The latter's debauchery and penitence were still topical in 1682-83 (the conjectured production date of Lee's play) and still beyond harsh satirical treatment (as Crowne's cudgling for the character Artall demonstrates); Lee's attack is therefore indirect and ambiguous, moving from "more or less direct" but highly complimentary allusion to Rochester (the eulogy of Posidore as the "Spirit of Wit") to the sardonic judgment on deathbed conversion (both of them spoken by Nemours himself) and a "reform" that is interpreted as merely another "piece of bait" to secure Marguerite.

5 JOHNSON, J. W. "Lord Rochester and the Tradition of Cyrenaic Hedonism, 1670-1790." Studies on Voltaire and the Eighteenth Century. Edited by Theodore Besterman. Vol. 153. Transactions of the Fourth International Congress on the Enlightenment, vol. 3. Oxford: Voltaire Foundation at the Taylor Institution, pp. 1151-67.

Places Rochester in the tradition of egoistic hedonism, first as practitioner, then as moral satirist of the tradition. His indoctrination is attributed preeminently to Saint-Evremond and Grammont, his most flagrant indulgences occurring between 1664 and 1671-72. He was a founding member of "The Ballers" in 1668 and, the following year, in Paris, became acquainted with members of the notorious Order of Sodomites. (His conversion to Catholicism--viewed as an attempt to escape the Protestant emphasis on damnation--occurred on an earlier trip to Italy.) "Upon His Drinking a Bowl" epitomizes this period of Rochester's life. By 1671-72, he had experienced the "practical consequences of too literal an application" of Cyrenaic hedonism. Sodom is the most telling expression of his disillusion with sensual gratification: fire and brimstone are to the sins of Sodom what the pox and death are to the Cyrenes, and the opening speech of Bolloximian parodies not only the beginning lines of Dryden's The Conquest of Granada, but the last lines of his own "Upon His Drinking a Bowl." Begun in 1671, probably as a collaborative effort (but still belonging in the Rochester canon), Rochester revised and completed it in 1676 while working on Valentinian, to which it bears "striking resemblances." The "Satyr against Reason and Mankind" represents a move away from hedonism to a "sceptically misanthropic version of Epicureanism" (see 1974.12);

having learned the benefits of pleasure in moderation, he has become interested in "rules of good and ill." The view of Rochester as one who defined happiness solely as the fulfillment of desire is misleading; his work as a whole depicts "the imperfect enjoyment"; desire fulfilled leads to boredom and death; satiety creates artificial desire. Rochester partially escaped this dilemma of hedonism, but he remains part of its tradition.

6 PAULSON, KRISTOFFER F. "Rochester and Milton: The Sound, Sense, and Sources of Pope's Portraits of Bufo, Atticus, and Sporus in An Epistle to Arbuthnot." PLL 12:299-310.

Traces the derivation of Pope's satirical portraits in the "Epistle" to specific passages in Rochester's Poems on Several Occasions and Milton's Paradise Lost. Pope's Atticus is specifically indebted to Milton's Belial, though Bufo and Sporus are no less parodies of fallen angels. Bufo descends from Rochester's characterization of Mulgrave (in "My Lord All-Pride") as a stuffed toad and as a hog given to rooting through the dung-hill of other poets' discarded works, the dung-hill becoming Bufo's dining table at which he is treated to the flattery of bad poets and also treats them to his frugal patronage. The "Rochesterian" qualities of Sporus are initially evoked by the consonantal echoes of the portraits of Bufo (and thus through that of Mulgrave) and Atticus: as the emblem of "the basic sin of pride" in Pope's "Epistle," Sporus suggests both the spitting toad and the hissing serpent. Prominent features of Sporus are also traced to Scroope's "The Answer" (which Pope found in Rochester's Poems) and to Rochester's "On the Suppos'd Author," from whose antithetical hero ("Made up of all these Halfs, thou cans't not pass, / For any thing intirely, but an Asse") Pope derived the contradictory character of the "amphibious" Sporus, "one vile Antithesis." Rochester's description of Scroope in the latter poem ("A lump deform'd, and shapeless wert thou born") is itself indebted to Milton's description of Death and may have prompted Pope to draw upon the associated Miltonic description of Sin for the portrait of Sporus. Pope's image of the "painted Child of Dirt that stinks and stings" may come from the stinging insect in the opening lines of Rochester's "On Poet Ninny."

7 ROOT, ROBERT L. "Rochester's Debt to Shadwell in 'Tunbridge Wells.'" N&Q 221 (May-June):242-43.

Notes that Rochester's precedent for associating the word "fribble" with a cuckold in "Tunbridge Wells" is Shadwell's Epsom Wells (1672), the source as well of the names of two "predatory gallants" in the poem (see 1968.4). Indeed, the plotline of Shadwell's play appears to have provided the basis for Rochester's treatment of a segment of Tunbridge society. See also 1981.9, but cf. 1982.16.

8 SITTER, JOHN E. "Rochester's Reader and the Problem of Satiric Audience." PLL 12:285-98.

Argues that, as poet, Rochester did not share the terms of the absolutist mythologies of his time--neither conservative nor apocalyptic--and that his task was therefore to neutralize their political associations, thereby depriving his readers of certain interpretive certainties. (This view is taken in a general way by Griffin [1973.4] and, with respect to expectations associated with particular forms, by Vieth [1972.12].) Rochester's neutralizing of language makes use of four strategies for upsetting the conventional solidarity of author and audience: (1) subversion of normative words, illustrated by the undermining of Humanist associations of the word "man" in the "Satyr against Reason and Mankind" and by the "linguistic cancelations" of "Upon Nothing"; (2) ironic redefinition of honorific terms, as "Woman's Honor" in the poem of that title, or "reason" (first as ignis fatuus, and then as "right reason") in the "Satyr"; (3) the use of obscenity as moral argument--for example, exposure, in "A Ramble in St. James' Park," of the prostitution of language by both Corrina and the speaker, whose self-delusion challenges the reader to respond actively to the poem; and (4) the creation of dramatic relativism through the qualification of the persona or the modification of the "truths" of a series of speakers in a poem (see 1968.4). Both techniques are found in "A Letter from Artemisia," where Artemisia connects her function as poetess to that of prostitute, and where the sequence of speakers constitutes a "relativistic framework" that prohibits the reader's complete acceptance or rejection of any one of them.

9 TREGLOWN, JEREMY. "Rochester and Davenant." N&Q 221 (December):554-59.

Cites several passages in Davenant's works that would have impressed Rochester and possibly inspired lines of the "Satyr against Reason and Mankind." Specifically mentioned are Davenant's criticism of pride in reason and his image of an idealized teacher (in "To My Friend Mr. Ogilby"); his condemnation of human treachery (in a song from The Cruelty of the Spaniards in Peru); his attack upon academic pride (in "To Henry Jarmin"), and the image of prelapsarian intellect (in "To the Lord Cary of Malvezzi"); and the depiction of humans as more savage than animals (in the stag-hunt episode of Gondibert). Another Davenant allusion is noted in Rochester's song "Upon His Leaving His Mistress"; here the "universal influence" of Celia's physical dispensations echoes the spiritual impartiality of Gondibert, who dispenses his heart to "all the Sex" "like an universal Influence." Rochester's song may also allude to Donne's "Sweetest love, I do not goe, / For weariness of thee." The allusions in Rochester's song function parodically to criticize the idealistic postures of seventeenth-century love poetry. See also 1973.11. For more on Rochester's relation to Davenant, see 1934.6-7.

10 _____. "Rochester: Three Forgotten Letters." MLR 71:19-25.

Reprints, from the mid-eighteenth-century magazine the Museum, three letters of Rochester to his wife (see also 1980.7). The three letters are taken from a selection of seven, only two of which (addressed to Rochester's son) had been printed before their appearance in the Museum.

11 VIETH, DAVID M. "Rochester and the Restoration: An Introductory Note and Bibliography." PLL 12:260-72.

Rejoicing in the growing interest in Rochester's works, Vieth nevertheless laments its indifference to matters of "basic scholarship" and its "extravagantly differing" interpretations of his poems, a consequence of oversimplifying them, failing to recognize their place in a tradition of Absurdist writing to which "the major authors of the period" belong. Rochester's contribution to this "unofficial" literary lineage, "Rochesterian irony" (see also 1968.4), may earn him the title of "England's most minor major poet." The list of "Recent Rochester Studies," which supplements the "Checklist . . . 1925-1967" in The Complete Poems and Griffin's "Additions to Vieth's 'Checklist . . .'" (1973.4), consists of sixty-three annotated items, including dissertations, editions, and reprints.

12 WHITE, ISABELLE. "'So Great a Disproportion': Paradox and Structure in Rochester's A Satyr against Reason and Mankind." Kentucky Philological Association Bulletin, pp. 15-23.

Extends and refines Griffin's relation of the structure of the Satyr to the rhetorical form of the paradox (1973.4), arguing that the poem is related to both explicit and implicit paradoxes emerging from the speaker's perception of himself (the speaker participates in the faults he judges) and his awareness of the human condition, and challenging popular attitudes toward reason and wit. Rochester's paradoxes (unlike Donne's) and the tensions of his poetic technique (cf. 1969.6) remain unresolved; they must be accepted as a reflection of the logical disorder of his world and testimony of his dissociated sensibility. Reprinted: 1984.6.

13 WILCOXON, REBA. "The Rhetoric of Sex in Rochester's Burlesque." PLL 12:273-84.

Argues that Rochester's use of obscenity alters the accustomed working of burlesque, described as a synthesis created by the dialectic of form and content. Rochester's burlesque does not create such a synthesis: it uses "the decorum of genres, while violating, in the cause of advancing its own 'truth,' the decorum of content," the effect being an alternating of philosophical perspectives. Rochester uses obscenity to ridicule the idealism of conventional genres; but naturalistic sex is also satirized. Thus in "Fair Chloris . . . ," obscenity makes a joke of pastoral innocence; but the burlesque of pastoral returns to modify this judgment: Chloris is innocent--responding to natural sexual arousal; in yet another sense, however, she is guilty, since her dream expresses her unconscious desire. Similarly, the

"Mock Song" uses obscenity to show the folly of Scroope's sentimental love song to Cary Frazier, but not to naturalize her sexual appetite; and in "By all love's soft, yet mighty powers," it is sexual uncleaniness that exposes the false illusions of romance, and then is itself criticized in the light of a standard of hygienic love. Finally, in "A Ramble in St. James's Park," obscenity inverts the conventions of panegyric (shown by comparison with Waller's "On St. James's Park") and panegyric inverts obscenity, implying a world where such profanation does not exist.

1977

1 EDWARDS, A. S. G. "The Authorship of Sodom." PBSA 71:208-12.
  Argues from the incomplete state of an extant manuscript (Portland PwV40) of Sodom and from a complete three-act version in another manuscript (see 1951.2) that the play--"a libertine jeu d'esprit"--was not undertaken by its author to be finished and that the complete manuscripts of the play (six of them are mentioned) are products of other hands. At least three writers, independent of one another, are thus postulated: (1) the author of the fragmentary text common to all the manuscripts; (2) a writer who completed the three-act version; and (3) a writer who completed the five-act version that achieved circulation in other manuscripts. If this line of reasoning is valid, the argument concludes, Sodom "cannot be confidently incorporated into the canon of any single author." For more on the Princeton MS, see 1976.2. For attribution of the play to Fishbourne, see 1946.1; for attribution to Rochester, see 1976.2.

2 NOKES, DAVID. "Lisping in Political Numbers." N&Q 222 (May-June):228-29.
  Notes several of Alexander Pope's "unlikely" ascriptions of poems in his copy of A New Collection of Poems relating to State Affairs (1705). Pope ascribed "Rochester's Farewel, 1680" and "On the Young Statesman: By the Earl of Rochester" to Dorset, and denied Rochester's authorship of "Tunbridge Wells." He also completely inked out two obscene couplets of "On King Charles: By the Earl of Rochester; for which he was banish'd the Court, and turn'd Mountebank," testimony to his opinion of Rochester's "very bad turn of mind."

3 O'NEILL, JOHN H. "An Unpublished 'Imperfect Enjoyment' Poem." PLL 13 (Spring):197-202.
  Uses the song "Bless me you stars! for sure some sad Portent" to establish the order of composition of five published poems cited by Quaintance (1963.1) as specimens of the motif called "the imperfect enjoyment," one of them Rochester's "Naked she lay, claspt in my longing Arms." (The manuscript sources attribute also "Bless me you stars" to Rochester, though Vieth rejects it in his edition.) Because Rochester's poem is the only one of the

of the five that was not borrowed by the poet of "Fruition was the Question in Debate" (another poem in the series), it is presumed not to have existed before the latter, which is believed to be the fourth in the series. On the other hand, "Bless me you stars" does borrow from "Naked she lay."

4   VIETH, DAVID M. "Divided Consciousness: The Trauma and Triumph of Restoration Culture." TSL 22:46-62.

Finds in Rochester's poems two of the innovative structures produced by the "divided consciousness" said to characterize the Restoration: entrapment of the reader between irreconcilable or unmediated extremes; and the poem that attempts to prove that nothing is something, a project in which meaning is reversed. The first structure is illustrated by the irresolvable choices of "The Disabled Debauchee" and the stalemated attractions of libertinism and Hobbism in "The Satire against Reason and Mankind."

5   VIETH, DAVID M., and PROBYN, CLIVE T. "Errata and Acknowledgement." Scriblerian 9 (Spring):147-48.

Lists six substantive errors in Probyn's transcription (1975.6) of the Doble MS text of "The Disabled Debauchee."

1978

1   BEAL, PETER. "Ben Jonson and 'Rochester's' Rodomontade on His Cruel Mistress." RES 29 (August):320-24.

Attributes to Jonson the "Rodomontade" beginning "Trust not that thing called woman," accepted by Vieth (1968.4) as possibly Rochester's, and provides evidence that variant versions of the eight lines in question circulated in manuscript commonplace books both before and after its printing in the 1640 edition of Jonson's Works. For an earlier recognition of the Jonsonian source (if not an argument for attribution to Jonson), see 1969.1.

2   ELIAS, RICHARD. "Political Satire in Sodom." SEL 18 (Summer): 423-38.

Argues that satirical attacks on the sexual licentiousness of Charles's court disguised a more pointed assault on its political designs, and, to illustrate this thesis, examines references in Sodom to political events and public figures of the 1670s. Although the farce cannot, with certainty, be attributed to either Rochester or Fishbourne (cf. 1946.1), the date of its composition can be pushed back to before 1676, seven years prior to Fishbourne's earliest known literary activity. Specifically, Boloxinian's dispensing with punishments for sexual crimes and his encouragement of sodomy at court (letting "conscience have its force of liberty") play upon phrases in Charles's Declaration of Indulgence, borrow key terms from the ensuing debate over it, and in general voice the Country party bias that regarded the arbitrary use of royal prerogative as a metaphor for the imposition of popery into England. The division within Boloxinian's "Councill" further suggests North's division of the Cabal ministry into papist and "fanatic" factions. As a member of the latter, Buckingham guided the Declaration through the Privy Council, the function assigned to Borastus, the "Catamite of Honor" in the farce. What begins, then, as freedom <u>of</u> nature becomes freedom <u>from</u> nature, a position that contradicts not only Rochester's theriophilic argument for freedom within nature, but the legitimate basis of monarchal rule.

3 FARLEY-HILLS, DAVID. <u>Rochester's Poetry</u>. Totowa, N.J.: Rowman & Littlefield, 238 pp.

Argues that Rochester believed that metaphysical order had failed and that poetry was the orderly way of asserting that disorder. One therefore finds at the same time in his poems both the shaping presence of convention and an attack upon those conventions that sanction metaphysical order. For instance, manipulation of the conventions of anti-Platonic poetry--in "Song of a Young Lady to Her Ancient Lover" and "Fair Chloris in a Pigsty Lay"--permits those conventions to inquire more seriously into the relations of men and women. In "Love and Life," libertine conventions undercut the solemnity of the search for meaning in time, but in so doing assert formally the possibility of order in a meaningless universe. Rochester utilizes the comic juxtaposition of burlesque to control its destructive tendencies in "A Ramble in St. James' Park" and in the lampoons. In the satires, he attempts to construct a coherent world out of the chaos to which burlesque would reduce the real one. "A Satire upon Reason and Mankind" achieves coherence only at the cost of contradiction; but by articulating the conventional theme that all is nothing, "Upon Nothing" effects its own triumphant negation. Order and coherence are achieved in a sort of <u>discordia</u> <u>concors</u> in the "Letter from Artemisia," where the stronger the force of disruption described, the greater the degree of its absorption by the structure of the poem. See also 1974.5.

4 MC FADDEN, GEORGE. <u>Dryden: The Public Writer: 1660-1685</u>. Princeton: Princeton University Press, pp. 158-76.

Traces certain literary contacts between Dryden, Rochester, and Robert Howard. Dryden seems to echo lines 6-7 of the "Satyr against Reason and Mankind" in a line of the preface to <u>All For Love</u>: "this wretched creature, who is so proud of a reasonable soul . . ."; Rochester's "wisdom" and "certain instinct" in the "Satyr" become Octavius's unsatisfactory statecraft and Antony's sensual enjoyment of the world.

5 PAULSON, RONALD. "Rochester: The Body Politic and the Body Private." In <u>The Author in His Work: Essays on a Problem in Criticism</u>. Edited by Louis L. Martz and Aubrey Williams. New Haven: Yale University Press, pp. 103-21.

Speculates on the correspondence between Rochester's physical actions and literary expression. The obscenity of his poems is the private half of a private-public analogy. "The Sceptor Lampoon" compares war and lust; peace-loving Charles's scepter and sexual organ are equated, and these are in turn compared to the equating of warlike Louis's scepter and sword. Rochester's figure restructures the terms: Louis's public act of warmaking is reduced to the private act of whoring; Charles's private lust becomes as meaningless as the public act of war. Vehicle and tenor are mutually substitutive; public and private are inseparable. "The Disabled Debauchee" elevates private debauchery to the level of public heroism; but then this distinguishable vehicle and tenor merge in the images of lovemaking as destructive, frenzied activity. Public and private become a "mutual travesty." The "brave youth" who may meanly "shrink" from heroism becomes, in "The Imperfect Enjoyment," the speaker's sexual organ, which can succeed with whores but "shrinks" from true love. Personal impotence is a synecdoche for the public issue, as the king's body (body politic) is manifest in "the microcosm of the body-Rochester." Looked at the other way round, Rochester made a symbol of himself, and, after 1676, began to extend poetry into life by performing his alternative selves, each transforming the private into the public man. Rochester's relations to the king were both filial and (as Charles had been a "son" to Rochester's real father) fraternal; thus, his attacks on the king are attacks on himself, and in joining the Opposition, he supported the replacement of Charles's brother by a bastard son. In finally returning to his mother and Ditchley, the private and public were completely severed.

6 SELDEN, RAMAN. "Butler and Rochester: Low-Style Satire." In *English Verse Satire: 1590-1765*. London: George Allen & Unwin, pp. 92-100.

Treats the "low satire" written by Rochester and Butler as an effect of the materialist undermining of traditional values. Butler's low view of man was a cynical treatment of Baconian rationalism, Rochester's an intensification of Hobbesian naturalism; hudibrastic style has affinities with Horace's "low and familiar way"; Rochester's is an animation of Juvenal's rhetoric with Horace's first-person speaker, a device that he developed by counterposing multiple points of view. The result expresses Rochester's ambiguous attitude toward Augustan orthodoxies.

7 WHITLEY, RAYMOND K. "Rochester: A Cosmological Pessimist." *ECS* 4 (Summer):179-92.

Discusses Rochester's satire in the light of the poet's acceptance of inconsistent value systems--specifically, the personal hedonism justified by Hobbesian empiricism and traditional religious morality. As a consequence, social satires like the "Letter from Artemisia," "The Heroical Epistle in Answer to Ephelia," and the "Epistolary Essay from M. G. to O. B." are implicitly philosophical; they view vice not merely as individual failing, but as cosmological disruption; the satirical butts in these poems express Rochester's own ambiguous attitude toward egotism. (Bajazet's celebration of the "sensational life of the moment" is the principle from which Rochester's "Love and Life" springs, and M. G.'s poetic credo was long understood as Rochester's.) In his more explicitly philosophical satires--"Upon Nothing" and "A Satyr against Reason and Mankind"--this combination of traditional moral absolutes produces profound pessimism. Behind the satire on human endeavor in "Upon Nothing" stands a deity--"the great united What"--both product and producer of Nothing. If there is Nothing in God and the cosmos, there must be Nothing in human affairs; everything is reduced to the metaphysical level of the "whores' vows." Rochester expects no end of human worthlessness, no correction from his satire. A similar pessimism, proceeding from "the dislocation of value"--though focused more sharply on mankind--is found in the "Satyr." Here, Rochester uses the new philosophy to criticize the reason of the traditional moral thinker, and then uses the moral absolutes of the latter to criticize the conception of man produced by the former. Although the "Epilogue" of the "Satyr" attempts to provide an escape from the complete pessimism of this argument, the possibility of its realization is virtually nonexistent.

1979

1 CARVER, LARRY. "The Texts and the Text of Sodom." PBSA 73, no. 1:19-40.
  Agrees with Edwards (1976.2) that the Princeton five-act manuscript version of Sodom may be "the best" text of the play, but questions his claim that its authority is demonstrable and his evaluation of the authority of seven other extant manuscripts of the play (see also 1977.1). Though all eight manuscripts are collaterally related and though all are "corrupt to some unknown degree," certain inferences concerning their dates and probable relationships are possible: the Bibliothèque Nationale MS and the Hamburg Staats MS--both "almost certainly" deriving from the lost 1684 printed version of Sodom--may be dated as late as the early eighteenth century; the Victoria and Albert MS and the Vienna MS "almost certainly" come from the same scriptorium and were probably compiled in the mid-1690s; the Nottingham Library MS is also early; and the British Museum MS (probably eighteenth century) is perhaps related to the lost 1689 printed edition of Sodom. Since none of these manuscripts emerges as an authoritative text, only one course, it is argued, is open to an editor of the play: construction of an eclectic text based on "informed and calculated conjectures." The manuscript that would form the basis of such a text is the five-act Princeton Manuscript.

2   DOWNIE, J. A. "The Rose Alley Ambuscade Again." Scriblerian 11 (Spring):128-29.

   Supplies a bit of near-contemporary information from the MS jottings of Edward Harley, second earl of Oxford, that divides the responsibility for Dryden's beating between Rochester (cf. 1939.5) and the duke of Buckingham.

3   MOEHLMANN, JOHN F. "An Introductory Essay: The Language of John Wilmot, Earl of Rochester." In A Concordance to the Complete Poems of John Wilmot, Earl of Rochester. Troy, N.Y.: Whitston Publishing Co., pp. i-xxvi.

   Examines four elements of Rochester's language as an approach to the study of his world and poetry: diction, allusion, rhetoric, and rhyme. Rochester's diction is characterized by infrequency (except for ironic purposes) of conventional poeticisms and foreign words, and frequency of colloquial, vulgar words—often compounded and alliterated ("salt-swoln," "broad-built")—expletives, and obscenities (both scatological and venery). His allusions, most commonly the names of actual persons, attest to his preoccupation with spatial and temporal immediacy. Rochester's rhetorical repertoire includes most of the "turns" of neoclassical wit (devices associated with antithesis like chiasmus and zeugma); hyperbole, personification, and extended metaphor are expecially frequent as the natural forms in which his passion and his ambivalence toward abstractions found expression. Also characteristic is the employment of a "'listing' technique" (articulus), especially effective in conveying a sense of disorder, and the frequency of the triplet (occurring on the average of once every twenty lines). Rochester's rhymes are, generally speaking, careful and subtle; they compliment the sense and are rarely dull. See also 1974.10.

4   OBER, WILLIAM B. "The Earl of Rochester and Ejaculatio Praecox." In Boswell's Clap and Other Essays: Medical Analyses of Literary Men's Afflictions. Carbondale: Southern Illinois University Press, pp. 233-52.

   Explores the relationship between Rochester's "The Imperfect Enjoyment" and the destruction of the king's dial in the Privy Garden as evidence for a theory of the poet's ambivalent sexual identity. Ejaculatio praecox in adults "commonly reflects" an ambivalence toward the sexual object (i.e., a difficulty in choosing between a male and female partner). Caught in this conflict, the psyche may retreat to a form of urethral aggression toward a consciously desired, but unconsciously rejected female (identified with some aspect of the mother). Rochester's destruction of Charles's "Pyramidical Diall" was in effect an act of self-destruction, the destruction of "a symbolic hermaphrodite"—male in form, female in function; the vandalism was both revenge for paternal castration threats and denial of unconscious feminine identification. For another psychoanalytical reading of "The Imperfect Enjoyment," see 1973.4. See also 1963.1.

5 PASCH, THOMAS K. "Concentricity, Christian Myth, and the Self-Incriminating Narrator in Rochester's A Ramble in St. James's Park." ELWIU 6 (Spring):21-28.

Argues that the structure, biblical metaphors, and persona of Rochester's "Ramble" produce an order and meaning that are mutually inconsistent, forcing the reader to reevaluate his relation to the poem and thereby "to participate in the poetic process" (see 1968.4 and 1972.12). The structural order of the poem is concentric, the balancing of two pair of contrasting scenes around a fixed center (ABCBA): the sexual promise of lines 1-42 (A1) is balanced by sexual despair in lines 133-66 (A2); the three beaus of lines 43-86 (B1) are paired with Corinna's three sexual partners in lines 105-32 (B2); lines 87-104 (C), the physical and philosophical center, state the narrator's positive values: the libertine principle that lust is natural, but passionless whoring is unnatural. But the validity of the libertine creed is denied by the concentric structure, which consists in a pattern of biblical metaphor: Creation, Fall, Redemption, Last Judgment. Ideally, according to this system of imagery, Corinna (Eve) should return unsatisfied from her whoring, to the narrator, whose love should redeem her in a Christ-like manner. But the redemptive cycle is incomplete; Corinna has not returned from her beaus; and the Christ-like narrator becomes a wrathful judge of sexual frustration who drives Corinna from the Eden of the park to the hell of the country. The narrator, then, incriminates himself; as the presiding deity of the poem, he makes himself its "ego center" from which the reader may regard the significance of the concentric structure and the biblical metaphors as attempts to spare his ego by altering the perception of reality. But Corinna does not engage in sex with fools unfeelingly (cf. 1973.4); the narrator is self-deceived. See also 1976.8.

6 ROBINSON, K. "Rochester and Semonides." N&Q 224 (December): 521-22.

Identifies the ancestress of Rochester's Chloris, the "pig-girl" in "Fair Chloris in the pigsty lay," as the "pig-woman" in the satire of Semonides of Amorgos.

7 _____. "Rochester's Dilemma." DUJ, n.s. 40, 71 (June):223-31.

Defines the ethical-epistemological dilemma underlying Rochester's life and thought, his inability to surrender one of the two value systems to which he was rationally or intuitively drawn: the nominalist, appetitive values of materialism, and the absolutist values of traditional philosophy. The dilemma is illustrated in several of Rochester's poems. The opening lament of man's estate in the "Satyr against Reason and Mankind," for instance: is the speaking "spirit free to choose" to be a beast? To do so would necessarily destroy his indestructible spirit. Rochester neither denies nor asserts the existence of the spirit. The translation of Seneca's "Troades" appears to assert the finiteness of existence; yet the very passion of this outburst expresses an uncertainty about its tenets. In "Upon Nothing," Rochester's cause and effect argument that life is nothing and leads to nothing requires the postulate of a first cause. The materialist cannot do without a teleology: "something" does not return to nothingness. Rochester's predicament also underlies the love poems, where his nominalist commitment rejects (but reluctantly) the longed for stability of a loving human relationship. His "reduced moral stature" provided little in the way of sensual compensation; "pleasure became a debt." Materialist assumptions reduced traditional values to physical terms; yet he continued to hanker after these values.

8 TREGLOWN, JEREMY. "The Dating of Rochester's 'Scaen.'" RES 30 (November):434-36.
Assigns the date April 1676 to Rochester's scene for Robert Howard's The Conquest of China and to Howard's letter to Rochester, the basis of all attempts to date the "scaen." The scene was dated 1672 by Prinz (1927.2) and Pinto (1953.3 and 1962.2) and 1678 by Wilson (1937.8). Since Howard's affairs in the Exchequer came under investigation shortly after his receipt of Rochester's scene and throughout 1676 and 1678, the new date explains why Howard abandoned his play.

9 WILCOXON, REBA. "Mirrors of Men's Fears: The Court Satires on Women." Restoration 3 (Fall):45-51.
Argues that Restoration satire of women and sex expresses not mysogyny but male anxiety, projected as fear of venereal disease (in Rochester's "On the Women about Town" and "I Rise at Eleven"), of sexual insatiability--a female "disease" causing sexual deviance and inducing a sense of inadequacy in males (as in Sodom and "Signor Dildo"), and as reminders of "inevitable decline" as a result of age and disease. See also 1975.5.

10 _____. "Rochester's Sexual Politics." In Studies in Eighteenth-Century Culture. Edited by Roseann Runte. Vol. 8. Madison: University of Wisconsin Press, pp. 137-49.
Argues that Rochester opposes either male or female dominance in sexual relationships, and rejects sex as a means to political or social power. The images of Rochester as both sexual athlete and slave to love are ironic roles: the brutal language of the former (in "To the Postboy," "The Disabled Debauchee" and "The Imperfect Enjoyment") invite our condemnation, and the courtly conventionality of the early lyrics is frequently subverted by reversals of tone or logic (as in the conclusions of "What cruel pains Corinna takes" and "To My More Than Meritorious Wife"). The satire of sexual dominance is directed not only at the male (the happy sultan, in the "Heroical Epistle . . . to Ephelia"), but also at the female who is willing to surrender herself as an object--the nymphomaniac Phyllis (in "The Mock Song") as well as the satyromaniac. The double-edge of this satire is epitomized in Rochester's dildo image and in the well-

matched combat between male and female wits. "A Letter from Artemisia" sets male and female dominance side by side (the victimizing of Corinna by a wit is the Fine Lady's justification for her tyranny over men; Artemisia's definition of ideal love is close to Rochester's own view: sex as pleasure involving rational choice. The antithesis of the Fine Lady and Corinna is exemplified by the female speaker of the "Song of a Young Lady to Her Ancient Lover." The poem is not addressed to an old man (he is the "Ancient person of my heart"); it is a meditation upon a future condition, "the lover's dream of the sensual forever melded with the affectionate."

1980

*1 BROOKS, DAVID, ed. Lyrics and Satires of John Wilmot, Earl of Rochester. Sydney: Hale & Iremonger, 148 pp.
   Cited in 1984.5.

2 O'NEILL, JOHN H. "Rochester's 'Imperfect Enjoyment': 'The True Veine of Satyre' in Sexual Poetry." TSL 25:57-71.
   Interprets Rochester's "Imperfect Enjoyment" as a satire against pride (of the flesh) in order to prove that obscene poetry in the Restoration is not, as Swift suggested, a deviation from the mainstream of humane learning, but part of the central tradition of "general satire," the "true veine of sature." Rochester's poem juxtaposes the minor genre of the imperfect enjoyment poem to a broader literary tradition which follows the course of pride from illusory self-sufficiency to total isolation. The latter enters the poem in an allusion to The Faerie Queene, I.viii-ix; after his imprisonment in the dungeon of Pride, the arms of the Red Cross knight (emblem of his martial potency), are "shronk up like withered flowres," and in the following confrontation with Despair he almost destroys himself; similarly, when Rochester's persona--who proudly believed that his sexual power separated him from other men--finds that he shares the common limitations of sexual capacity, his pride produces a disintegration of personality that separates his penis ("shrunk up and sapless, like a withered flower"). The allusion to Spenser--evoking a familiar theme of pride--enables the reader to perceive his own ironic involvement with the persona.

3 PATTERSON, JOHN D. "Another Text of Rochester's 'To the Post Boy." Restoration 4 (Spring):14-16.
   Reprints, from British Library MS Harley 7312, a text of "To the Post Boy" to which is joined, as a continuation, the lines of the poem called "One Writing against His Prick." See also 1963.2.

4 _____. "Does Otway Ascribe Sodom to Rochester?" N&Q 225 (August):349-51.

Argues that Otway, in "The Poet's Complaint of His Muse," refers to Rochester not as "Lord Lampoon" and/or "Monsieur Song," but as the stinking, poxed, and spiteful author of Sodom at the head of the Muse's train. It is unlikely that Otway would have hesitated to name Fishbourne (see 1946.1) if he believed him the author of the indecent farce. On the other hand, if the second figure in the muse's train ("that blundring Sot") is identified as Settle, whom Rochester had described as "blundering" and coupled with a reference to Otway in "An Allusion to Horace," there is reason to believe that the latter might recall Rochester's epithet for Settle had he just described the earl. See Robinson's comment on this note at 1982.8.

5 SHEEHAN, DAVID. "The Ironist in Rochester's 'A Letter from Artemisia in the Town to Chloe in the Country." TSL 25:72-83.

Establishes an ironic point of view in Artemisia's expression of her temerity as a poet (she is in fact "perversely defiant of conventions) and in her idealistic definition of love. From this point of view Artemisia's attitude toward the Fine Lady appears unambiguously disapproving (cf. 1972.14 and 1973.4); moreover, she rejects the latter's preference for fools as lovers much as Waller rejected Suckling's praise of ignorance in "Against Fruition" (I). Obviously, then, she also disapproves of the Fine Lady as an "Impertinent." One positive norm emerges from Artemisia's irony: realistic love, love based on knowledge, not deception. The importance of Artemisia's irony becomes apparent when Rochester's poem is compared to Swift's "The Lady's Dressing Room"; in the latter poem, the curious lover Strephon is like the "men of wit" the Fine Lady condemns as lovers; and Swift's narrator, who advises Strephon to find joy in illusion, is like the Fine Lady. But the meaning of Swift's poem is left unclear; it wants the ironic context of Artemisia's point of view.

*6 STRAGE, MARK. "The Writer's View." In The Durable Fig Leaf: A Historical, Cultural, Medical, Social, Literary, and Iconographical Account of Man's Relation with His Penis. New York: William Morrow, pp. 196-254.
Cited in Scriblerian 14 (Autumn 1981).

7 TREGLOWN, JEREMY, ed. Introduction to The Letters of John Wilmot: Earl of Rochester. Oxford: Basil Blackwell, pp. 1-40.

Comments on the thought and style of Rochester's letters and supplies relevant biographical information on the poet and his chief correspondents: his wife, Savile, and Elizabeth Barry. The edition reprints all the extant letters (those by as well as to Rochester), including five by the countess dowager to her sister-in-law (on her son's illness) and the Latin text of Charles Blount's letters to "Strephon." For the countess's letters to her grandson, Edward Henry Lee, see 1974.7.

8 _____. "Scepticism and Parody in the Restoration." MLR 75 (January):18-47.

Illustrates the Restoration court poets' fascination with parody, pointing out in particular Rochester's use of literary adaptation as a way of keeping several attitudes simultaneously in play in a poem. Rochester's "Dialogue between Strephon and Daphne," for instance, treats pastoralism ironically in order to satirize "the insensitivity of men or the falsehood of women, or vice versa, or both." His "Phyllis, be gentler I advise," plays off a view of time as malignant fate against Herrick's "impersonal motion of the 'glorious' sun." "The Fall" sets the transient pleasure of the real present against the unlimited pleasure of prelapsarian Eden and the Golden Age. Also provided is an index of "Mock Songs and Answer Poems" printed in Miscellanies in the Bodleian Library, published between 1660 and 1680. Listed are poems containing "a substantial, easily recognizable allusion in its opening lines to an earlier well-known poem whose attitude it in some way clearly modifies." Four poems attributed to Rochester are included: "I swive as well as others do," mocking a song by Scroope; "Woman's Honor," mocking Herbert's "Love"; "Against Constancy," parodying a tradition of idealistic love poems that begin "Tell me no more"; and "'Tis not that I am weary grown," which echoes Donne's "Sweetest love, I do not go." See also 1976.9, 1973.11, and, for other examples of Rochester's parody, 1967.3 and 1974.5.

9 VIETH, DAVID M. "'Pleased with the Contradiction and the Sin': The Perverse Artistry of Rochester's Lyrics." TSL 25: 35-56.

Finds in Rochester's lyrics the "extremes-with-out-a-mean" structure described in 1972.12. (The validity of this view is demonstrated in a note citing readings of the "Satyr" since 1972.) Here, the model of this open-ended structure is metaphor, the differences between the tenor and vehicle of which are never finally canceled by their similarities. The tenor in "A Song of a Young Lady to Her Ancient Lover" is the literal finality of age, the vehicle the mythical rejuvenation of love; the lady's efforts to arouse her lover are art on the literal level, nature on the mythical. But these levels are not brought together: human identity is not repeated like the cycle of seasons. In the song "Absent from thee," the speaker presents two unacceptable alternatives: intellectual unhappiness in the presence of the mistress, emotional unhappiness in his absence from her. The reader grasps this psychological perversity by translating it into a religious expression of "the spiritual paralysis of sin and despair." The secular tenor relies upon its religious vehicle for comprehension; but the vehicle comes to assume "roughly equal status" with the tenor. "The Mistress" expresses the disjunctive terms architectonically as well as thematically, but its conclusion only partially reconciles the thematic extremes. In "Upon Leaving His Mistress," the irreconciled extremes of two expressions of Celia's sexual power achieve a closure, but not without "ideological stalemate." These conflicts bring into focus the central consciousness of the poems--sometime the speaker, sometime Rochester, but always the reader. This sense of self--"something new" in the seventeenth century--may be Rochester's chief gift to Western culture. But Rochester's lyrics also present continuity: their "semiparodic" use of earlier song constitutes a "creative misreading" that makes literary ancestry accessible.

10 WALKER, ROBERT G. "Public Death in the Eighteenth Century." RS 48 (March):11-24.

Claims that Burnet's Life of Rochester (and Robert Parson's funeral sermon) inaugurated the eighteenth-century tradition of public (or publicized) death. By making his repentence to a priest who was also a journalist, Rochester was able to offer assurance of the sincerity of his conversion, exhorting Burnet to make the very account of his death the "fruit" of his repentance. Rochester's public death became a powerful weapon for Christian apologists in the eighteenth century. For the theological implications of Rochester's public death, see 1982.15.

1981

1 COPE, KEVIN L. "The Infinite Perimeter: Human Nature and Ethical Mediation in Six Restoration Writers." Restoration 5 (Fall):58-75.

Considers Rochester's attempts to bridge the gap created by dualistic thought in the earlier century--Cartesian matter and spirit, for instance, or Baconian nature and the supernatural. For the Restoration, the trick was to make man the bridge between the material and the spiritual without assimilating him in either. Rochester's attempt, in "A Satyr against Reason and Mankind," fails by trapping man in naturalism; if speculative reason drew man beyond the human sphere, "right reason," which is reduced to instinct, errs in the opposite direction. It would take the subtler "trimming" of Dryden's "The Medal" and "Religio Laici" to steer between these extremes.

2 GILL, JAMES E. "Mind Against Itself: Theme and Structure in Rochester's Satyr Against Reason and Mankind." TSLL 23 (Winter):555-76.

Places Rochester's "Satyr" in the context of theriophilic thought in order to reveal its treatment and enactment of problems of reflexivity; read in this way, its paradoxes appear constructive--not disjunctive, as Vieth (1972.12) maintained--its inconsistencies--in Griffin's view (1973.4)--unified. One way theriophilic argument attacks pride in human reason is by representing the action of reason in considering itself: the very attempt to prove that animals are superior to men is an exercise in rational self-criticism--though not necessarily a useless one. Rochester's satirist (who is more reflexive than Boileau's) sets up an ideal of right reason, but in the very discursive act of doing so demonstrates its inferiority to the spontaneous way that animals know: he simultaneously asserts and demonstrates the capacities and incapacities of human reason. Thus the facile division of a "libertine" section of the "Satyr," internal in its focus, and a "Hobbesian" section, exposing the social failure of reason, is "a source of the poem's cohesion." The epilogue of the poem emphasizes this reflexivity. The satirist now imagines possible exceptions to the satiric hypothesis: if deviousness is essential to human beings, why can it not be employed unselfishly? "Sheer contrariety and deviousness render possible what is improbable." The final paradox, then ("Man differs more from man . . ."), speaks of "the internal divisions within man" as well as of "the hypothetical differences among men."

3 KRISHNAN, R. S. "Methodized Art: Neoclassical Theory and Formal Verse Satire." Ph.D. dissertation, University of Nebraska, 319 pp.

Attempts to establish the correlation between neoclassical theory of satire and the practice of formal verse satire in the eighteenth century. A chapter is devoted to analysis of selected satires of Rochester. The study concludes that what Dryden called "modern" satire was the result of a conscious incorporation of prevailing poetic theory into the classical satiric tradition. See also DAI 42 (1981):2142-43A.

4 NOTZON, MARK JOSEPH. "Scepticism and Satire: A Study of the Art of John Wilmot, The Earl of Rochester." Ph.D. dissertation, Indiana University, 84 pp.

Interprets Rochester's poetry in the context of seventeenth-century skepticism, a cultural phenomenon that made paradox and contradiction a rule of human thought and behavior, and that criticized reason in order to check its power and expose human pretension. Rochester, who was greatly influenced by Hobbes's skepticism, was a "radical sceptic," totally negating reason. His satires are a rhetorical counterpart to skeptical discourse. See also DAI 42 (1982):3166A.

5 PATTERSON, JOHN D. "Rochester's Second Bottle: Attitudes to Drink and Drinking in the Works of John Wilmot, Earl of Rochester." Restoration 5 (Spring):6-15.

Investigates attitudes toward drinking expressed in Rochester's writings. His praise, in a letter to Savile, of the "second bottle" (see also 1952.1) associates wine with true friendship and honesty; it was therefore a rare indulgence among courtiers. The expressed preference for wine over women in the early song "Love a woman? You're an ass!" is perhaps conventional; nevertheless, wit or mental procreation is described as a higher pleasure than sexual procreation, and alcohol stimulates the former; in "To a Lady in a Letter," however, Bacchus and Chloris are balanced as the means of raising "pleasure to the top." Wine is also an anodyne--in "Upon His Drinking a Bowl," for instance, where drinking is a way of varying the mechanical pleasure of the present. In "The Disabled Debauchee," drinking is the basis of a demoniac religion, an idea that may have inspired Oldham's "A Dithyrambic, Suppos'd to be spoken by Rochester."

6 ____. "The Restoration Ramble." N&Q 226 (June):209-10.
Argues that the word "ramble" in Restoration literature has a sexual meaning; Johnson's definition of the verb, "to rove loosely in lust," comes close to it. The "ramble poem," a minor genre, is typically narrated by a plain-speaking man in search of sexual stimulation. Rochester's "A Ramble in St. James's Park," the first datable use of the title (1673), is an example. Johnson's use of the word as the title of his periodical implies that the sexual element had disappeared by 1750.

7 ROBINSON, KEN. "A New Verse Portrait of Rochester." Restoration 5 (Spring):2-5.
Finds a satiric portrait of Rochester in an eighty-six-line passage (quoted in full) of a poem entitled "The Court Burlesqu'd" (beginning "I Sing a merry Monarch's Fame"). The poem, which is printed in The Posthumous Works . . . by Mr. Samuel Butler (1715), alludes to many well-known incidents in Rochester's life and, in identifying his poetic trademark as a "P, or C, in e'ery Line," unintentionally accounts for the numerous false attributions of obscene poems to the earl. No attempt is made to reattribute "The Court Burlesqu'd," and the composition date of June 1679-July 1680 is only tentatively advanced. For a consideration of other lampoons on Rochester, see 1963.2.

8 ROTHSTEIN, ERIC. In The Routledge History of English Poetry. Edited by R. A. Foakes. Vol. 3. Restoration and Eighteenth-Century Poetry: 1660-1780. Boston: Routledge & Kegan Paul, pp. 31-33, 42.
Defines the Restoration as a period in which history had so muddied traditional values and loyalties that men were forced to turn to the inescapably real. Thus Rochester's satires treat human relations as "functions of the will to power"; his love poems reveal that power-seeking in love.

9 SELDEN, RAMAN. "Rochester, Shadwell and Mr. Fribble." N&Q 226 (June):210-11.
Finds that lines 114-48 of "Tunbridge Wells" are indebted to Shadwell's Epsom Wells for more than the two names "Cuff" and "Kick," noted by Vieth (1968.4). Rochester's "fribble" (or "trifler"), the surname of Shadwell's cuckold (and therefore properly beginning with a capital), makes the passage an extended allusion to the play. See also 1976.7 and cf. 1982.16.

1982

1 CARVER, LARRY. "Rascal Before the Lord: Rochester's Religious Rhetoric." ELWIU 9 (Fall):155-69.
   Reopens the question of Rochester's attitude toward orthodox Christianity, opposing Wilcoxon's view that Rochester simply rejected it (1974.12) and taking generally the side of Pinto (1962.2) and others on the question: Rochester, through his various personae, may seem to banish Christian orthodoxy; nevertheless, his verse "everywhere" reveals "an excessive preoccupation with and acceptance" of it. Rochester's religious rhetoric is a rhetoric of negativity, his response to the gap between what should be and what is. He uses language to defeat language in a poem like "Written in a Lady's Prayer Book"; that very effort, however, demonstrates the effectiveness of language. Rochester desired the ideal, which in the human sphere is necessarily debased; he therefore pursued it through the negative, the realm of the unlimited—extending possibility by creating "his own negative." Since no man can worship God as He ought to be worshiped, better to worship Him negatively. All his poems, then, are paradoxical encomia, a praise of impiety that is really pious. The speaker in "Rochester Extempore" turns "self-debasement into self-enhancement"—negative into positive; wit both separates Rochester from God (but affirms His existence) and binds himself to Him. The rhetorical stance of the speaker of "To the Postboy" is similar, a perfecting of sin in order to become God's perfect servant. (This reading suggests an alternate punctuating of the final line of the poem: "The readiest way? My Lord's, by Rochester." The way to Hell is also the way to Heaven.)

*2 DANCHIN, PIERRE. "A Late Seventeenth-Century Miscellany—A Facsimile Edition of a Manuscript Collection of Poems, Largely by John Wilmot, Earl of Rochester." Cahiers Elisabéthains: Etudes sur la Pré-Renaissance et la Renaissance anglaises. 22: 51-86.
   Cited in Restoration 7 (1983):79.

3 EVERETT, BARBARA. "The Sense of Nothing." In Spirit of Wit: Reconsiderations of Rochester. Edited by Jeremy Treglown. Hamden, Conn.: Archon Books, pp. 1-41.
   Argues that Rochester's closeness to the materiality of the Restoration world threw him back on an idealism that is abstract and negative; his commitment to the social forms of that world thus became a way of breaking those forms; his peculiar "art of extremity" is the achievement of "arriving at the point where something comes to an end." Rochester's irony, then, has no intention behind it; his typical lovers are ghosts who haunt a time that is never "Now"—even "The Maim'd Debauchee" looks forward to "the pleasure of looking back at the pain of having suffered." His obscenity, his use of unprintable words, signifies his arrival at the extreme of verbal and emotional nothingness.

4 GREENSLADE, BASIL. "Affairs of State." In Spirit of Wit: Reconsiderations of Rochester. Edited by Jeremy Treglown. Hamden, Conn.: Archon Books, pp. 92-110.
   Considers Rochester's distaste for political concerns. Lacking both the means of political power (he was wholly dependent on court favor) and experience of the city, his royal service was personal. He was an alien in the newly politicized society which, he felt, was destroying social intercourse. His satire touches state affairs, then, in either a very personal way (the "Sceptre" lampoon on Charles) or in the most general ethical terms (the upright statesman in the "Satyr against Reason and Mankind"). On these grounds it appears unlikely that the programmatic "History of Insipids" is his.

5 KAUFMAN, ANTHONY. "Civil Politics--Sexual Politics in John Crowne's City Politiques." Restoration 6 (Fall):72-80.
   Suggests that the character Florio in Crowne's City Politiques represents Rochester, the embodiment of one aspect of the Restoration--wit and charm combined with self-loathing and misanthropy--"a man in conflict." Florio's awareness that his piety is a mask reminds one of Rochester's ambiguous sense of his own reformation. Florio, a Tory, parts with his friends at court in order to pose as a Whig; Rochester too associated with Whigs later in his life. Crowne's relationship with his former patron "appears to have been uneasy." Cf. 1968.4.

6 LOVE, HAROLD. "The Text of 'Timon.'" Bibliographical Society of Australia and New Zealand: Bulletin 6:113-40.
   Cited in 1984.5.

7 PORTER, PETER. "The Professional Amateur." In Spirit of Wit: Reconsiderations of Rochester. Edited by Jeremy Treglown. Hamden, Conn.: Archon Books, pp. 58-74.
   Deals with the criticism (going back to Pope) of Rochester as an amateur or dilletante poet. In avoiding professional publication, Rochester was true to his rank; nevertheless, he was no amateur at versification, and his indifference to the marketplace allowed him to experiment. He was classical by temperament, and classicism means "keeping technique in the foreground." If his verse questions the existence of art, it must, to make its case, be supremely artistic. In eschewing professionalism, Rochester became a disinterested poet, able to make a virtuosity of disengagement. His poetry offers no absolute beyond its own existence; its presence--like that of much twentieth-century poetry--proceeds from an interest in its own language.

8 ROBINSON, KEN. "Does Otway Ascribe Sodom to Rochester? A Reply." N&Q 227 (February):50-51.
   Objects to Patterson's literal reading of Otway's lines on the author of Sodom (in "The Poet's Complaint of his Muse") as a reference to Rochester's syphilitic repulsiveness (1980.4). These

lines, it is maintained, are written in a tradition that metaphorically describes aesthetic ugliness as physical disease. The author of Sodom takes precedence in the Muse's train simply by virtue of the rankness of his play.

9 _____. "Rochester's Income from the Crown." N&Q 227 (February): 46-50.

Attempts to put straight the record of Rochester's income from the crown. This derived from two sources: an annual pension of 500 pounds in recognition of his being Henry Wilmot's son, first paid in 1661, and an annuity of 1,000 pounds which came with Rochester's appointment as gentleman of the bedchamber, the first warrant for which was issued in October 1667. Payments from both sources were always in arrears; the Treasury computed the arrears on the pension at 3,375 pounds to the end of 1671, and on the later annuity at 1,500 pounds to June 1670. It does not seem to be the case (although one cannot be certain) that these irregularities are evidence of the king's disfavor with Rochester; if anything, the record indicates that Charles indulged him. But the crown was a notoriously undependable paymaster, and absences from the country were convenient excuses for postponed payments. On one occasion in 1669 payments were stopped for a year, until Rochester paid his poll money. In 1672, two letters to Rochester, one by Robert Howard, secretary to the treasury, the other by Thomas Clifford, Lord of the treasury, testify to his efforts to pursue his claims for payment on both sources of income.

10 ROGERS, PAT. "An Allusion to Horace." In Spirit of Wit: Reconsiderations of Rochester. Edited by Jeremy Treglown. Hamden, Conn.: Archon Books, pp. 166-76.

Focuses on minute differences between Rochester's "Allusion" and Horace's satire I.x, producing both detailed commentary on the former and evidence of its proto-Augustan linguistic context. Rochester's most obvious divergences from Horace stem from the absence, in the "Allusion," of an authentic pretext: Horace's satire is a contribution to a larger textual whole; its verbal gestures correspond to an "ongoing dialogue." Rochester must supply this pretext rhetorically. Dryden is therefore identified with recent productions of his plays, a complexity Rochester deals with by tense management. Rochester's lexical choices present the language before its Augustan solidification. "Patron" had not yet acquired the opprobrious connotation it has in Johnson's definition and so does not deflect criticism away from Dryden to Mulgrave. Does "refined" (Etherege) suggest "over-refined," as it does in Swift? "Poet Squab" suggests unfledged; "dry-bob" implies impotence in matters both venereal and satirical.

11 SELDEN, RAMAN. "Rochester and Shadwell." In Spirit of Wit: Reconsiderations of Rochester. Edited by Jeremy Treglown. Hamden, Conn.: Archon Books, pp. 177-90.

Argues that Rochester's admiration of Shadwell rests on the latter's "refreshingly unelaborate and natural" manner, compared to Dryden's laboriousness. Evidence of this attitude, though not unequivocal, is cited in Tunbridge Wells for its expression of the unaffected vigor of the lower classes (see also 1981.9, but cf. 1982.16). Rochester might also have felt a certain affinity for the philosophy expressed in Shadwell's The Libertine, which bears some similarity to that expressed in "The Satyr against Reason and Mankind."

12 TIERNEY, THOMAS PATRICK. "Satire on Mankind: The Nature of the Beast." Ph.D. dissertation, Loyola University of Chicago, 216 pp.
Analyzes the subgenre of "satire on mankind" as a context for examination of the works of Boileau and Rochester. Four types of satiric attack are noted: direct assertion; animal comparison and perspectives; extreterrestrial perspectives; and cosmic perspectives. See also DAI 42 (1982):5133A.

13 TREGLOWN, JEREMY. "'He knew my style, he swore.'" In Spirit of Wit: Reconsiderations of Rochester. Edited by Jeremy Treglown. Hamden, Conn.: Archon Books, pp. 75-91.
Identifies the characteristic quality of Rochester's style as a peculiar complexity of tone, the balancing of detachment and engagement with an appearance of effortlessness: e.g., the contemptuous criticism of heroic prosiness in the sharp, flexible couplets of "Timon" and the close observation (involvement) that contradicts the aloof narrative stance of "Tunbridge Wells." Rochester's allusions to other poems (see 1973.11 and 1980.8) also affect his tone: "Sab: Lost" is "a reversal of Milton's Comus"; "The Imperfect Enjoyment," a "Lost Opportunity" poem, evokes a minor genre called "the lucky minute" poem.

14 TROTTER, DAVID. "Wanton Expressions." In Spirit of Wit: Reconsiderations of Rochester. Edited by Jeremy Treglown. Hamden, Conn.: Archon Books, pp. 111-32.
Interprets the "paradox" that Rochester offered to recant in the "Satyr against Reason and Mankind" as his rejection of the doxa or received opinion of the time, tension between which and his own opinion was the generating force of his satire. The Latitudinarian Edward Stillingfleet's sermon alluding to satire like Rochester's and Rochester's possible retaliation to it (see 1971.4) or to a similar sermon by Glanvill constitute a mobilizing of forces in society. In departing from the "spiritual and intellectual consensus," then, satire is a political threat. The particular doxa Rochester undermined in the "Satyr" (as in his life) was Latitudinarian, one which aimed to establish social stability by discouraging swearing and the gratuitous verbal abuse of lampooning. Dryden's endorsement of the inoffensive Horatian (as opposed to the violent Juvenalian) mode of satire and his view of satire as a branch of heroic poetry that gives the sat-

irist a public role represent his way of "recanting" the "paradox." If Rochester tried to find such a role, he was unwilling to give up the pleasure of gratuitous provocation. "Timon" and "Tunbridge Wells," both of which make the satiric protagonist a victim who "re-acts" out of remorse to social phenomena, deal with this problem. Rochester's "Satyr" plays upon this controversy between a witty "aesthetic of gratuitousness" and its Latitudinarian criticism. It was shaped by circumstances.

15 WALKER, ROBERT G. "Rochester and the Issue of Deathbed Repentance in Restoration and Eighteenth-Century England." SAB 47 (January):21-37.

Pursues further (see 1980.10) the subject of deathbed repentance the efficacy of which became a matter of theological debate following the publicity attached to Rochester's death through Burnet's Life of the earl and Parson's funeral sermon. Earlier in the seventeenth century, Anglican ministers took a conservative stand on this issue; Jeremy Taylor, for instance, maintained that repentance must leave the sinner time for "holy living"; "sorrow for sins" is only the "title page" of the "volume of duty" which is true repentance. Some softening of this position can be seen in statements on the question (even before Rochester's death) by John Tillotson and Isaac Barrow. The former believed that deathbed repentance was "very difficult," "very rare"; nevertheless, he regarded Rochester's public death as so powerful a polemic weapon that he was willing to accept it as the exception that proves the rule. After Rochester's death, this tolerant attitude increases (though acceptance of deathbed conversion is "never unanimous") until, in the nineteenth century, death becomes secularized, the scene of present rather than future concerns.

16 WEINBROT, HOWARD D. "Rochester's 'Fribble' Revisited." N&Q 227 (December):523-24.

Cites instances of the word "fribble" (and its derivatives) in the Tatler, Spectator, and other eighteenth-century works (including Garrick's mock-heroic Fribbleriad) to establish the meaning: "male sexual inadequacy." The word has this lowercase sense in Rochester's "Tunbridge Wells" and in Shadwell's Epsom Wells and not that of "trifler," as Selden (1981.9) argues. See also 1976.7.

17 WILDERS, JOHN. "Rochester and the Metaphysicals." In Spirit of Wit: Reconsiderations of Rochester. Edited by Jeremy Treglown. Hamden, Conn.: Archon Books, pp. 42-57.

Argues that Rochester's poetic vision is not limited to Hobbesian one-dimensionality but that he is as aware of "the multiple nature of man" as the metaphysical poets. "Against Constancy" and "Absent from Thee," for instance, are products of a divided mind, the speaker of the first unable wholly to embrace the sort of life he appears to recommend, that of the second betraying his beloved at the very moment he pledges his fidelity to her; the effect of "A Song of a Young Lady to Her Ancient Lover," combining attraction and revulsion, arises from "a disjunction between its sentiments and its language." Are the companion poems by Rochester and his wife ironic or not, or if ironic, consciously so or not? Rochester is as aware of these complexities as his predecessors Donne or Marvell were.

18 WINTLE, SARAH. "Libertinism and Sexual Politics." In Spirit of Wit: Reconsiderations of Rochester. Edited by Jeremy Treglown. Hamden, Conn.: Archon Books, pp. 133-65.

Finds Rochester's libertine attitudes toward women disturbing, at once challenging older patriarchal attitudes and reacting to an envisioned sexual equality in a problematic or intuitively orthodox way. A number of his poems consider the implications of female sexual liberation. The vision of sexual equality in "To a Lady in a Letter," for instance, leads not to mutuality, but to solitariness. This sense of isolation is also the effect of "Signor Dildo" and "Fair Chloris in a pigsty lay," where women are sexually independent of men. Even in Paradise, as described in "The Fall," sexual equality is less than ideal--bleakly contractual; in the post lapsarian world, on the other hand, women are the more sexually dependable and therefore more threateningly powerful. The speaker of "A Song of a Young Lady to Her Ancient Lover" takes over the male role almost completely--even his hypocrisy. In "A Ramble in St. James' Park," an idea of sexual freedom (female lust) deriving from libertine speculations on nature conflicts with a more traditional notion of social order when Corinna goes off with her three pretenders to distinction. Here female nature violates the basic categories of social discourse.

1983

1 HAMMOND, PAUL. "Was Rochester an Artist?" Cambridge Quarterly 12:56-66.

Questions the "simple assumption" of Rochester's artistry made by contributors to Treglown's Spirit of Wit (see, e.g., 1982.13). Rochester's tone is complex, tempting the reader to take him too seriously. He lacked any serious view of politics, lacked any real authority to judge publicly literary matters, lacked clarity of judgment, "grip," and discipline. It may be that he lacked the respect of "human constructs" necessary to take art seriously. An exception among the contributors is Trotter (see 1982.14).

2 MEANS, JAMES A. "Pope and Rochester." N&Q 228 (February):34.

Maintains that lines 319-22 of Pope's portrait of Sporus (in "An Epistle to Dr. Arbuthnot") are indebted to the following lines in Scroope's epigram on Rochester: "Sit swelling in thy hole like a vexed toad, / And full of pox and malice, spit abroad."

1984

1 COUSINS, A. D. "The Context, Design, and Argument of Rochester's A Satyr against Reason and Mankind." SEL 24 (Summer):429-39.

Reads the Satyr in the context of libertine thought implicit in Rochester's love poems--which analyze the impulse to pleasure in terms of "unreason" and power--and his satires--which pursue this human disorder into Restoration society where it is institutionalized. The Satyr differs from these poems in seeking a "solution" to discord in "right reason," the basis of a real restoration of order. Life, it argues, may be both libertine and ordered if lived according to right reason, which is "subversively redefined" to harmonize with the impulse to pleasure. But a second argument suggests that disorder is natural to human beings. Order, then, is the cooperation of right reason with human meanness, and seems possible only as a personal (as opposed to an interpersonal) achievement. The good man is rare, but not impossible, as the epilogue reveals.

2 NUSSBAUM, FELICITY A. "'That Lost Thing, Love': Women and Impotence in Rochester's Poetry." In The Brink of All We Hate: English Satires on Women, 1660-1750. Lexington: University Press of Kentucky, pp. 57-76.

Argues that love is an unattainable ideal in Rochester's poems, and that women, therefore, possess a power that the poet fears. But feminine power produces here "monuments" to masculine impotence, not antifeminist denunciation: Rochester's narrators confront their desires, mocking those who seek the ideal as well as those who deny it. The poems are unresolved and invert readers' expectations. "A Ramble in St. James's Park" makes a conventional curse of women serve as a conventional retribution of the scorned lover; "The Imperfect Enjoyment" mocks a love that creates both rapture and despair; the faded wife of the host in "Timon" "embodies woman's ability to inspire love and create impotence." Rochester acknowledges the power of women and the impotence of men in order to gain the power of wit and language. See also 1979.9.

3 ROBINSON, KEN. "The Art of Violence in Rochester's Satire." In The Yearbook of English Studies. Edited by C. J. Rawson. Modern Humanities Research Association, vol. 14:93-108.

Describes Rochester's methods of controlling cruelty and violence in satire. The violence of his invectives is almost, but not quite, gratuitous; it is delicately balanced by less fervid tones in "The Imperfect Enjoyment" and justified as an appropriate punishment for Corinna in "A Ramble in St. James's Park." Lampoons, which assume rather than appeal to audience agreement, use violence to frustrate the victim's reply ("My Lord All-Pride," "On Poet Ninny"), represent the victim with character-like generality, and enact formally the poet's struggle to maintain stability. Impromptus (like that on Charles II) suspend cruelty in an ambivalence of superficial playfulness. Rochester's epigrams, however, "operate at the limits of what can be made acceptable through wit," and seek the reader's complicity in cruelty (in perceiving Cary Frazier's lust as the reduction of men to living dildoes; in making gratuitous disgust itself the literal truth of Mrs. Willis). Rochester's violence lacks moral force; its moral neutrality is a peculiar expression of his skepticism.

*4 VIETH, DAVID M. Rochester Studies, 1925-1982: An Annotated Bibliography. New York: Garland, 174 pp.

5 WALKER, KEITH, ed. Introduction to The Poems of John Wilmot, Earl of Rochester. Oxford: Basil Blackwell, pp. ix-xx.
    Reviews the highlights of Rochester's life and poetic reputation and sets forth the editorial principles of this admittedly "untidily" punctuated edition of the poems. On the method of determining copy-texts and on their selection, Walker follows Vieth (1968.4). He removes, however, from Vieth's list of "doubtful" poems "Trust not that thing called woman" ("now known to be by Ben Jonson") and restores to it "Why do'st Thou shade the lovely face" and "The Heaven drinks each Day a Cup." The poems are arranged by genre and supply complete tables of editorial variants from copy-texts. The volume includes a list, by Michael Tilmouth, of musical settings for nine of Rochester's poems.

6 WHITE, ISABELLE. "'So Great a Disproportion': Paradox and Structure in Rochester's A Satyr against Reason and Mankind." Restoration 8 (Fall):47-55.
    Reprint of 1976.12.

7 ZIMMERMAN, HANS-JOACHIM. "Simia Laureatus: Lord Rochester Crowning a Monkey." In Functions of Literature. Edited by Ulrich Broich et al. Tübingen: Niemeyer Verlag, pp. 147-72.
    Cited in Restoration 8 (1984).

1985

1 RAWSON, CLAUDE. "Systems of Excess." TLS, 29 March, pp. 335-36.
    Discriminates between Rochester's poetic qualities and those of Augustan satirists like Pope and Swift. Rochester's wit is uniquely "lordly," a matter of metrical "ease" that frequently spills over into excess (unlike Pope's ease, which implies containment). The commanding force of his style makes him an unlikely choice for author of the "yokel couplets" of Sodom. Excess, or "hyperbolic fantastication," also prevents Rochester's obscenity from becoming pornographic; like Rabelais' enormities, it is preoccupied with itself rather than its subject. In general, his sensualism is a physical exhaustiveness that urged him to systematize a metaphysical exhaustiveness; his "impotence" becomes "an

energy in its own right" (as in "The Disabled Debauchee"). This essay reviews 1984.4 and 1984.5.

Index to Butler

Ache!, 1858.1
A Hermit at Hampstead, 1857.1
A., J. T., 1850.1
Allen, Don Cameron, 1946.1
Anderson, Paul Bunyan, 1947.1
Anthony-Johnston, R., 1869.1
Arouet, François Marie, 1733.1
Asrelsky, Arnold, 1971.1
Astry, Sir James, 1704.1; 1779.1; 1863.1
Aubrey, John, 1704.1; 1898.1; 1921.1; 1933.2; 1936.1; 1966.5; 1971.12; 1976.1
Avellaneda, 1863.2

B., A., 1857.2
Bacon, Francis, 1951.2; 1972.5; 1976.2; 1978.1; 1983.1, 3
Baldwin, Edward Chauncy, 1911.1
Bates, William, 1868.1
Bauer, Josephine, 1948.1; 1969.2
Bede, Cuthbert, 1881.1
Belleau, Remy, 1870.1
Bensly, Edward, 1935.1
Bentley, Christopher, 1973.1
Bentley, Norma E., 1944.1-2; 1945.1; 1946.2; 1948.2; 1969.4
Blair, D., 1870.1
Bloom, Edward A. and Lillian D., 1979.1
Blunden, Edmund, 1928.2
Boileau, Nicholas, 1693.1; 1931.1
Bond, Richmond P., 1932.1; 1972.4
Boxberger, Rudolf, 1876.1
Boyce, Benjamin, 1955.1
Boyle, Robert, 1965.3; 1969.1
Brinkley, Roberta Florence, 1955.2
Brodsley, Laurel Harriet Chilk, 1970.1; 1972.1
Brooks, Harold F., 1940.1
Brunn, Sv., 1969.1; 1974.1
Buckingham, George Villiers, duke of, 1928.3; 1945.1; 1947.1
Büeler, Sigisbert, 1939.1
Burton, K. M. P., 1958.2
Butler, Samuel
-life, 1704.1; 1759.1; 1779.1; 1793.1; 1820.1; 1853.1; 1854.1; 1881.1-2; 1884.1; 1895.1; 1898.1; 1912.1; 1923.2; 1944.2; 1967.3; 1973.7
--ancestry, 1924.1; 1966.4
--early life, 1924.1; 1966.4-5
--education, 1779.1; 1820.1; 1921.1; 1924.1; 1952.2-3; 1966.4
--later life, 1852.1; 1928.3; 1933.2-3; 1971.12
--royal gifts, 1928.3; 1940.1; 1944.1
--theatrical interests, 1928.3; 1948.2
--visits abroad, 1928.3; 1931.1; 1945.1
-mind and thought, 1929.2; 1933.1; 1937.1; 1944.2; 1951.2-3; 1953.1; 1954.2; 1955.3; 1967.1, 3; 1969.3; 1970.6; 1973.6-7; 1974.3, 6; 1976.5; 1979.2; 1981.1-2; 1983.3; 1984.3

—as Augustan, 1933.1; 1951.2; 1952.1; 1955.3; 1971.1; 1978.1
—as empiricist, 1933.1; 1967.3; 1970.6; 1974.6
—as humanist, 1952.1; 1972.3
—as literary critic, 1928.1; 1933.1; 1946.1-2; 1951.2; 1961.2; 1967.3; 1970.5; 1974.6
—as modern, 1928.1; 1951.2-3; 1955.2; 1969.3; 1976.5
—as rationalist, 1901.1; 1933.1; 1944.2; 1951.2; 1954.2; 1963.1; 1979.2
—as satirist, 1895.1; 1901.1; 1910.1; 1911.1; 1925.1; 1928.1; 1929.2; 1952.1; 1955.2; 1963.1; 1967.3; 1971.3, 9, 11; 1976.5; 1977.1; 1978.1; 1983.3
—as stylist, 1928.2; 1952.1; 1953.2; 1955.2; 1963.1; 1970.3; 1971.9; 1973.7; 1974.5; 1977.1; 1978.1
—medieval character of, 1903.1; 1912.1; 1925.1
—method of composition, 1928.4; 1948.1; 1967.1; 1969.2; 1972.2
—on ancient learning, 1951.2; 1952.1-2
—on astrology and pseudoscience, 1929.1; 1933.1; 1973.5; 1976.2; 1982.3; 1983.1-2
—on bourgeois values, 1944.2; 1963.1
—on politics, 1933.1; 1944.2; 1951.2; 1974.6
—on religion, 1923.2; 1933.1; 1944.2; 1951.2; 1974.6; 1979.2
—on science, 1944.2; 1951.2; 1961.1; 1965.3; 1969.1; 1972.5; 1973.5; 1974.6; 1983.1, 3
—on theriophily, 1970.3; 1973.6; 1976.5
—on women, 1912.1; 1923.2; 1933.1; 1974.5; 1976.4-5; 1982.2; 1984.2

—skepticism of, 1923.2; 1967.3; 1972.5; 1983.3
—wit of, 1899.1; 1923.2; 1951.2; 1952.1; 1953.1; 1955.2; 1970.3; 1971.5
-works by or attributed to
--<u>Character of the Rota upon Mr. Milton's Book</u>, 1947.1; 1982.1
--<u>Character of the Rump</u>, <u>The</u>, 1947.1; 1982.1
—characters, 1911.1; 1948.1; 1952.2; 1953.2; 1954.2; 1955.1; 1958.1-2; 1963.1; 1965.1; 1968.1; 1969.5; 1970.1-2; 1971.1, 10; 1972.6; 1973.6; 1976.5
-"Ambitious Man, An," 1948.1
-"Anabaptist, An," 1976.5
-"Astrologer, An," 1973.5
-"Atheist, An," 1974.6
-"Bawd, A," 1948.1
-"Drunkard, A," 1948.1
-"Fifth Monarchy Man, A," 1951.3
-"Hermetic Philosopher, An," 1973.5; 1975.2; 1982.3
-"Hunter, A," 1958.1
-"Hypocrite, An," 1958.1
-"Hypocritical Nonconformist, An," 1975.2
-"Lawyer, A," 1948.2
-"Master of Arts, A," 1948.1
-"Modern Politician, A," 1951.2; 1975.2
-"Morose Man, A," 1948.1
-"Pedant, A," 1958.1
-"Quibbler, A," 1961.2
-"Railer, A," 1948.1
-"Schoolmaster," 1948.2
-"Self-Conceited Man, A," 1948.1
-"Self-Conceited or Singular, The," 1948.1
-"Small Poet, A," 1946.2; 1961.2; 1975.2
-"Undeserving Favourite, An," 1976.5
-"Vapourer, A," 1948.1
-"Virtuoso, A," 1973.5
--"Cydippe to Acontius," 1982.1
--"Dildoides," 1982.1

Index to Butler

--"Doctor and His Wife's Pin Money, The," 1948.1; 1969.2
--"Elephant in the Moon, The," 1869.1; 1879.1; 1901.1; 1925.1; 1958.2; 1961.1; 1965.3; 1969.1; 1970.5; 1972.5; 1973.5; 1974.1, 5; 1981.1-2; 1983.1, 3
--Hudibras, 1733.1; 1744.1; 1779.1; 1793.1; 1819.1; 1853.1; 1854.1; 1857.2-4, 6, 8, 10; 1858.1; 1863.1-2; 1866.1-2; 1868.1; 1870.1; 1874.2; 1875.1; 1882.1-5; 1901.1; 1902.1; 1904.1; 1905.1; 1907.1-3; 1910.2-3; 1911.1; 1920.1; 1923.2; 1928.2; 1929.2; 1944.2; 1951.3; 1952.1; 1953.1; 1955.1; 1956.2; 1957.1; 1960.2; 1965.3-5; 1966.1-3; 1967.3; 1969.5; 1970.1-3, 5; 1971.1-5, 7-8, 11; 1972.1, 3, 7; 1973.5-6; 1974.3, 5, 7; 1975.1; 1976.1-2, 4-5; 1977.2; 1979.1, 5; 1981.3; 1982.2-4, 1983.2; 1984.2-3
-as allegory, 1715.1; 1860.1; 1903.1; 1923.1; 1952.1; 1953.2; 1955.4; 1956.2; 1958.3; 1971.1
-as burlesque, 1692.1; 1693.1; 1744.1; 1779.1; 1903.1; 1931.1; 1932.1; 1937.1; 1953.2; 1970.1, 3; 1971.5; 1972.4; 1979.3
-as mock-heroic, 1793.1; 1912.1; 1932.1; 1953.1-2; 1963.1; 1967.3; 1970.1; 1971.3; 1975.1; 1976.3; 1981.3
-as satire, 1903.1; 1911.1; 1925.1; 1932.1; 1944.2; 1952.1; 1956.2; 1958.2; 1965.4; 1967.3; 1970.1; 1971.7, 11; 1973.5-6; 1974.3; 1976.4-5; 1979.3-5
-borrowings from, 1923.2; 1932.2; 1951.1; 1967.2; 1970.5; 1974.4; 1980.1
-dates of composition and publication, 1910.2-3; 1923.1; 1928.3; 1929.1; 1933.2; 1943.1; 1955.3; 1966.2-3; 1967.3; 1969.4; 1971.12
-"Heroical Epistle of Hudibras to Sidrophel, An," 1929.1; 1965.3; 1966.3; 1967.3; 1983.1
-illustrations of, 1850.1; 1857.1, 5-7, 9, 11; 1873.1-4; 1875.1-3; 1876.2; 1877.1; 1937.1; 1965.4; 1971.8; 1972.3; 1984.1
-imitations of, 1821.1; 1925.1; 1932.1; 1937.1; 1956.1; 1971.6
-rhyme and meter in, 1692.1; 1693.1; 1899.1; 1908.1; 1925.1; 1932.1; 1954.1; 1971.2; 1977.1
-Sidrophel, 1874.1; 1929.1; 1933.1; 1965.5; 1973.5; 1976.2; 1981.2; 1984.1
-Sir Hudibras, model for, 1715.1; 1884.1; 1903.1; 1923.2; 1933.2; 1943.1; 1955.1; 1967.3; 1971.4; 1972.1
-origin of name, 1867.1-3; 1935.1-2; 1979.1
-sources of, 1850.2; 1858.2; 1901.1; 1920.1; 1923.2; 1931.1; 1971.4; 1975.3
-spurious second part of, 1821.1; 1902.1; 1910.2; 1929.1; 1932.1; 1966.3
-"The Ladies Answer," 1971.11
-translations of, 1733.1; 1939.1
--Letter to Sir George Oxenden, 1933.2-3; 1967.3; 1971.12
--"Lord Roos His Answer to the Marquesse of Dorchester's Letter," 1936.1; 1982.1
--Mercurius Menippeus ("Memoirs of the Years 1649 and 50"), 1982.1
--Mola Asinaria, 1933.1; 1951.2; 1982.1
--"Nero," 1928.3; 1948.2
--"No Jesuit E'er Took in Hand," 1973.1

--notebook and commonplace book, 1895.1; 1908.2; 1928.4-5; 1933.1; 1944.2; 1945.1; 1946.1-2; 1947.1; 1948.1-2; 1951.2; 1952.2; 1953.2; 1954.2; 1958.1; 1969.2; 1971.1; 1972.2; 1973.6; 1979.2; 1983.1, 3
--"Occasional Reflections on Dr. Charleton's Feeling a Dog's Pulse at Gresham College, An," 1965.3, 1983.1
--"Priviledge of Our Saints in the Business of Perjury, The," 1974.7
--prologue and epilogue to Queen of Aragon (by Habington), 1928.3
--Rehearsal, The (collaboration in), 1928.3; 1947.1; 1982.1
--"Repartees between Cat and Puss at a Caterwauling," 1928.3
--"Satirical Epistle to a Bad Poet," 1928.3; 1931.1
--"Satyr on Our Ridiculous Imitation of the French," 1961.1
--"Satyr upon Critics Who Judge of Modern Plays by the Rules of the Ancients," 1928.3
--"Satyr upon Modern Critics," 1971.9
--"Satyr upon Plagiaries," 1971.9
--"Satyr upon the Imperfection and Abuse of Human Learning," 1971.9
--"Satyr upon the Licentious Age of Charles the 2nd," 1971.9; 1974.5; 1981.2
--"Satyr upon the Royal Society," 1965.3; 1973.5; 1983.1
--"Satyr upon the Weakness and Misery of Man," 1981.2
--"Speech made at the Rota," 1901.1
--"To the Memory of the Most Renowned Du-Vall," 1931.1; 1951.2; 1961.1
--Transproser Rehears'd, The, 1947.1; 1982.1
--Two Letters, One from John Audland . . . the Other,
William Prynne's Answer, 1820.1; 1951.2
--"Two Speeches made in the Rump Parliament," 1901.1
--"Upon a Hypocritical Nonconformist," 1901.1
B., W. C., 1866.1
Byron, George Gordon, Lord, 1854.1; 1967.2

C., A. B., 1857.3
Carbery, Lord, 1852.1; 1873.2
Catlett, La Rue Scott, 1971.2
Cervantes, Miguel de, 1863.2; 1903.1; 1910.1; 1923.2; 1931.1; 1975.1; 1979.4
Chew, Beverly, 1902.1; 1910.2; 1926.1
Cleveland, John, 1874.2; 1910.1; 1929.1; 1933.3; 1955.1; 1960.2; 1963.1; 1966.1; 1970.2; 1971.12; 1973.2
Clough, Ben C., 1920.1
Coleridge, Samuel Taylor, 1955.2
Colvil, Samuel, 1821.1; 1937.1
Connelly, Kenneth Amor, Jr., 1953.1
Cope, Kevin L., 1981.1
Courthope, W. J., 1903.1
Cousins, A. D., 1981.2
Cowley, Abraham, 1903.1; 1966.1
Craig, Hardin, 1923.1
Cunningham, Peter, 1852.1
Curtiss, Joseph Toy, 1929.1
C., W. A., 1874.1

Daves, Charles Warner, 1965.1; 1970.2
Davies, Paul C., 1970.3
De Beer, E. S., 1921.1; 1928.3; 1969.4
De Morgan, A., 1857.4
Dennis, John, 1693.1; 1744.1
De Quehen, A. H., 1967.1; 1969.2 1972.2; 1973.7; 1979.2; 1982.1
Desconocido, 1850.2
Deva, 1857.1, 5-7, 11
Donne, John, 1895.1; 1920.1; 1946.1-2; 1947.1; 1963.1
Donovan, J., 1973.2; 1974.2
Dowden, Edward, 1901.1

Dryden, John, 1692.1; 1693.1; 1744.1; 1895.1; 1903.1; 1928.3; 1947.1; 1951.3; 1956.2; 1961.2; 1969.1; 1970 1; 1981.1-2
Duffett, G. W., 1935.2
D'Urfey, Thomas, 1821.1; 1863.1; 1937.1

Eade, J. C., 1984.1
Edwards, Thomas R., 1971.3
Elton, Oliver, 1899.1
Engler, Balz, 1979.3
Erasmus, 1952.2
Erskine-Hill, H. K., 1965.2
Evelyn, John, 1969.1

Farley-Hills, David, 1974.3
Flecknoe, Richard, 1970.2; 1975.3
F., P. H., 1857.7

Garnett, R., 1895.1
Genuine Remains in Verse and Prose, The, 1759.1
Gibson, Dan, Jr., 1933.1
Gilfillan, George, 1854.1; 1858.1
G., J. A., 1867.1
Glanvill, Joseph, 1961.1; 1972.5; 1978.1
Granger, Bruce Ingham, 1956.1; 1971.6
Gratiae Ludentes, 1850.2
Greg, W. W., 1928.4
Grey, Zachary, 1744.1; 1793.1; 1850.1; 1868.1; 1874.2; 1907.4; 1935.1; 1965.4; 1966.3; 1969.4
Guez de Balzac, Jean-Louis, 1973.1

Hall, John, 1929.2; 1933.3
Hall, Joseph, 1965.2
Hancock, C. V., 1921.1
Harder, Bruno, 1900.1
Hazlitt, William, 1819.1
Henri, 1857.8
Hill, Christopher, 1969.3
Hill, Richard, 1921.1
Hindle, C. J., 1936.1
Hobbes, Thomas, 1857.1; 1933.1; 1951.2; 1963.1; 1974.5-6; 1978.1

Hogarth, William, 1850.1; 1857.9, 11; 1873.1-4; 1877.1; 1937.1; 1965.4; 1970.1-4; 1971.8; 1972.3; 1984.1
Hooke, Robert, 1929.1; 1965.3; 1969.1
Horne, William C., 1971.4-5; 1972.3; 1982.2; 1983.1-2
Howard, Edward, 1858.1; 1928.3
"Hudibrastics," 1928.1

"Imitations of Hudibras," 1821.1
Ingleby, C. M., 1882.1-2; 1882.5
Irving, George Vere, 1867.2

Jack, Ian, 1952.1; 1957.1; 1960.1; 1979.5
Jaffe, Nora Crow, 1977.1
J., C. J., 1857.9
Jefferey, Leonard, 1873.2; 1924.1; 1954.2; 1966.4
Johnson, Reginald B., 1893.1
Johnson, Samuel, 1779.1; 1903.1
Jonson, Ben, 1867.2; 1935.1-2; 1955.3
Jump, John D., 1972.4

Keenan, Hugh T., 1967.2
Kelly, Ann Kline, 1974.4
Ker, W. P., 1955.3
Korshin, Paul J., 1982.3
Krynski, Stanislaw, 1962.1
Kulischeck, Clarence L., 1951.1; 1954.1

La Courreye, Catherine Clotilde, 1968.1
Laelius, 1867.3
La Fontaine, Jean de, 1974.1
Lamar, René, 1924.1; 1928.1, 4-5; 1948.1; 1952.2; 1954.2; 1969.2; 1982.1
Landon, Michael, 1976.1
Langston, F. W., 1881.2
Laprevotte, Guy, 1972.5
Leigh, Richard, 1947.1
L'Estrange, Sir Roger, 1715.1; 1821.1; 1860.1; 1868.1; 1973.2
Leyburn, Ellen Douglass, 1953.2; 1956.2
Lilly, William, 1874.1; 1929.1; 1965.3

Lobzowska, Maria, 1973.3
Longueville, William, 1948.2; 1966.5; 1979.2; 1982.1
Lowndes, William T., 1866.2; 1882.3
Lucan, 1974.5
Luke, Sir Samuel, 1779.1; 1903.1; 1933.2; 1943.1

Malcolm, E. H., 1875.1, 3; 1876.2
Marvell, Andrew, 1895.1; 1947.1; 1971.12
Mayhew, A. L., 1907.1
Mayhew, T., 1857.10
Meston, William, 1821.1; 1937.1
Miller, Ward Searing, 1955.4; 1958.3
Milton, John, 1867.3; 1947.1; 1972.7
Miner, Earl, 1969.4; 1974.5
Mitford, John, 1853.1
Moffett, William, 1821.1
Mortland, Donald Eugene, 1971.6

Nash, Treadway Russell, 1793.1; 1966.3
Natan, Alex, 1952.3
Neel, Jasper Philip, 1975.1
Neile, Sir Paul, 1929.1; 1965.3; 1969.1
Nelson, Nicolas Harding, 1971.7; 1976.2
Nevo, Ruth, 1963.1; 1970.3
N., G., 1857.11
Nicolson, Marjorie Hope, 1965.3; 1972.5; 1974.1
"Note on Samuel Butler . . . and Jonathan Swift, A," 1958.1
Nussbaum, Felicity A., 1984.2

"Oldys's Notes on Hudibras," 1863.1
Oldys, William, 1704.1; 1863.1
Oxenden, Richard and George, 1933.2-3; 1967.3; 1971.12

Palmer, A. Smyth, 1907.2-4
Paradise Lost, 1733.1; 1972.7
Parker, Samuel, 1944.2; 1947.1; 1948.2; 1979.2; 1982.1

Paulson, Ronald, 1965.4; 1970.4; 1971.8
Pepys, Samuel, 1965.3
Pope, Alexander, 1895.1
Powers, Doris C., 1971.9
Previte-Orton, Charles Williams, 1910.1
Prideaux, W. F., 1910.2
Prior, Matthew, 1821.1; 1937.1
Prynne, William, 1820.1; 1933.1

Quinn, John David, 1971.10
Quintana, Ricardo, 1929.2; 1933.2-3; 1951.2; 1970.6

Rabelais, François, 1923.2; 1931.1; 1952.2; 1955.3
Ramsay, Alexander, 1846.1
Rawson, C. J., 1970.5
Richards, Edward Ames, 1937.1
Richards, Gertrude R. B., 1943.1
Rimbault, Edward F., 1873.1
Rix, Joseph, 1866.1-2
Robbins, Alfred F., 1910.3
Robinson, Ken, 1983.3
Rochester, earl of, 1693.1; 1951.3; 1974.3, 5; 1978.1
Rolle, Sir Samuel, 1974.2
Rosenbach, A. S. W., 1948.2
Rosewel, Sir Henry, 1933.2
Rothstein, Eric, 1981.3
Rowlands, Samuel, 1974.4
Royal Society, 1929.1; 1933.1; 1961.1; 1965.3; 1969.1; 1972.5; 1973.5; 1974.6; 1981.2; 1983.1
Rump, 1958.3; 1971.4-5; 1983.2
Russell, Sir Thomas, 1924.1
Rymer, Thomas, 1928.1, 3; 1970.6

Saintsbury, George, 1908.1
Satire Menippee, 1733.1; 1901.1; 1971.1
Scarron, Paul, 1693.1; 1931.1; 1932.1
Scott, Paulette Maier, 1974.6
Sedley, Sir Charles, 1982.1
Seidel, Michael A., 1971.11; 1979.4-5
Selden, John, 1901.1; 1946.1; 1955.4

Selden, Raman, 1978.1
Session of the Poets, 1928.3
Smith, Harold Wendell, 1951.3
Smith, William Francis, 1912.1
Snider, Alvin, 1984.3
Solly, Edward, 1873.1-3; 1875.2; 1877.1; 1879.1; 1882.2-5
Spence, Alexander C., 1961.1
Spenser, Edmund, 1867.1; 1935.1; 1952.1; 1975.1; 1979.4
Sprat, Thomas, 1945.1; 1951.3; 1961.2; 1965.3; 1972.5; 1981.2
Staves, Susan, 1979.5
Stephens, F. G., 1873.4; 1875.3; 1876.2
Stubbe, Henry, 1961.1; 1965.3; 1972.5
Sutherland, James, 1969.5
Sutherland, W. O. S., 1965.5
Swartchild, William G., III, 1966.1
Swift, Jonathan, 1854.1; 1901.1; 1932.2; 1951.1-2; 1954.1; 1955.2; 1956.1; 1958.1; 1974.3-4; 1977.1; 1980.1

Taine, Hippolyte A., 1863.2
Tanswell, J., 1860.1
Taylor, John, 1867.2
Temple, Sir William, 1974.1
Thorson, James Llewellyn, 1966.2-3; 1969.4; 1973.4; 1974.7
Thyer, Robert, 1759.1; 1965.1, 3; 1982.1
Tillotson, John, 1974.6; 1979.2
Totten, Charles Frederick, 1972.6; 1975.2
Trumbull, John, 1937.1; 1956.1; 1971.6

Vaughn, Thomas, 1974.6
Veldkamp, Jan, 1923.1-2
Vieth, David M., 1977.2
Voltaire. See Arouet, François Marie

Wagner, Joseph B., 1973.5; 1982.4
Walker, Hugh, 1925.1
Waller, A. R., 1905.1; 1908.2; 1928.5; 1948-1

Waller, Edmund, 1858.1; 1961.2; 1981.2
Walter, James F., 1976.3
Ward, C. A., 1884.1
Ward, Edward (Ned), 1821.1; 1937.1
Wasserman, George R., 1970.6; 1973.6; 1976.4-5
Webster, C. M., 1932.2
Wedgwood, C. V., 1960.2
Wendell, Barrett, 1904.1
West, Albert H., 1931.1
White, Robert B., Jr., 1980.1
Wilders, John, 1967.3; 1969.4; 1973.7
Wilding, Michael, 1966.4-5; 1971.12; 1972.7; 1975.3
Wilkins, John, 1965.3; 1969.1
Williams, Sparks Henderson, 1874.2
Williamson, George, 1961.2
Wood, Anthony à, 1704.1; 1779.1; 1820.1; 1928.3; 1947.1; 1976.1; 1982.1
Wood, Isaac, 1850.1

Yardley, E., 1907.4
Yeowell, J., 1858.2
Young, Edward, 1853.1

Index to Rochester

Adlard, John, 1974.1; 1976.1
Alcock, Thomas, 1942.1
Allen, Don Cameron, 1964.1
Arouet, François-Marie, 1733.1; 1934.1
Ashton, Colonel Edmund, 1963.2
Aubrey, John, 1898.1
Auffret, Jean, 1959.1

Babler, C. F., 1952.1
Baine, Rodney M., 1946.1
Balfour, Sir Andrew, 1935.6
Beal, Peter, 1978.1
Behn, Aphra, 1963.1; 1974.4
Beljame, Alexandre, 1881.1; 1937.5; 1948.1
Belleau, Rémy, 1963.1
Bender, Robert M., 1967.1
Berlind, Bruce P., 1957.1
Berman, Ronald, 1964.2
Blount, Charles, 1934.8; 1935.6; 1964.1; 1980.7
Boileau, Nicholas, 1691.1; 1693.1; 1733.1; 1779.1; 1937.1; 1943.1; 1949.1; 1968.4; 1969.2, 7; 1981.2; 1982.11
Brooks, David, 1980.1
Brooks, Elmer L., 1973.1
Brooks, Harold, 1935.1-2; 1938.1; 1949.1; 1969.1
Brooks, John H., 1980.2
Brown, Tom, 1707.1; 1973.6
Bruser, Fredelle, 1946.2
Buckingham, George Villiers, duke of, 1895.1; 1931.1, 3; 1935.4; 1948.2; 1955.4; 1960.3; 1963.2; 1978.2; 1979.2

Bullough, Geoffrey, 1932.1
Burnet, Gilbert, 1680.1; 1926.1; 1935.4, 6; 1937.5; 1939.1; 1964.1; 1974.9; 1980.10; 1982.15
Burton, K. M. P., 1958.1
Butler, Samuel, 1693.1; 1951.1; 1978.6

Carver, Larry, 1979.1; 1982.1
Charleton, Walter, 1968.3
Clark, John R., 1973.2
Clarke, Charles Cowden, 1871.1
Clarke, Reginald Dennis, 1971.1
Clifford, Martin, 1960.3
Collier, Jeremy, 1974.2, 11
Cope, Kevin L., 1981.1
Courthope, W. J., 1903.1
Cousins, A. D., 1984.1
Cowley, Abraham, 1940.1; 1951.3; 1965.2; 1973.11
Crabbe, George, 1940.1
Crocker, S. F., 1937.1
Crashaw, Richard, 1973.11
Crayle, Benjamin, 1969.5
Crowne, John, 1982.5

Dale, Donald A., 1937.2-4; 1939.1
Danchin, Pierre, 1982.2
Danielsson, Bror, 1967.2
Davenant, William, 1934.7-8; 1976.9
Davies, Paul C., 1969.2-3; 1970.1; 1972.1; 1974.2
Davison, Dennis, 1973.3
De Beer, E. S., 1936.1
Defoe, Daniel, 1974.8

Dennis, John, 1693.1
Des Barreaux, Jacques Vallée, 1937.1
Descartes, Rene, 1974.4
Donaldson, Ian, 1972.2
Donne, John, 1942.2; 1952.2; 1976.9; 1980.8; 1982.17
Dorset, Charles Sachville, earl of, 1707.1; 1935.4; 1965.2; 1977.2
Downie, J. A., 1979.2
Dryden, John, 1881.1; 1903.1; 1921.1; 1931.2; 1939.2, 5; 1940.1; 1951.1; 1957.3; 1961.1; 1963.2; 1973.3-4; 1974.6; 1975.1; 1976.5; 1978.4; 1979.2; 1981.1, 3; 1982.10-11, 14
Duclos, Paul-Charles, 1956.1
Duncan, Ronald, 1940.1
Duncan-Jones, E. E., 1972.3
Durfey, Thomas, 1975.7

Eccles, John, 1968.2
Edwards, A. S. G., 1974.3; 1976.2; 1977.1
Elias, Richard, 1978.2
Ellis, Frank H., 1965.1
Elton, Oliver, 1899.1
Emslie, Macdonald, 1954.1
Erickson, Don Lowell, 1975.1
Erskine-Hill, Howard, 1966.1
'Espinasse, Paul G., 1934.1
Etherege, George, 1925.1; 1939.6; 1958.3; 1963.2; 1965.2; 1974.4; 1982.10
Everett, Barbara, 1982.3

Fabricant, Carole, 1972.4; 1974.4; 1976.3
Fane, Sir Francis, 1968.2
Fishbourne, Christopher, 1946.1; 1978.2
Farley-Hills, David, 1972.5; 1974.5; 1978.3
Field, P. J. C., 1970.2
Fletcher, John, 1926.3; 1935.3; 1937.6-7; 1968.2
Forgues, Emile Durand, 1857.1
Freke, John, 1965.1; 1970.4
Fujimura, Thomas H., 1958.2

Garnett, Richard, 1895.1
Giddey, Ernest, 1964.3
Gill, James E., 1981.2
Glanvill, Joseph, 1982.14
Grabo, Norman, 1962.1
Graves, Wallace, 1964.4
Gray, Philip, 1938.2
Greene, Graham, 1931.1; 1935.3; 1974.6
Greenslade, Basil, 1982.4
Griffin, Dustin Hadley, 1969.4; 1973.4

Halifax, George Savile, marquess of, 1955.4
Ham, Roswell J., 1925.1; 1933.1
Hamilton, Anthony, Comte de Grammont, 1713.1; 1926.1
Hammond, Paul, 1983.1
Hanson, Laurence, 1953.1
Harley, Robert and Edward, 1934.5; 1979.2
Harris, Brice, 1931.2; 1932.2; 1935.4
Hartmann, Cyril Hughes, 1955.1
Hayman, John, 1968.1
Hayward, John, 1926.1; 1934.2; 1937.5
Herbert, George, 1973.11; 1980.8
Hobbes, Thomas, 1903.1; 1934.9; 1935.6; 1964.1; 1973.9, 11; 1974.1, 12; 1978.6-7
Hogan, Patrick G., 1952.2
Hook, Lucyle, 1956.2; 1960.1; 1968.2
Horace, 1972.13; 1975.4; 1978.6; 1982.10, 14
Howard, Edward and Robert, 1937.8; 1963.2; 1978.4; 1979.8; 1982.9
Howell, James, 1964.5
Hume, Robert D., 1976.4
Huntley, Frank Livingstone, 1939.2
Hyde, Laurence, 1936.1

Iglesias, John H., 1971.2
Isaacs, J., 1927.1

Jerome, Judson Blair, 1955.2
Johnson, James William, 1974.7; 1976.5

Johnson, Joseph A., Jr., 1973.5
Johnson, Ronald Wayne, 1973.6; 1975.2
Johnson, Samuel, 1779.1; 1892.1; 1912.1; 1969.7; 1972.5; 1981.6; 1982.10
Jones, R. T., 1975.3
Jordan, Robert, 1973.7
Juvenal, 1857.1; 1939.2; 1972.9; 1978.6; 1982.14

Kaufman, Anthony, 1982.5
Knight, Charles A., 1970.3
Krishman, R. S., 1981.3

Lane, Jane, 1950.1
La Rochefoucauld, 1937.1
Lawrence, W. J., 1935.5
Lee, Edward Henry, 1974.7
Lee, Nathaniel, 1935.3, 5; 1972.9; 1976.4
Legouis, Pierre, 1937.5; 1954.2
Levin, Harry, 1942.2
Loane, George G., 1934.3-4
Longueville, Thomas, 1903.2
Love, Harold, 1972.6; 1982.6
Lucretius, 1691.1; 1974.1
Lutrell, Narcissus, 1935.7; 1940.2; 1956.2

McFadden, George, 1978.4
Mackie, J. L., 1954.3
McVeagh, John, 1974.8
Main, C. F., 1960.2
Marvell, Andrew, 1953.3; 1954.2; 1970.4; 1972.3, 10; 1973.3, 7; 1982.17
Means, James A., 1983.2
"Memoirs of the Life and Character of the Late Earl of Rochester . . . ," 1707.2
Milton, John, 1976.6; 1982.12
Miner, Earl, 1974.9
Moehlmann, John Frederick, 1974.10; 1979.3
Moncada, Ernest J., 1964.5
Montaigne, 1937.1
Moore, John F., 1943.1
Motteaux, Peter Anthony, 1968.2
Mulgrave, John Sheffield, earl of, 1685.1; 1956.2; 1960.3; 1963.2; 1975.5; 1976.6; 1982.10
Munker, Dona F., 1975.4
Murdock, Kenneth B., 1939.3
Murphy, John A., 1973.8

Needham, Francis, 1934.5
Newport, Francis, 1946.3
Nicoll, Allardyce, 1921.1
Nokes, David, 1977.2
Norman, Charles, 1954.4
Notzon, Mark Joseph, 1981.4
Nussbaum, Felicity, 1984.2

Ober, William B., 1979.4
Oldham, John, 1707.1; 1935.1; 1953.7; 1963.2; 1969.7; 1972.5; 1981.5
O'Neill, John H., 1975.5; 1977.3; 1980.2
Otway, Thomas, 1925.1; 1931.1; 1960.2; 1963.2; 1980.4; 1982.8

Paden, W. D., 1953.2
Palmer, Melven Delmar, 1960.3
Parker, Samuel, 1954.2; 1973.3
Parson, Robert, 1980.10; 1982.15
Pasch, Thomas K., 1979.5
Patterson, John D., 1980.3-4; 1981.5-6
Paulson, Kristoffer Frimann, 1968.3; 1971.3-4; 1972.7-8; 1976.6; 1978.5
Pepys, Samuel, 1937.4; 1939.1
Pinto, Vivian de Sola, 1934.6-9; 1935.6; 1937.5; 1939.4; 1940.2; 1953.3-4; 1954.5; 1955.3; 1956.3; 1957.2; 1960.4; 1961.1; 1962.2-3; 1964.6-8; 1965.2; 1970.4
Pope, Alexander, 1903.1; 1940.1; 1960.3; 1966.3; 1969.7; 1975.1; 1977.2; 1982.5; 1983.2; 1985.1
Portsmouth, Louise de Keroualle, duchess of, 1940.2
Porter, Peter, 1982.7
Powers, Doris C., 1971.5
Powley, Edward B., 1934.10
Prinz, Johannes, 1926.2; 1927.2; 1937.5
Probyn, Clive T., 1975.6; 1977.5

Quaintance, Richard E., 1962.4; 1963.1
Quarles, Frances, 1967.3

Radclyffe, Edward, 1957.3; 1973.8
Rawson, Claude, 1985.1
Reich, Wilhelm, 1974.1
Righter, Anne, 1967.3
Robinson, K. E., 1973.9-10; 1975.7; 1979.6-7; 1981.7; 1982.8-9; 1984.3
Rochester, Anne, dowager countess of, 1974.7; 1980.7
Rochester, Elizabeth, Countess of, 1955.1
Rochester, John Wilmot, earl of
-life and reputation, 1680.1; 1685.1; 1713.1; 1820.1; 1857.1; 1863.1; 1898.1; 1926.1; 1927.2; 1935.6; 1937.5; 1953.4; 1956.1; 1962.2; 1972.5; 1974.1, 6; 1975.3; 1979.4; 1982.9; 1983.1
--affair at Epsom Wells, 1937.5; 1941.1; 1970.1; 1975.7
--alias Dr. Bendo, 1942.1; 1967.3; 1974.6
--alias "Sabinus," 1973.8
--alias Strephon, 1934.8; 1935.6
--as courtier, 1713.1; 1903.2; 1935.6; 1948.2; 1982.4
--as Duke Nemours, 1935.3; 1976.4
--as husband, 1937.5; 1974.6; 1980.7
--as patron, 1881.1; 1927.2
--atheism, 1964.1
--conversion, 1680.1; 1927.3; 1935.6; 1937.5; 1939.3; 1964.1; 1974.1, 6, 9; 1976.4-5; 1980.10; 1982.15
--duel with Mulgrave, 1937.5
--grand tour, 1927.1; 1935.6; 1956.3
--marriage, 1943.2; 1955.1; 1974.6
--political interests, 1936.1; 1937.5; 1955.1; 1982.4-5
--relations with Elizabeth Barry, 1713.1; 1925.1; 1931.1; 1974.6; 1980.7

--role playing, 1713.1; 1942.1; 1967.3; 1978.5
--Rose Alley affair, 1881.1; 1937.5; 1939.5; 1940.2; 1951.1; 1954.2; 1979.2
-mind and thought, 1680.1; 1934.9; 1939.3; 1951.1; 1953.3-4; 1972.1; 1973.4; 1981.1
--deism, 1934.8
--as "explorer of reality," 1935.6; 1953.4; 1957.2; 1966.1
--Hobbesian influence, 1903.1; 1934.9; 1935.6; 1943.1; 1958.2; 1960.2; 1973.9, 11; 1974.1, 6; 1981.4; 1982.16
--liberalism, 1972.1; 1974.2
--libertinism and hedonism, 1976.5; 1982.18; 1984.1
--psychology, 1973.4; 1974.1; 1975.3; 1979.4
--religious views, 1939.3; 1963.2; 1982.1
--skepticism, 1863.1; 1969.4; 1974.8; 1975.1; 1980.8; 1981.4
--theriophily, 1936.2; 1972.2; 1973.11; 1981.2; 1982.12
--the senses, 1943.1; 1951.1; 1955.2; 1961.3; 1964.2; 1974.4
-literary considerations
--as Augustan, 1961.1, 3; 1963.2; 1966.1; 1969.3, 6; 1972.1, 6, 11; 1973.4-5; 1978.6; 1982.9
--as lyricist, 1927.2; 1936.2; 1962.4; 1963.1; 1973.5; 1980.9
--as satirist, 1707.1-2; 1903.1; 1927.2-3; 1936.2; 1940.1; 1953.3; 1962.3; 1971.1-2; 1972.6; 1973.6; 1978.6; 1980.1; 1981.3-4, 8; 1982.4, 12; 1984.3; 1985.1
--borowings from, 1970.2; 1972.3
--burlesque, 1693.1; 1976.13; 1978.3
--editions, 1935.7; 1937.2-4; 1938.2; 1939.1, 4; 1947.2; 1950.2; 1953.1-2, 5; 1956.4; 1959.2; 1963.2
--formal satire, 1949.1; 1960.2; 1971.5; 1981.3
--imitations and translations, 1691.1; 1936.2; 1949.1;

Index to Rochester

    1965.2; 1967.3; 1969.7;
    1972.13; 1982.10
--influences on, 1937.1; 1969.2;
    1973.11; 1976.9
--irony, 1966.1; 1970.1; 1972.12;
    1973.9; 1976.11; 1982.3
--language and style, 1758.1;
    1974.10; 1975.4; 1976.8;
    1979.3; 1982.7, 10, 13
--manuscripts, 1921.1; 1927.2;
    1932.2; 1951.2; 1954.1;
    1956.4; 1959.2; 1963.2;
    1967.2; 1972.6; 1982.6
--metaphysical qualities, 1952.2;
    1964.3; 1982.17
--obscenity, 1971.1; 1975.8;
    1976.8, 13; 1980.2; 1981.7
--parody, 1973.6; 1980.8
--persona, 1960.3; 1963.2;
    1966.3; 1967.3; 1968.3;
    1973.6
--pornography, 1707.1; 1927.2;
    1940.1; 1964.2; 1975.8
--printed texts and canon of,
    1926.1; 1927.2; 1934.2;
    1937.2-4; 1938.2; 1939.1, 4;
    1947.2; 1950.2; 1953.1-2, 5;
    1956.4; 1959.2; 1963.2;
    1966.2; 1968.4; 1984.5
--sexuality, 1964.2; 1971.7;
    1973.4; 1974.4; 1975.3, 5;
    1976.13; 1979.10; 1980.2;
    1982.17; 1984.2; 1985.1
--the reader, 1966.1; 1967.3;
    1975.2; 1976.8; 1979.5;
    1983.1
--wit, 1707.1; 1955.2; 1961.3;
    1971.3; 1973.5; 1985.1
-works by or attributed to
--"Absent from thee I languish
    still," 1952.2; 1973.4;
    1980.9; 1982.17
--"Advice, The," 1973.11
--"Alexander Bendo's Bill,"
    1926.;1; 1942.1; 1973.6;
    1974.6
--"All my past Life is mine no
    more" ("Love and Life"),
    1934.9; 1960.4; 1967.3;
    1973.11; 1974.12; 1978.3, 7
--"Allusion to Horace, An," 1939.

    5; 1949.1; 1963.2; 1971.5;
    1972.9, 13; 1973.5; 1974.9
    1980.4; 1982.10
--"An Age, in her Embraces past"
    ("The Mistress"), 1960.4;
    1974.9; 1975.4; 1980.9
--"Answer, The," 1963.2; 1976.6
--"By all love's soft, yet mighty
    powers," 1976.13
--"Commons' Petition, The," 1935.1
--"Could I but make my wishes in-
    solent," 1934.5
--<u>De Rerum Natura</u> (translation
    from), 1691.1; 1974.12
--"Dialogue between Strephon and
    Daphne," 1980.8
--"Disabled [or "Maim'd"] Debau-
    chee, The," 1956.1; 1961.1, 3;
    1972.10; 1973.4; 1974.4-5;
    1975.2, 6; 1977.4-5; 1978.5;
    1979.10; 1981.5; 1982.3;
    1985.1
--"Disappointment, The," 1963.1;
    1975.7
--"Dispute, The," 1960.1
--"Ephelia to Bajazet," 1963.2
--"Epistolary Essay from M. G. to
    O. B.," 1955.2; 1960.3; 1963.2;
    1964.8; 1966.1, 3; 1972.6;
    1973.4; 1974.8; 1978.7
--"Fair Chloris in a Pigsty Lay,"
    1973.6; 1974.9; 1976.13;
    1978.3; 1979.6; 1982.18
--"Faith and Reason," 1934.6-7
--"Fall, The," 1980.8; 1982.18
--"Familiar Epistle to Mr. Julian
    . . . , A," 1963.2
--"Fling this useless Book away"
    ("Written in a Lady's Prayer
    Book"), 1944.1; 1973.11;
    1982.1
--"Fruition was the Question in
    Debate," 1939.6; 1963.1
--"History of Insipids, The,"
    1857.1; 1899.1; 1965.1;
    1970.4; 1982.4
--"Imperfect Enjoyment, The,"
    1955.2; 1963.1; 1972.10;
    1973.4, 6; 1974.4-5; 1975.7-8;
    1977.3; 1978.3, 5; 1979.4, 10;
    1980.2; 1982.13; 1984.2-3

--"Impromptu on Charles II," 1934.1-4, 10; 1984.3
--"In Defence of Satyr," 1941.1; 1963.2; 1970.1
--"Insatiate Desire," 1947.1
--"Insulting Beauty, you mispend," 1956.5
--"I swive as well as others do" ("Mock Song"), 1963.2; 1976.13; 1979.9; 1980.8
--"Leave this gaudy gilded stage," 1973.11
--"Letter from Artemisia . . . , A," 1953.1; 1955.2; 1958.3; 1967.3; 1968.3; 1969.3; 1972.6, 12, 14; 1973.4, 6; 1974.4-5, 8; 1976.3, 8; 1978.3, 7; 1979.10; 1980.4
--letters, 1926.1; 1927.2; 1937.5; 1941.2; 1951.3; 1976.10; 1980.7
--"Lorraine you stole" ("Impromptu"), 1974.3
--"Love a Woman, You're an Ass," 1940.1; 1981.5
--"Love bade me hope, and I obeyed," ("Woman's Honour"), 1973.11; 1976.8; 1980.8
--<u>Lucina's Rape</u>. See <u>Valentinian</u>
--"Maim'd Debauchee, The." See "Disabled Debauchee"
--"Must I with patience ever silent sit," 1954.2
--"My Lord All-Pride," 1963.2; 1976.6; 1984.3
--"Oh, that I could by some chymic art" ("The Wish"), 1947.1
--"One Writing against His Prick," 1980.3
--"On Poet Ninny," 1963.2; 1976.6; 1984.3
--"On Rome's Pardons," 1963.2
--"On the Court Ladyes," 1931.2; 1932.1; 1973.1
--"On the Suppos'd Author of a Late Poem in Defence of Satire," 1963.2; 1976.6
--"On the Women about Town," 1960.1; 1979.9
--"On the Young Statesman," 1935.4; 1977.2

--"Phyllis, be gentler I advise," 1980.8
--"Plain-Dealing's Downfall," 1976.1
--"Posted on Whitehall Gate." See "Impromptu on Charles II"
--"Quoth the Duchess of Cleveland to Counselor Knight," 1975.5
--"Ramble in St. James' Park, A," 1960.1; 1972.8; 1973.6; 1974.5; 1976.8, 13; 1978.3; 1979.5; 1981.6; 1982.18; 1984.2-3
--"Rochester's Extempore," 1982.1
--"Rochester's Farewell," 1935.2; 1954.2; 1959.1; 1977.2
--"Sab: Lost," 1973.8; 1982.12
--"Satyr against Reason and Mankind, A," 1733.1; 1779.1; 1937.1; 1943.1; 1949.1; 1951.1; 1953.2; 1958.1-2; 1960.2; 1961.1, 3; 1966.1; 1967.1; 1968.3; 1969.2-3, 6; 1970.2-3; 1971.4-5; 1972.3, 7, 12, 14; 1973.4, 6, 9-11; 1974.2, 5, 8-9, 12; 1975.2; 1976.5, 8-9; 1977.4; 1978.3-4, 7; 1979.7; 1980.9; 1981.1-2; 1982.4, 11, 14; 1984.1
-"epilogue" to, 1953.2; 1956.3; 1958.2; 1969.2; 1971.4; 1972.7; 1975.2
-sources (or originality) of, 1937.1; 1943.1; 1949.1; 1956.3; 1958.2; 1969.2
--"Satyr on Charles II, A" ("Scepter Lampoon"), 1958.4; 1974.4; 1978.5; 1982.4
--"Scaen" (for <u>The Conquest of China</u>), 1921.1; 1926.1; 1937.8; 1979.8
--"Session [or "Trial"] of the Poets, A," 1931.1, 3; 1933.1; 1946.3; 1963.1-2; 1975.7
--"Signor Dildo," 1946.3; 1973.6; 1975.5; 1979.9; 1982.18
--"Since Death on all Lays his Impartial Hand," 1939.6
--<u>Sodom</u>, 1946.1; 1951.2; 1964.4; 1969.5; 1974.1; 1976.2, 5; 1977.1; 1978.2; 1979.1, 9; 1980.4; 1982.8; 1985.1

174

Index to Rochester

--"Song of a Young Lady to Her Ancient Lover," 1967.3; 1973.2; 1974.4-5; 1978.3; 1979.10; 1980.9; 1982.17-18
--"Tell mee noe more of Constancy" ("Against Constancy"), 1953.6; 1954.1, 3; 1964.7; 1973.11; 1980.8; 1982.16
--"Thou damn'd Antipodes to common sense," 1963.2
--"Timon," 1857.1; 1938.1; 1949.1; 1963.2; 1968.3; 1972.6; 1973.4, 6; 1974.4; 1982.6, 13-14; 1984.2
--"To a Lady in a Letter," 1960.5; 1961.2; 1981.5; 1982.18
--"To forme a Plott," 1963.2
--"To His Mistress," 1967.3
--"To My More than Meritorious Wife," 1979.10
--"Too late, alas! I must confess," 1956.5
--"To the Post Boy," 1941.1; 1963.2; 1967.3; 1974.9; 1975.2; 1979.10; 1980.3; 1982.1
--"Trial of the Poets for the Bays, A." See "A Session of the Poets"
--<u>Troades</u> (translation from), 1691.1; 1934.8; 1966.1; 1974.12; 1979.7
--"Trust not that thing called woman" ("A Rodomontade on His Cruel Mistress"), 1969.1; 1978.1; 1984.5
--"Tunbridge Wells," 1857.1; 1954.2; 1963.2; 1972.2, 6; 1973.3, 6-7, 11; 1974.5; 1976.7; 1977.2; 1981.9; 1982.11, 13-14, 16
--"T'was a dispute 'twixt heav'n and Earth," 1934.5
--"Upon His Drinking a Bowl," 1976.5; 1981.5
--"Upon His Leaving His Mistress," 1976.9; 1980.8
--"Upon Nothing," 1779.1; 1871.1; 1892.1; 1899.1; 1956.1, 3; 1961.1, 3; 1962.1; 1966.1; 1967.3; 1968.3; 1971.3, 6; 1973.4; 1974.8, 9, 12; 1975.1; 1978.3, 7; 1979.7
--<u>Valentinian</u>, 1921.1; 1926.1, 3; 1935.3, 5; 1937.6-7; 1956.2; 1968.2; 1972.1; 1974.1; 1976.5
--"Very Heroical Epistle in Answer to Ephelia, A," 1963.2; 1966.1; 1967.1; 1978.7; 1979.10
--"What cruel pains Corinna takes," 1979.10
--"While on those lovely looks I gaze," 1956.5
--"Written under Nelly's Picture," 1964.5
--"Young Gentleman, desirous to be a Minister of State, A," 1954.5; 1955.3-4

"Rochester and Dr. Bendo," 1942.1
Rogers, Pat, 1982.10
Root, Robert J., 1976.7
Rosa, Salvator, 1956.3
Rothstein, Eric, 1981.8
<u>Rump</u>, 1935.1
Rymer, Thomas, 1691.1

Saint-Evremond, Seigneur de, 1707.2; 1926.1; 1936.1; 1976.5
Savile, Henry, 1935.6; 1937.5; 1939.5; 1941.2; 1946.3; 1980.7
Scroope, Sir Carr, 1941.1; 1963.2; 1970.1; 1975.5; 1976.13; 1980.8; 1983.2
Sedley, Sir Carr, 1941.1; 1963.2; 1970.1; 1975.5; 1976.13; 1980.8; 1983.1
Selden, Sir Charles, 1964.6; 1965.2; 1973.6, 8
Selden, Raman, 1972.9; 1978.6; 1981.9; 1982.11
Semonides, 1979.6
Settle, Elkanah, 1931.3; 1933.1; 1937.8; 1946.3; 1963.2; 1980.4
Shadwell, Thomas, 1946.3; 1973.10; 1976.7; 1981.9; 1982.11, 16
Sheehan, David, 1980.5
Silverman, Stuart, 1971.6; 1972.10
Sitter, John E., 1976.8
Smith, Harold Wendell, 1951.1

175

Sprague, Arthur Colby, 1926.3
Spenser, Edmund, 1980.2
Sprat, Thomas, 1949.1; 1951.1
Sternhold, Thomas, 1973.11
Stillingfleet, Edward, 1971.4; 1982.14
Strage, Mark, 1980.6
Street, G. S., 1892.1
Suckling, John, 1980.5
Swift, Jonathan, 1968.3; 1969.3; 1973.6; 1975.1, 4; 1980.2, 5; 1985.1

Taine, H. A., 1863.1; 1937.5
Taylor, Jeremy, 1982.15
Thacker, Godfrey, 1960.1; 1964.6
Thomas, D. S., 1969.5
Thorpe, James, 1947.1-2; 1950.2; 1951.2
Thorpe, Peter, 1969.6; 1972.11
Tierney, Thomas Patrick, 1982.12
Todd, William B., 1953.5
Tonson, Jacob, 1956.5; 1961.2
Treglown, Jeremy, 1973.11; 1976.9, 10; 1979.8; 1980.7, 8; 1982.13
Trotter, David, 1982.14

Vieth, David M., 1951.3; 1953.6-7; 1955.4; 1956.4-5; 1957.3; 1958.3-4; 1959.2; 1960.5; 1961.2; 1963.2; 1964.8; 1966.2-3; 1967.2; 1968.4; 1972.12; 1976.11; 1977.4-5; 1980.9; 1984.4
Voltaire. See Arouet, François-Marie

Waller, Edmund, 1936.1; 1965.2; 1968.1; 1976.13
Walker, Keith, 1984.5
Walker, Robert G., 1980.10; 1982.15
Walmsley, D. M., 1931.3
Walpole, Horace, 1758.1
Watts, Isaac, 1960.4
Weinbrot, Howard D., 1969.7; 1972.13-14; 1982.16
Weitzman, Arthur J., 1973.12; 1974.11
Whibley, Charles, 1912.1

White, Isabelle, 1976.12; 1984.6
Whitefield, Francis, 1936.2
Whitehall, Robert, 1934.5
Whitley, Raymond K., 1978.7
Wilcoxon, Reba Grey, 1971.7; 1974.12; 1975.8; 1976.13; 1979.9-10
Wilders, John, 1982.17
Wilkinson, C. H., 1935.7
Williams, Charles, 1935.8; 1937.5
Williamson, George, 1927.3; 1961.3
Wilson, J. Harold, 1937.6-8; 1939.5-6; 1941.1-2; 1943.2; 1944.1; 1946.3; 1948.2
Wintle, Sarah, 1982.18
Wolseley, Robert, 1685.1; 1820.1; 1956.2
Wood, Anthony à, 1820.1; 1940.2; 1965.1
Wycherley, William, 1974.4

Zimmerman, Hans-Joachim, 1984.7

DEC 1 3 1989